Stories of Love,

Courage & Compassion

to Nourish Your Spirit

& Sweeten Your Dreams

A FIRESIDE BOOK
Published by Simon & Schuster

CHOCOLATE

for a

WOMAN'S
HEART
&
SOUL

KAY ALLENBAUGH

FIRESIDE
Rockefeller Center
1230 Avenue of the Americas
New York, NY 10020

First Fireside Edition 1998

FIRESIDE and colophon are registered trademarks
of Simon & Schuster Inc.

Manufactured in the United States of America

1   3   5   7   9   10   8   6   4   2

Library of Congress Cataloging-in-Publication Data
Chocolate for a woman's heart and soul / [compiled by] Kay Allenbaugh.
p.   cm.
Previously published separately as: Chocolate for a woman's soul, and
Chocolate for a woman's heart.
1. Women—Religious life.   I. Allenbaugh, Kay.   II. Chocolate for a
woman's soul.   III. Chocolate for a woman's heart.
BL625.7.C465   1998
291.4'32—dc21   98-40620   CIP
ISBN 0-684-85785-5

These titles were previously published separately.

Permissions Acknowledgments appear on page 511.

*D*edicated to

the contributing authors

whose "chocolate" stories

light the way for

women around the world.

CONTENTS

III

FEEDING A WOMAN'S HEART

IV

MAXIMUM EXPOSURE

V

PATHFINDERS

VI

FREE AT LAST

VII

MOMENTS OF TRUTH

VIII

THE ANIMAL CONNECTION

IX
ACTS OF KINDNESS

X
A DEEPER REFLECTION

XI
SERIOUSLY FUNNY

PART TWO: *Chocolate for a Woman's Soul*

XII
FINDING LOVE IN ALL THE RIGHT PLACES

XIII
DIVINE ASSISTANCE

XIV
A WOMAN'S INTUITION

XV

SOARING THROUGH BARRIERS

XVI

THE COURAGE TO MOVE ON

XVII
CROSSROADS

XVIII
GOING THE DISTANCE

XIX

GO WITH YOUR PASSION

XX

A NEW WAY OF BEING

XXI

TENDERNESS AND COMPASSION

XXII

LEARNING TO LAUGH AT OURSELVES

INTRODUCTION

*S*haring stories is something that women do best! Inspirational stories, in particular, touch that inner part of us that says "yes" to life. At the same time, such stories encourage us to reach out, take risks, face challenges, and taste all the richness of our personal adventures and everyday experiences.

I am honored to be part of an expanding group of dynamic women, now more than 150 strong, who have shared their favorite real-life stories brought together in this special edition of *Chocolate for a Woman's Heart & Soul.* Many of these contributors are motivational speakers, spiritual leaders, consultants, therapists, and bestselling authors. Who better to offer compassion and sustenance than women who delight in lifting up and encouraging others?

Some of their stories will make you laugh, others will make you cry, but all of them will lead to self-discovery as you explore the relevance of each story's message in your own life. Many of these true tales will give you just the boost you need, while others will be perfect for a special friend, sister, daughter, or mother.

Why chocolate? Because women and chocolate are made for each other! We've never needed science to tell us that chocolate releases those "feel-good" endorphins. We've known that all along. Just like the rich taste of chocolate, the stories here will bring you a warm sense of satisfaction deep down inside. You can almost taste the love that abounds within these pages, the thought-provoking moments of truth.

Ever since I was inspired—divinely, I believe—to create the Chocolate series, I've been moved to deepen my spiritual path. As I've embraced my role as a teller and keeper of stories for and by women, I've discovered much about myself in a very short period of time. Never before have I been put to the test in so many ways. Never before have I been so excited and scared at the same time. Like many of the women you will read about here, I've had to learn to trust myself and tap into my intuition during challenging situations.

My wish for you is that these rich stories serve as a catalyst —as they have for hundreds of thousands of women who have already found the Chocolate stories—so that you can move through your own fears, follow your intuition, discover love, and identify your own personal greatness.

Women from all over the country, and even all over the world, have contacted me with their own stories about how *Chocolate for a Woman's Heart* and *Chocolate for a Woman's Soul* have boosted their spirits and touched their lives. Now it's your turn to treat yourself to these tales or share their gift of inspiration with someone you love. Open up this book the way you would a box of chocolates, and sample the delicious morsels within. And rejoice in the shared experiences of women as their stories warm your heart and feed your soul.

Kay Allenbaugh

PART ONE

CHOCOLATE

for a

WOMAN'S HEART

I

DIVINE INTERVENTION

*"You block your dream
when you allow your fear
to grow bigger than your faith."*

—MARY MANIN MORRISSEY

BACK-SEAT DRIVER

My *father died when I was ten years old. I used* to wake up and hear my mother crying. Angry at my father for dying, I told myself that I would never get married and let a man hurt me like my mother was hurting.

Life went on. As I grew older, my youth leaders said that I would grow up and find a young man whom I would want to marry. The hurt from my father's death was still too fresh for me to take that prediction to heart.

One night in prayer, I explored my strong feeling that I didn't think I could ever let myself love someone who could hurt me. If I was intended to marry, how could I lower my barriers enough to be receptive? As I prayed, I asked for help. I felt a great calm and peace come over me.

After graduating from high school, I went to the University of Arizona. Coming home from a party, a nice young man offered me a ride. I knew him only through mutual friends. We were getting acquainted through small talk when we pulled up to a stoplight.

"This is the man you will marry!" a voice from the back seat said. I turned around to see who was sitting in the back. No one was there.

"Did you just hear someone?" I asked my companion. "No," he replied.

I continued to think about what I'd heard. I realized it was an answer to my prayer so very long ago!

Eight months later, I married that young man. We have been married twenty-four years and have six beautiful children.

I still marvel that my childhood prayer was answered like

clockwork at the perfect moment. I heard one more comment from the "back seat" that fateful night. The Divine voice said, "You asked me to tell you."

ANAMAE ELLEDGE

A DREAM COME TRUE

Following World War II, I was living the American dream—a cozy cottage, Betty Crocker in the kitchen, rambling roses on the picket fence, a baby carriage in the nursery, a savings account, and Gold Bond stamps.

In the early stages of my second pregnancy, nasty telltale signs of impending trouble appeared one afternoon. I began bleeding heavily, and my doctor advised me to get myself immediately to the hospital, where he would meet me.

When I was propped up in the strange comfort of my hospital bed, my feet raised high and cold packs resting on my belly, Dr. Weiker told me he would wait for the lab report and decide on a plan of action the following morning. With a reassuring smile and friendly wishes for a good night, he left. Soon after that, my husband, edgy and nervous, went home to take care of our little boy.

Left to myself in the quiet of my cheerful hospital room, I speculated on what was happening in my body and wondered if I would lose the baby whose living presence I already loved and cherished. I forced myself to concentrate on stilling my worries and dwelling on only that which would be best for the baby. The dark night sky closed in on my room as I drifted peacefully off to sleep, ready for dreams to tell me a story.

An image of a small summer garden appeared in a dream. It was ablaze with tall white daisies and dazzling snapdragons. Blue skies and dappled sunlight enhanced the colors of the flowers. Just then a tiny girl came into my vision and walked toward me. She had soft golden-brown curls and light-brown eyes set wide apart in a round, adorable face. She was dressed in a white-and-blue gingham dress, with a white piqué Peter Pan collar and narrow white cuffs on puffed sleeves. The letters *ABC* were embroidered in bold bright-red yarn across the top of her dress. Suddenly her little face took on a sad expression, and from her rosebud mouth there issued a bell-like voice. "Mommy, Mommy, don't let them take me away from you!" she pleaded.

Voiceless, I screamed, unable to stop until I awoke—a hand on my shoulder gently shaking me back into reality. The kind face of a nurse loomed over me. "Don't be afraid," she said in a soothing voice. "Everything will be all right. Go back to sleep. No more nightmares. Good night."

I nodded sleepily and obediently closed my eyes, holding the vision of the little girl in my mind. No sooner had I drifted back into sleep than I found myself in the garden once more, and the tiny girl once again transfixed me with her eyes. She pleaded shrilly, "Mommy, Mommy! Don't let them take me away from you!"

That time I woke up to my own shouting, which soon turned to tears and a few moments of uncontrolled sobbing. Once again the nurse appeared, put her arms around me, and quietly talked me back into the peaceful quiet of my room. Dawn came slowly, erasing the shadows of the dark night and filling me with a sense of purpose and a strange knowing of untold secrets.

My doctor appeared early in the morning, all dressed in surgical greens, a mask dangling from his handsome face. "All set for the D and C," he announced. "The lab reports indicated you've miscarried. We'll clean you out, and in three months you can start thinking again about having a baby," he concluded, matter-of-factly.

"I'm pregnant," I announced. "I'm not going to have a D and C, and furthermore," I added triumphantly, "I'm going to have a little girl in seven months."

He looked at me in surprise, remarking that he'd always thought I was a sensible, rational person with both feet on the ground. I should put fanciful thoughts out of my mind and get on with my life. We argued back and forth for quite a while, until finally he gave in to my request for a new pregnancy test before hauling me off to the operating room. He departed with an injured air to the set of his squared shoulders. I went back to sleep.

Several hours later, he walked into my room, no longer dressed in greens. He stood at the foot of my bed, shaking his head, and said, "Well, you were right! You *are* pregnant. You must have aborted a twin."

When I answered his question as to how I knew I was pregnant, he looked even more puzzled than during our previous argument. He shook his head, gave me a hug, and left. I suppose what I told him—my dreams of a little girl—was just too much for his scientific mind and medical training. I never told my story to anyone else, but I promised myself that one day I would tell it to my daughter. I was quite certain I would have a girl!

Seven months later, almost to the day, I gave birth to a healthy little baby girl, with a tiny round face and golden fuzz for hair. My doctor could only shake his head again and, in a somewhat exasperated tone of voice, mumble something under his breath about "Women . . . their dreams . . . their intuition . . . their spooky ways."

Happily, I took my daughter home, marveling at her light-brown eyes, which seemed to stay locked onto mine, telling me things I needed to know.

The first baby present to arrive in the mail was sent by a good friend of mine who lived in New York City. She knew nothing about the circumstances of my daughter's birth. When I opened the gaily wrapped box and gently parted the protective layers of crisp tissue paper, I lifted out a white-and-blue gingham dress with a white piqué Peter Pan collar and white cuffs on puffed sleeves. The letters *ABC* were embroidered in bold bright-red yarn across the top.

URSULA BACON

SMALL MIRACLES

*I*t was a breathless July day. *Humidity clung in foggy clouds on windows and dripped down perspiring fore-heads.* In sauna-like conditions, the annual baseball playoff game was in progress. Anxious parents stuck to metal bleachers, and tension escalated as the championship game approached.

Adam was the littlest guy on his team. All season, he'd been hitless. Sitting on the bench gave him time to think about things and to remember his big brother Neal, his hero.

Four summers earlier, Neal had died in an accident. Adam missed him, especially now with his team needing help. He wished his big brother were here to root him on.

Adam's team was behind 5–4 with two outs as the game drew to a close. When Adam heard his name called, he walked hesitantly up to bat. The outfielders moved in when they saw the little batter step up to the plate. Adam swung at the first pitch. "Stee-rike one!" called out the umpire. The second wobbly swing brought "Stee-rike two!" Hope dwindled as fans and teammates gathered their things to leave.

But wait! Hold everything! Our hearts were in our throats as we noticed something happening with Adam. A look of confidence crossed his face as he gripped the bat, waiting for the final pitch. Was it the spirit of his brother encouraging him on? Was it Adam wanting to show Neal he could do it? In that magical moment, Adam's third swing connected with the ball! He quickly found himself standing on first base, dazed and triumphant. Fans and teammates jumped to their feet, cheering! Maybe Neal was there after all!

That's all it took to get the team fired up. Encouraged by Adam's moment of glory, the next few batters got hits also. Soon Adam touched home plate with the winning run. The moment he crossed the plate, the crowd heard Adam yell "Yes!"

The little guy with big courage taught us some important life
lessons:

- *Yes* to small miracles!
- *Yes* to heroes and the example they set!
- *Yes* to never giving up!
- *Yes* to stepping up to bat in life!

JILL AND CANDIS FANCHER

A WISE MAN, A MENTOR, OR AN ANGEL?

My hands rushed to my face, and I sobbed with joy. After five attempts, I had finally won the title of Miss Hawaii. Flashbulbs flickered like little lightning bolts, congratulations echoed from the crowd. After the festivities had wound down, I headed to my dressing room, alone. I saw him then. A man in his forties with a quiet, kind face, dressed in bland colors and smoking a pipe. He was portly, with gentle brown eyes framed by eyeglasses and wispy hair combed straight back. The aroma of his cherry pipe tobacco was instantly comforting.

"Congratulations! You deserved to win," he said.

How did he know that? "Who are you?"

"My name is George." His smile disappeared, and his eyes turned serious. "We need to talk, Donna. Ten o'clock tomorrow at the coffee shop."

I was tempted to laugh at first, but my curiosity won out. He wasn't menacing, just sure of himself. I nodded yes.

"I sensed your hesitation, and I do intend to justify my actions by passing on a message to you."

"OK—let's hear it."

"To fulfill your destiny, Donna, you must leave the Hawaiian Islands next year."

This time I couldn't help laughing. "I love it here."

George sighed. "All right, then, you leave me no choice but to predict three incidents that will occur before we have breakfast tomorrow."

Now what? I thought, and opened my mouth to speak, but George put up his hand.

"Your car will be towed, your kitchen's leaky pipes will burst, and the noiseless third step in your apartment will begin to creak."

By the next morning, everything George predicted had happened. My car wouldn't start, my roommate was in tears because the kitchen pipes were leaking badly, and as I climbed the stairs to my room, I heard a creaking sound, which came from the third step. Over breakfast, I asked how he knew so much about me.

I thought I detected a squint in one eye as he smiled. "We rarely listen to our intuition—our inner voice that tells us what to do. For instance, I know I'm supposed to be in your life, to watch over you and be around when you need me. You must now search for your own truth."

And search I did. I went on to compete in the Miss USA pageant in Miami and lost. The next year I moved to Los Angeles, and I struggled for seven years to become an actress. Meanwhile, George and I talked frequently on the phone or met when he came to L.A. Trying to stay thin and beautiful, I became bulimic and hooked on diet pills. I was alone and miserable, and contemplating suicide, when the phone rang. It was George. He said, "You've got a lot of work to do. Don't you dare think about checking out."

"How did you know?" I asked, dumbfounded.

"I'm leaving Oklahoma. I'll be in L.A. this afternoon, and then we'll talk."

That day, George convinced me to believe in myself again. "Your life will change at thirty. Hang in there for a few more years."

Age thirty sailed in, and I still wanted off this earth. I had hit rock bottom—emotionally, financially, spiritually, and mentally. On March 1, 1978, I boarded a DC-10 from Los Angeles to Hawaii, to emcee a Miss Hawaii pageant. The plane exploded on takeoff, and I was the last to escape the rear section of the flaming aircraft. Transported to a medical triage, I asked where the nearest phone was. This time I called George.

He said, "It has changed, Donna. You can finally see the big picture. It's time to get out of your own way—time to help others."

I didn't understand completely, but I ended up waiving my right to sue the airline and became an envoy for the dead and burned passengers. I fought for better safety regulations and was grilled in court for hours by the big guns representing the airline. After it was over, I stepped down from the witness stand, drained and again alone. When I reached the courthouse parking lot, George was leaning against my car, smoking his pipe.

"I just got to town," he said. "Let's get an ice cream and walk on the sand."

Watching the sun set over Santa Monica Beach, I babbled countless questions and George patiently answered every one. I felt restored by his philosophy, insight, and truth.

"Understand," he said, "we all have fears, but our destiny is to conquer them." I knew at that moment that I would go on to teach survival skills.

"George, please tell me," I begged, "will I marry, have children, and be happy?"

He looked out over the sea and spoke in measured words. "You'll have a daughter late in life, and oh, yeah, she'll be a pistol. She'll have your energy and will be a leader. The bonding between you and your daughter will be miraculous." A smile lit up his face. "And, Donna, she'll come to you."

"What exactly do you mean by that?" I asked.

"The truth is inside you. Trust yourself. Pursue your destiny with power."

It was later that I learned I was not destined to give birth. I put in for an adoption, only to be overlooked by the birth mothers year after year. I worried that single moms over forty were not on their agenda.

George passed away suddenly, from cancer. I was devastated. I never got to say good-bye. The last time I spoke to him, George had said, "Your daughter is coming—and I'll be there."

Three more years passed before I got a call from Las Vegas. My prayers had been answered. I was ecstatic. A birth mother and father chose me. I had six short weeks to deal with the mounds of paperwork required for the adoption.

I named my baby Mariah. Seventy-two hours after her birth, the final papers were ready to sign. The birth mother was pushing Mariah in her bassinet down the brightly lit hospital corridor, and she said indignantly, "I smell pipe smoke. Can you imagine that—and in a baby nursery?" My heart flip-flopped and I was frozen to the spot as I watched her dart from room to room, searching for the offender. When she returned, she said, "That's odd—there's no one here. I know I smelled cherry tobacco. Did you?"

Tears welled up in my eyes and streamed down my cheeks. "Yes."

"Donna, what's wrong?" she asked.

"I don't know if you believe in the spiritual world, but there was a man named George who was always there for me in my times of great need. He told me years ago, just before he died, I would have a daughter and he'd be here when that happened. George smoked cherry tobacco in his pipe."

My birth mother stared at me wide-eyed and said, "I chose you because I feel this child is going to become a leader and I can't give her what she needs, but you can."

She bent over the bassinet and lifted the baby up to me. I smiled down at Mariah and murmured to her, "What do you think, darling? Was George a wise man, a mentor, or an angel?"

DONNA HARTLEY

TURNING POINT

There's a very fine line between having a nightmare and having a dream.

Cruising along Interstate 55, Mom and Dad were on their way to a trailer show in St. Louis. At one point, they were following a motor home. As a long time RVer, Dad sees things on the road that others don't see. "That motor home isn't tracking properly," he said to my mom. "There's a slight wobble in the left rear wheel."

Knowing how dangerous a loose wheel could be, and fearing the worst, he decided to alert the driver. He pulled toward the front of the motor home and said, "Rose, why don't you get the driver's attention? See if you can get them to pull over." Mom began to wave at the woman driving the motor home and to point toward the rear of her RV. The woman ignored her.

A bit frustrated by the woman's refusal to respond, Dad considered it might not be worth the effort to get them to stop. He dropped back to take another look at their rear wheel, and shook his head. "That's not safe. Their wheel could fall off and the motor home would tip over. At sixty mph, it would kill them. If I have to, I'll run them off the road."

As providence would have it, there was a truck weigh station just ahead. If it was necessary to run someone off the road, Dad knew this would be the place to do it. He drove his car closer and closer to the motor home, honking his horn, while Mom motioned to the driver to pull over. The woman had little choice but to comply.

Dad stopped the car to get out. Now he was the one in danger. Running a stranger off the road simply isn't a wise thing to do in the nineties. Mom said, "It might be better if I get out with you, dear. We'll appear less threatening that way." By now the man on the passenger side of the motor home, who had been sleeping, was walking toward Dad. Pointing to Mom and Dad, his wife said, "Those people just ran us off the road."

Dad, keeping his distance, raised his hands where they could be seen. He said, "You might be pretty angry for what I just did. I'm an RVer too. I know I'd be angry. Before you do anything, just walk to the back of your motor home and take a look at your left rear wheel."

Not quite knowing what to make of my folks, the man walked with some hesitation toward the back of his motor home. He looked at the wheel, then removed the hubcap. Two lug nuts fell to the ground. Realizing the wheel had been close to falling off, he was visibly shaken. He walked up front and told his wife about the possible disaster they had just avoided.

She burst into tears and hugged both my parents, clinging tight. Finally able to talk, she said, "Last night I dreamed that I was driving down the road and lost control of our motor home. It began weaving back and forth wildly. I shouted to my husband, and he turned to me just as we began to roll over. I woke up with a start and lay in bed shaking, because it had seemed so real."

My dad had demonstrated that if we pay attention, each of us has opportunities daily to divinely influence the lives around us.

Seize those opportunities.

Thwart nightmares.

Be a dream weaver.

REV. DEBORAH OLIVE

DIVINE ASSISTANCE

*S*everal years ago, I visited a young mother at home.
The doctors said she had just a few days to live, as the
cancer she had battled so courageously had advanced
throughout her body.

Seeing her during those last days had been particularly hard
for me. Sally was one of the most beautiful people I have ever
experienced. Long before she had cancer, I remember watching
Sally leave church one Sunday morning and thinking: She is too
gentle for this world. She had a purity about her.

Dealing with her cancer was the fight of her life. She had
done everything that her church teaches. She had done everything she learned in her Native American tradition. She had
done everything that medical science offered her—surgery, chemotherapy, radiation, and even a bone marrow transplant.
Nothing stopped the cancer. Sally began to accept that she
would soon make her transition.

I remember getting ready to go visit her to say good-bye and
be with her. It was a very hard thing for me to do. While
putting my makeup on, I heard a voice say, "Tell her about the
angels." And I immediately said, "No way! She doesn't want to
hear that. She's already pretty angry as it is."

While I drove to her home, that voice kept saying, "You tell
her about the angels." And I thought: I will not. Yes, I talk to
angels, but I've never seen one. I'm not going to tell her about
the angels this morning.

Having made that decision, I walked into her home. And it
happened. Even though the lights were dimmed, the room
glowed with a brilliant radiance—a radiance that had no apparent source. I had never been in so awesome a presence! I went
to my knees the moment I walked into that room. I didn't
think, I just went down in honor and respect. All my resistance
against speaking of angels vanished.

Sitting there in silence, I felt an absolute sense of peace. Sally looked over at me, and I saw anger in her eyes. She asked me, "Why?" That's a tough question to answer for a dying woman in the prime of her life, with two beautiful sons and a husband she cherished.

I told her the only truth I knew: "I don't know. I do not know. But I need to tell you something very important. When you're ready to make your transition, the angels will come for you, and your most beloved relatives will be there with you. You don't have to be afraid. You will see a great light."

She looked over at me, and the anger disappeared. Her face became as radiant as the room. "Then it's begun," she whispered. "It's already started." And she went back into peaceful silence.

At Sally's memorial service, I shared with her relatives my reluctance to tell her about the angels. "Well, maybe we should tell you what happened while you were visiting Sally that morning," one of them responded. They had left Sally alone for a few hours, knowing I was coming. While they ate lunch at the kitchen table, a garbage truck went by, making its regular pickups. They noticed that something fell off the back as the truck drove off. Out of curiosity, they went outside to see what it was.

What they found was as powerful as Sally's illuminated room. What they found reinforced the persistent message I'd heard while getting ready to see Sally for the last time. What they found convinced me of what I knew but could not see. The book that fell out of the passing garbage truck was titled *Angels on Assignment*.

REV. MARY OMWAKE

> *"Women never have young minds.*
> *They are born three thousand years old."*
> —SHELAGH DELANY

EARTH ANGEL

I teach Reiki, an ancient system of hands-on healing. In the advanced classes, I instruct my students to send healing energy to others at a distance, or even backward in time. Esoteric concepts to be sure, but nonetheless quite possible.

While driving through Montana with a friend on our way to a seminar, I was lost in thought as I watched one rolling hill after another melt into the overcast sky. There were few cars on the open road, so we were surprised to see the flashing lights up ahead in the distance. "Oh, no, an accident," I said to myself. We slowed down, and as we passed the scene of chaos I gasped. A car had rolled over completely, and its contents were strewn all over the grass lining the highway. Paramedics were just lifting a person on a stretcher into the ambulance. "Dear God," I prayed, "please help them." I remembered my Reiki training and started to send healing energy back in time to arrive at the moment of the accident. I prayed that my work might have some good effect.

All of a sudden, I felt the familiar sensations of healing energy running up and down my spine, much stronger than ever before. It was as if I had been plugged into a light socket, the electrical sensations were so intense. I'm lucky my friend is driving, I thought. Seconds later, my eyelids became heavy and my head slumped forward as I slipped into a dreamlike state. In this condition of altered awareness, I went back in time, watching the car roll. Immediately, as if someone had hit Rewind on the scene, I was in spirit form, inside the car, moments before the vehicle careened out of control. I felt a sickening lunge as the car began to flip. In my spirit form, I held the woman as she rolled and held her closer as the car rolled again. Infinite tenderness and love seemed to flow through me and out of my hands.

My awareness shifted back to the car I was riding in. I felt a tremendous heat flaming through my abdomen and in the small of my back. "Feel this," I mumbled to my friend. He reached over and put his hand on my back. "Wow!" He kept driving as I slipped back into the "dream."

I heard a voice echoing as if we were underwater. The voice became clearer. "This is her sister. Tell her I love her." I felt a huge presence of love flow through my heart and course through my veins. The moment of altered awareness ended, and I burst back into the present time.

Something transformational had happened within me. Tears of joy welled up in me, so great had been the love I'd just felt. By now we were miles past the accident. "She's OK," I told my friend as I dried my eyes. I just knew.

We arrived at a beautiful ranch nestled in an old pine forest, where we would be studying a Native American perspective on healing and living in balance. I became absorbed in the workshop activities, as the incident on the road faded into a memory. Two days into the seminar, however, a remarkable announcement was made by the seminar leader. "We are pleased to announce," the facilitator said, "that one of your fellow students will soon be joining you. Janine was in a bad accident on her way here." I stopped eating. With my fork still in midair, I listened intently. "Her car rolled over two and a half times, but miraculously she was unhurt. She has only minor cuts and some bad bruises." "My God," I said to myself. "She's the one."

When I introduced myself to Janine, I held back tears and told her what I'd "seen." Somewhat shyly—because I didn't know how she'd take it—I mentioned the message from her sister. She looked at me, her eyes widening. "I felt like angel hands were holding me," she said simply. "And yes, my sister did pass away some time ago. I've always felt she was with me." We looked into each other's eyes, soul-to-soul and saw the connection that bridges time and space.

Some things defy explanation and logic. Sometimes we just intuitively know. Down to my core, I know that my prayer was answered. I had a special opportunity to influence and protect the life of another being. I got to experience the profound honor of momentarily being an earth angel.

ANN ALBERS

> *"Change doesn't happen in the middle.*
> *It only happens when we venture over to the edge*
> *and take one small step after another."*
> —Karen Sheridan

OUR TEACHERS COME IN MANY FORMS

Our chauffeured bus meandered lazily along the country road, heading to a vineyard for a charity auction to benefit the Salvation Army. A group of us from a local business club rode together. Looking out the window to watch the sun peeking through the continuous stream of birch and maple trees was relaxing.

The low hum of many private conversations could be heard throughout the bus. My husband, Eric, and our friend Phyllis and I were huddled together in the back. Our exchanges quickly went from casual conversation to "How are you *really?*"

I found myself once again pouring out my fear of public speaking. With my first book about to be published, I knew it was my job to publicly promote it. I questioned why I had put myself in this predicament. My book included inspirational stories from speakers around the country—women who couldn't wait to get in front of a group and empower others. I thought they were the natural ones to talk with the media, sharing their uplifting messages from the book, thus letting me off the hook. But God had a bigger vision for me! It was as if He had played a joke on me. In reality, the author needs to be "out there" speaking to groups too. Listening to His guidance had taken me this far down the path, and now there was no turning back. I had to grow!

Aware of my inner struggle, Phyllis pulled out a small velvet bag, loosened the tassel bow, and told me to reach in and choose a card at random. The affirmation card I selected read: *"Breakthrough . . . You will be changed at depth . . . You will not recognize yourself."* We laughed, yet we wondered about the message. Was a big change coming my way? Did I hold any stock in this process? We nestled back in our seats, keeping our thoughts to ourselves.

At that moment, I felt a power surge in my heart. It was a distinct physical sensation of being filled up. "It's the craziest thing!" I told Phyllis. "My body feels like it just got a dose of confidence!"

An hour later, at the vineyard, we sat at picnic tables covered with red-and-white checkered tablecloths and ate our box lunches. The coordinator of the event introduced the fund-raising auctioneer.

The bidding for a case of Merlot wine was going at a snail's pace when my husband shouted out to the auctioneer, "I'll give you one hundred dollars."

With no response from the quiet crowd, I shouted out, "I'll give you two hundred dollars." My confident tone surprised both me and Eric. The crowd roared as they observed our banter as we competed for the same case of wine.

"We're in this together, babe," Eric said with a laugh. But my enthusiasm to use my newfound voice could not be contained. We got ourselves a case of wine for far more than we needed to pay for it.

The auctioneer pulled me up front with him, knowing my enthusiasm would be contagious to potential bidders. I found myself speaking with and leading a group that had become responsive to my spontaneity. The bidding back and forth increased and influenced others to give to a good cause. Where had this new freedom come from—not only to speak but to shout in joy in front of a group? I believe I was being shown that I could indeed do what I feared I could not. It was as if God was saying, "Your fear of speaking is not serving you well. I'm always here to support you. Release the fear, and go forward in joy."

Our teachers come in many forms. It's amazing what happens when we put ourselves in an open, learning, receptive mode. Selecting an affirmation card felt unfamiliar, yet the "perfect" message I got was just the boost I needed to learn and grow.

You see, God filled me up right where I was. I may not always hear an important message in the most conventional way. The lyrics in a song on the radio may give me what I need at a special time. Or the words in a greeting card from a friend may inspire me. A powerful quote from an ancient teacher may stir my soul, or I may discover my next life step as the wind brushes my cheek while I hike in the woods.

With many radio and TV shows behind me, amazing things have happened since that turning point when I stepped through the doorway of fear into a world of trust. I now remember God's words to us all: "If you knew who walked with you, how could you be afraid?"

KAY ALLENBAUGH

II
GROWTH
SPURTS

"Like yourself now. Be ten years ahead of your friends."

—JENNIFER JAMES

> *"There is no power on earth that can withstand the power of love.*
> *By loving our enemies*
> *we turn them into friends."*
> —STELLA TERRILL MANN

ANGEL OF THE LORD

I kept an eye on the disheveled young man dressed in black leather who stood near the chapel. As a security guard for a hospital in Georgia, I checked people out, particularly those who looked suspicious. When I asked this young man if I could help him, he told me he was waiting for someone. I made a mental note to keep close tabs on him. Returning later to look for him, I found him gone.

A while later, I patrolled the hospital corridors and saw that young man fast asleep on a pew in the chapel. He no longer looked to be a threat. He looked like a wet puppy brought in from the cold November day. As I watched him sleep, I remembered what my mom had told me as a child: "No matter who you come in contact with, no matter how ragged they look, treat them kindly—they could be an angel of the Lord."

I asked Easter, my co-worker and friend, to help me. We dug in our purses, pooled our change, and bought a lunch from the cafeteria for this shabby stranger. I set the food tray beside him, tucked a pillow under his head, and covered him with a blanket —careful not to wake him.

When he awoke the next morning, I had gone home from work. He found Easter and asked her who had been so kind to him the night before. He was surprised to learn that this act of kindness had come from a black security guard.

His expression was one of despair and confusion as he confessed, "I've never been around a black person before. Everything my friends taught me about blacks is untrue. I was told they are out to cut your throat. That doesn't make sense. I've got to sort out some things."

Because of our special encounter, we each got to see each other with acceptance rather than judgment. For this young man to recognize me as a person and for me to recognize his need for compassion changed both our lives forever. A moment of healing allowed us never to see things as we did before. This experience caused me to ask, "What if we looked upon each person we met as an angel of the Lord?"

You never know when an act of kindness will draw people together. With some apprehension, this scruffy stranger took off his worn jacket, rolled up his shirtsleeve, and revealed to Easter a startling tattoo symbolizing who he used to be. It read: *Ku Klux Klan*.

ARLINE CRAWFORD BURTON

JUST A HAIR MORE LOVE

I *always had a difficult relationship with the wavy,* thick patch of black that crowned my small head like a jester's hat. Footloose and free-spirited, it chose a new course with each sunrise. It tumbled down my forehead one day and curled cavalierly backward the next. I should have loved its impetuous nature, its fearless embrace of change, its sparkle and shine. Instead I have done battle with my hair for almost four decades, shamelessly attempting to break the spirit of those now silver-streaked locks. Despite endless coaxing, cajoling, and threats, I could never get those wild things to work together to produce what could be viewed as a hair style. Bereft of all hope, I yielded smoldering dissatisfaction to outright disdain for my hair.

I, who always believed in the underdog . . . I, who still gave loose change to men wandering skid row . . . I, who woke up smiling with the conviction that every day offered new promise . . . I, who bought cookies, candy bars, wrapping paper and losing raffle tickets from every child who rang the doorbell . . . I, who thought my earnest study of various spiritual traditions testified to my personal evolution—I could not love my own hair.

In desperation, I began to meditate about it. I burned incense. I held a smudging ceremony in my bathroom. I knelt before the Hair Goddess and begged for mercy. Then it happened—a pure and direct connection to the Divine. The Hair Goddess spoke:

My child, long have I waited for you. Coveting thy neighbor's hair is wrong. Hair spray, mousse, and the blow dryer are all false gods. Inner peace and wisdom are attained by honoring the wildness of your hair. Do not resist it; embrace it.

With that the Hair Goddess faded. I called out to her, but she said no more. And so I began the long journey toward loving my hair. When I got frustrated, I apologized; when I flew into a rage and scowled in the mirror, I put myself in time out. Within a year's time I was having a love affair with my hair. I had a sophisticated hairstyle, and I reveled in the compliments I received.

One day I went to my usual salon for a little trim, and something went terribly wrong. Despite my instructions, my perfect hairstyle was snipped into thousands of lost locks on the floor. Too upset to speak, I drove home in a daze. Tears in my eyes, I knelt once more before the great Hair Goddess, seeking solace and answers. The goddess appeared and kissed me gently on the forehead. A smile began to play upon her lips, and she spoke: "This was only a test. Had this been a real hair emergency, you would have had a job interview tomorrow."

O. C. O'CONNELL

SOULMATING

When my son, Ryan, went off to college, I was confident I had instilled in him the qualities that would prepare him to be a good citizen of the world. Then I held my breath. Kids were kids. It was his first taste of freedom. He was going to screw up. It was inevitable.

I had no time for the "empty nest syndrome." I was preparing my lines for the kinds of calls we children of the sixties and seventies gave our parents. "Hiya, Ma! I'm in jail. . . . But it was just beer! They said it was legal on campus!" Stuff like that.

Two weeks later, Ryan came home to Houston, laundry bag in hand. When I asked him how he found college—other than filthy, judging from the amount of dirty clothes he had—he said, "Well, you know, Mom, there are some really, really weird people on campus."

I imagined perverts, druggies, gangsta-type seniors, HIV-positive coeds pursuing their MRS. I asked, "Like how weird?"

"Like nutzoid. Mike and Carl and I went over to Darcy's room to meet her roommate and some other freshman girls. We were all crammed in this room and talking, and this one girl starts singing! Bursts into song. Not soft, but loud. Like kinda drowning out what we were trying to say. It was weird."

"The songs were weird?"

"No, *she* was weird. She wouldn't give it a rest, either. She would just keep humming to herself, even while we were talking."

"Where was she from?"

"Houston. And she didn't even know her roommate, Mom! She was assigned to her room."

"Imagine that!" I said, remembering my own experience (wasn't that just last week?), when *all* our roommates were strangers.

"What kind of person wouldn't hand-pick their roommate?"

At this point I'm getting an uneasy feeling. He's acting a bit too assertive and sheepishly avoids eye contact.

"Ryan, by any chance did you make fun of that girl?"

Silence.

My skin crawled with goose bumps, and suddenly I envisioned myself in that room with those kids. I felt I knew them all, except for the singing girl. I certainly knew the razor-keen sense of humor my son possessed. He could give Robin Williams a run for his money. I felt the pain, embarrassment, and loneliness of the singing girl.

There were tears in my eyes. "Ryan, you've always been too picky about people. I think you said something to hurt this girl. Something that maybe didn't seem like much to you but to her was biting and dreadful. The minute you get back to campus, I want you to find that girl, and you apologize to her."

"Aw, Ma . . ."

Ryan went back to school on Sunday night, and he called me the next night. "Mom, you know the singing girl? She's gone! Her roommate told me that she left campus. Dropped out! Went back home and enrolled at the University of Houston. It's all my fault, Mom. I just know I hurt her, like you said."

The year passed, and Ryan came home from college, older and wiser. That summer, he worked long hours doing hard labor for his father and me in our swimming pool and spa business.

He and the crew delivered a spa to one of our customers, who telephoned my husband later that day and said, "My daughter saw a young man delivering our spa, and she would like to go out with him, but she's too shy to ask. Could you tell me who the tall blond boy is?"

"My son," my husband answered. "I'll be happy to pass along the message."

Ryan was puzzled. "I never saw a girl there. But I do remember somebody watching through the curtains at the bedroom window. Maybe that was her."

Ryan, who liked to make new friends, called Christy and

made a date. The following Saturday night, after meeting her parents, he walked Christy to his car. When they were about to pull away from the curb, Ryan turned to her and said, "You were the singing girl in Darcy's room."

"Yes, Ryan, I was."

"I'm so sorry for how I treated you."

"I know you are, Ryan."

When Ryan came home that night and told me the story, we both had tears in our eyes. I was flooded with that incredible feeling I get when I know my life has been divinely touched.

I looked at my son and said, "Ryan, you're going to marry that girl someday."

"I know, Mom," he said—and he did, several years later.

Of all the joys in my life, knowing that my son found his soul mate is the greatest of them all.

Just think if Ryan had not budged from his first impression. It reminded me of the saying I shared with him when this whole episode started: "Be careful," I had said. *What you focus on determines what you miss!*

CATHERINE LANIGAN

"I think the one lesson I have learned
is that there is no substitute for paying attention."
—DIANE SAWYER

MOVING THE MOON

I was sitting under a sycamore tree, reading, one late afternoon, while my daughter, too young to be a swimmer, wandered back and forth on the top steps of our pool. Suddenly she called out, "Mom, look! The moon!"

Wanting to be left to my reading, I said in a tone that I hoped conveyed this, "Honey, I can't see it from under this tree."

"That's okay," she said. "I'll move it so you can."

Move the moon? She had my attention. She began walking across the pool steps and, from her perspective, pulled the moon away from the tree.

"The moon follows me," she confided matter-of-factly.

Now, fully aware that this was one of those magic moments of motherhood, I closed the book and walked out from under the tree.

"Yes, I can see it now."

It was beautiful in the almost evening light—a near-full moon with one blurred edge.

"Thank you for showing me the moon," I said, and meant it.

"Why does the moon follow me?" she said, with the pleased self-assurance of a starlet.

I paused and reflected before I answered. With my first child, I would have rattled off scientific facts about perspective and perception. If my second child had asked about the moon following him, I would have said, "I knew that answer once. I think I remember where to look it up. I'll make a note of it. I'll get back with you on that."

But this child, this magic fairy being, who *knows* the moon is following *her*—what do I say to her? I knew that soon enough someone (probably a brother) would inform her roughly that the moon does *not* follow her. Or in the slow brutality of growing up it would gradually seep into her awareness that the moon couldn't be following her. And as she moved into adulthood, she would forget she had that magic and at some point, like me, forget all about the moon and even stop looking at it.

"Look! I'm making it jump up and down. See it?" she called out anew.

I was still in a reverie. Then—I am ashamed to admit it, but it happens to us mothers occasionally—I had a momentary lapse. After all, she was interrupting my great train of thought. She was saying, "Did you see me make the moon jump up and down?" and I responded, testily, too testily, "No, I didn't."

She stopped and looked at me inquisitively. "You didn't?" She was so pure—it slapped me in the face, and I recovered.

"Let me see it again," I said.

She jumped. I jumped. I saw it.

"You are right," I said. "It's jumping."

She smiled a brilliant smile of confidence.

Einstein said, "If you want your children to be brilliant, tell them fairy tales. If you want them to be very brilliant, tell them even more fairy tales."

I hope she always remembers that wondrous perspective and her magical ability to do amazing things. I know I will never forget, because for me, my magic fairy child will always move the moon.

SARAH JORDAN

HEALING WITH LOVE

Someone once asked me what was the worst thing I'd ever done, and I answered without hesitation: "I was so self-absorbed that I didn't nurture Rich enough when he was a baby." Rich is the second of my four children, born when I was nineteen years old. I certainly cared for him in all the physical ways a mother cares for her child. I fed him properly, changed his diapers, kept him clean, and ensured that he got the proper amount of sleep.

Still, if you're a parent, you know that's not enough. Usually, the intimacy is almost palpable when you watch a new mother and her infant gazing at each other. I loved my son, but our relationship lacked that bursting abundance of feeling. That sense of rapture, the connection, was missing. Frightened that I would never be able to live my own dream and become a teacher, I had turned myself off. I felt dead inside. I attended to Rich's needs meticulously, but in many ways I was simply going through the motions of motherhood.

At the age of six months, Rich developed a condition in which his body could not retain any nourishment. He ran very high fevers doctors could not control. No matter what we did, Rich continued to lose weight.

The time came when the doctor told me my baby was not likely to survive the night. In the early hours of the morning, I was sitting in a hospital room adjacent to where Rich struggled for life, tubes protruding from his tiny arms. An attending physician explained the severity of Rich's condition, trying to prepare me for the worst. Suddenly I realized I was watching our conversation from the other side of the room. What I had come to identify as "me," my everyday consciousness, was hovering in an upper corner, observing this sterile white room and the people in it in a way that was curiously unattached yet compassionate. I had read about out-of-body experiences but shrugged off those stories. Now I could clearly see the doctor speaking with a young, frightened mother: me.

At the same moment, I could sense my consciousness hovering in Rich's room. Gazing down at my baby, I was overcome with the realization that he was not starving for physical nourishment; rather, he needed the sustenance of the unconditional love I had denied him. His body hungered in that absence, unable to thrive.

In a flash, I found my consciousness back in my body, and I thanked the doctor for his words of condolence. Immediately I headed for Rich's room. Every sense in my body felt keenly aware and awake. As I approached the crib where he lay, my energy seemed to grow and expand to surround my ailing baby son. Suddenly I felt as if I were once again pregnant with my child. I completely enfolded Rich with my love, my being. Careful not to disturb the tubes, I reached into the crib and began stroking his face, reassuring my baby that I would never again deprive him of the love he needed. My heart opened completely. I connected with how much I loved him and wanted him in my life. I matured a great deal in those few minutes. For the remainder of the night, I sat next to Rich's crib, praying and feeling his soft skin against my hand.

Rich survived the night, and slowly the symptoms of his illness subsided. But doctors warned us about permanent neurological damage. When he was one year old, Rich still could not pull himself up. His arms and legs had little strength. In the weeks and months that followed, my husband, our parents, and I concentrated on nothing but pouring love into him. He grew stronger but didn't recover fully until he was almost three.

Years later, as I watched him play football in high school, I could hardly believe that as an infant this vital young athlete had been barely able to move his limbs. We each had experienced our own miracle. His was the miracle of physical healing. Mine was the miracle of moving past fear and doubt into a realm where I was free to love my son.

REV. MARY MANIN MORRISSEY

THE MIRACLE OF SELF-LOVE

Most of my life, I felt my dreams have been just out of reach. It seemed it took so much work to accomplish goals, and I was often left yearning for love or success. I was caught in a trap of working and getting nowhere. When my world appeared to be in complete disorder and I felt the depths of despair, I had been advised over and over again: *Love yourself.*

"How," I would ask, "do I love myself?" I didn't know. To me, loving yourself meant ending the pain with a new outfit or a hot fudge sundae. My mentors and counselors would quickly point out that such a remedy would last only as long as the experience of it lasted. I needed concrete steps to solve my dilemma, not vague advice.

Earning my bachelor's degree while working full time; raising my sons; getting divorced; and having major surgery weren't easy. But they were way stations toward my lifelong dream of living in Seattle.

The first step to my dream was to have a public relations career. What I found in Seattle were few jobs and hundreds of applicants. I struggled for four years, taking jobs on the fringe of public relations. Often I worked a full day, then volunteered and freelanced so I could improve my résumé. It was like holding two full-time jobs. I was deep into struggle and felt self-contempt for my inability to create the job and lifestyle I had dreamed of all those years.

After four years of this vicious circle, I was laid off my permanent job, with no immediate opportunities in front of me. I was scared and worried, yet I continued my "doing," going through the motions of job hunting for months—but with no results. Out of sheer desperation, I felt I had to give up the dream that had kept me going through most of my life.

Wanting to run away to a place of power and beauty, where I wasn't faced with the pain, I took some time away at my cousin's cabin on the ocean.

A remarkable thing happened there. For three days I did nothing but enjoy the scenery, meditate, and read. While checking my phone messages on the fourth day, I heard a call from an association with which I had interviewed months earlier. It was an offer for a public relations position. I realized then that "giving up" the struggle, trusting the process to allow goodness into my life, was the way I had loved myself.

What success I had ever experienced during my life had come to me with a great deal of struggle. This was the first demonstration that consciously letting go and trusting the outcome achieved something I longed for.

After two years, I was offered a wonderful job with the association's national headquarters, in Washington, D.C. It wasn't Seattle, but I didn't question the move, for I had learned that the best things in my life come to me without struggle or pain.

I would like to tell you that I have completely given up struggle, but I can't. Still, I have been blessed with patient friends, a loving family, and caring teachers, who listen to my frantic pleas when I forget I am the child of a loving Father.

I now believe "self-love" means going with ease and releasing the need to try and figure everything out by myself. I ask for help and then let go. I now regularly give God something to do.

JILL GOODWIN

III
FEEDING
A WOMAN'S
HEART

*"Love is a fruit in season at all times
and within reach of every hand."*

—MOTHER TERESA

SNAPSHOTS OF THE HEART

The 1962 August moon gleamed across the white hood of the Ford Fairlane as Jason weaved his car between the huge moss-laden oaks lining my driveway. Shy and silent, I sat close to the passenger door, twisting a piece of my stiffly sprayed brown hair. The car rolled to a stop beneath the security lights that illuminated my home, and for a moment, Jason let the engine idle. With an inaudible sigh, I stole a last look at the Elvis-like lips that complemented his perfectly sculpted nose. The date I had dreamed about all through high school was ending on a "see you next lifetime" note.

Jason squeezed my hand at the door. "We'll do it again, Linda, sometime."

The words I wanted to say clung to my tongue like peanut butter, and instead of encouraging him to ask me out again, I smiled and said, "Thank you for a nice evening."

As we said good night, he squinted in the glare of the bright porch light, then looked at me with eyes that glistened like emeralds. Each of my senses recorded the moment like a snapshot: the sticky summer air touching our clasped hands, moonlight lunging between the tall pines in my yard, a cricket symphony strumming around us. Even his cologne mingled with the smell of the woods and found its way into that snapshot.

After he'd gone, I turned off the lights, while my heart sank like a rock in water. "I blew my chance with Jason!" I cried out, and stood in the dark, leaning against the partially opened front door. As I listened to the low rumble of his car in the distance, I knew my phone would gather a mountain of South Georgia dust before he called again. That night, I swallowed a large, unpalatable lump of rejection.

For days I wallowed in self-disgust over the romance that might have been had I not hidden my true personality under a facade called "the perfect date." If Jason had been unpopular or less intelligent or had a face like Quasimodo, I wouldn't have been afraid to show him the real Linda. But he had been captain of the football and basketball teams, class president, and a DJ at our small-town radio station. Aside from being impressed with his abilities and popularity, I was enamored of his good looks and intimidated by his intelligence.

Thoughts of college soon helped me bury my emotional snapshot of Jason, along with my feelings of rejection.

Twenty-three years later, I saw him at a class reunion.

"You look terrific!" Jason said, hugging me. I remarked about the George Hamilton splashes of gray at his temples. We talked casually, but it wasn't long before an undertow of old fears made me uneasy, and I put a crowd of schoolmates between us.

One spring day in 1996, after surviving most of the adult crises chronicled by Gail Sheehy in her book *Passages,* I answered the phone, surprised to hear a strong masculine voice. He spoke my name with such gusto, I thought I had won the *Reader's Digest* Sweepstakes.

"Linda! Do you know who this is?"

"No," I said, searching a mental file of men in my past.

"This is Jason."

After my initial shock, Jason and I began to piece together our school days. Like a couple of spirited five-year-olds, we plunged into our sandbox of memories and laughed at the many humorous things we did back then. We discussed our lives, faults, and failures with refreshing honesty and began to build a friendship based on truth.

Then out of the blue Jason asked a startling question.

"Linda, do you remember our date after graduation?"

"Well, I remember your old white Ford."

"What happened to us? How did you view that date?"

I laughed. "You rejected me! You never called again."

"No, Linda. I'll tell you what really happened. I was inse-cure," he admitted. "You were aloof, and I came from the poor side of town. I wasn't good enough for you. I was afraid to see you again. But I've thought about you all these years!"

With the honey of his truth, my thirty-four-year-old wall of rejection crumbled like old cookies at the bottom of the Oreo box. I saw the real Jason for the first time—a sensitive, down-to-earth man with a heart of love, a man with fears like me.

It's midsummer now, and I've replaced my old snapshot of Jason with new ones—like the one my senses take each evening when a golden streamer of sunlight stretches across the wide river to Jason and me on the grassy bank. Or the one that records the rhythmic lapping of water against the sailboat as we hang our feet off the floating dock and watch the mid-river porpoise ballet.

Best of all is the picture of tender hugs, rich laughter, and the growing love of two friends who found the courage to make snapshots of the heart together.

LINDA DUNIVIN

THE PAJAMA CONNECTION

People *expected to hear I joined the Peace Corps to* live a life of service, or to help those less fortunate, or at the very least because I'd lost my mind. The truth is I craved adventure, and for someone on a budget that couldn't even qualify as shoestring, it seemed the most convenient way. That is how, at twenty-two, I came to live on a Guatemalan mountaintop, in a mud hut eighteen kilometers from the closest road. The day I moved in, the welcoming committee consisted of one pit viper curled up under the wood-and-rope-frame bed, which I hacked to death with a machete. Shortly afterward, a neighbor stopped by to point out which of the insects inhabiting my adobe walls would "do nothing" and which would "kill you for certain." After the snake incident, the ritual of holding a candle to the wall each evening and squashing scorpions and tarantulas with a hiking boot before retiring to bed seemed like small beans. Under these circumstances, I readily jumped at the invitation to join a male Peace Corps friend on a trek to the ancient Guatemalan capital of Antigua to watch the Super Bowl in an American bar.

Dressed for the long hike and bus ride in 115-degree desert heat, I'd worn a long sheath dress, which hung limply off my body, and tied my red hair in a bun on the top of my head. By the time we reached our destination, sunburned and dirty, we were more than ready to simply sit back and vegetate in front of the TV. It was then that my companion chose to inform me how awful I looked. "On top of which," he said, "that dress looks like a nightgown. You look like you're wearing pajamas." Thinking his teasing was funny, he turned to the crowd of other Peace Corps Volunteers and Americans around us, urging, "Come on, don't you think she looks like she's wearing pajamas?" Slowly the man sitting in front of me turned around and looked me square in the eyes. "I think you look absolutely beautiful," he said, before turning his attention back to the game. I was smitten.

Back in my little hut the next day, I hatched The Plan. Asking around before I left the city, I had discovered that his name was Frank. A fellow Peace Corps Volunteer, he lived in a village ten hours away from mine. My mission was to arrange a chance meeting in the capital, where Volunteers converged the first weekend of each month to receive their monthly living stipend. That way he'd have the opportunity to ask me out—because, as all proper Catholic girls who attended the correct parochial schools learned early in life, a young lady never makes the first move, and she certainly never invites a man on a date. Problem was, the one time I did see him after that, he didn't ask me out, and then I didn't see him again for six months. And so I did what I wish they'd advocate more often in those proper parochial schools: I broke the rules.

I wrote Frank a letter, inviting him to meet me in the capital for dinner the night before the annual Fourth of July party at the American Embassy. I started out by reminding him who I was, and ended by telling him I would send him a telegram closer to the date, letting him know when and where to meet me. "If you're not interested," I concluded, "just don't show up, and I will never bother you again." I made each and every one of the men present in the Peace Corps office read my letter. "What do you think?" I asked. "I want to make sure it doesn't sound too forward or crass." It's perfect, was the resounding reply. "I've waited my whole life to get a letter like this," one dear friend said. "Don't change a thing." So I held my breath, slipped it into his mail slot there in the office, and returned home.

By noon the next day, I'd made the eighteen-kilometer hike up and then back down my mountain: Because of a series of bizarre and unfortunate incidents involving three rattlesnakes, a chicken, and a slab of marble, I found myself hitching a ride back to the embassy to fill out a crime report. Being so near the Peace Corps office for the second time in two days, I figured it made sense to swing by and check to see if Frank had dropped in and read his mail. I strolled through the back door and almost walked right into him, sitting on the edge of the sofa reading my letter. As I watched, he leaned forward, pen in hand, and began writing a note. Realizing he didn't know I stood behind him, I stole in a little closer to read over his shoulder. That way, if the news was bad, I could beat a hasty retreat back out the door without having to bear the humiliation of being turned down in person. "Dear Ellen," his letter began, "You could send me a telegram anytime, anywhere, and I would immediately come to be with you." Tap, tap, tap . . . I poked his shoulder and, to his startled look, smiled and said, "Here I am!"

We walked hand in hand to Burger King—quite the luxurious restaurant in those parts—to plan our first date, one month in the future. Having established the time and place of our next meeting, as well as our coinciding views on Eastern religions and Western politics, we walked to my bus station and he kissed me on the cheek before waving goodbye. When I finally did make it home late that day, I settled down by candlelight to write a letter to a friend back in the States. At the end I added a postscript: "I just made a date with the man I'm going to marry."

Our dinner date in the capital on July 4th turned into a week of breakfasts, lunches, and dinners. Three weeks later—one week before our next planned meeting—a haggard co-worker trekked up my mountain to bring me a telegram. "Let's never spend this much time apart again," it said. "Love, Frank." And we didn't, arranging to travel and work in each other's villages one week every month. On Christmas Eve, in an ancient monastery in the same little town where he first told me I was beautiful, he bent down on one knee and asked me to marry him.

As darkness fell on that magical night, we found a quiet restaurant where we could celebrate our good fortune with wine and cheese and roast lamb—so different from our usual fare of beans and eggs. Christmas being a family holiday in Central America, we were the only guests at the inn until halfway through the meal, when an elderly couple came in and took the table right next to ours. Curious, we thought, that they would sit so close when there were empty tables everywhere. But then our attention turned, and we ceased to notice them. Finished with our meal, we stood to head back out into the night, when the old woman reached out and touched my arm. "Excuse me," she said, as she grasped my hand. "I hate to intrude on such a special night, but I must ask you a question. The two of you look so happy: is this a special occasion?" Frank beamed as he replied, nodding toward me. "Yes, ma'am, it is. Tonight I asked her to become my wife." The old woman turned her gaze to the old man, and the two of them smiled deeply. Then the elderly gentleman looked first at me and then at my husband-to-be. "Fifty years ago tonight, I did the very same thing," he said to Frank. "Our wish for you on this Christmas Eve is that you will always be as happy as we have been."

We were married that spring in Virginia, surrounded by family and cherished friends. In addition to a gift, one woman brought a two-year-old letter with a postscript: "I just made a date with the man I'm going to marry."

ELLEN URBANI HILTEBRAND

> *"If we won't feel our emptiness,*
> *we won't find the depths of love available to us."*
> —DEBORAH OLIVE

PAIRS AND SPARES

As a never-married over-thirty woman, I didn't care for weddings. No, it was stronger than that. I *hated* weddings. I would sit in the pew, watching the church fill up like the loading of the ark, two by two, all the while moaning under my breath, "Where's *my* other giraffe?" The only thing that made this particular wedding bearable was the obvious love the bridal pair had for each other.

The bride and I shared the same first name, which meant that the whole time she was taking her vows, I mentally took them with her—you know, just in case I never got to actually say them myself, or as a means of practice if someday I did marry. When the ceremony concluded, I noticed a handsome, smiling man about two rows back, all by himself. No ring on his left hand. Hmm. I knew vaguely that he worked at the radio station with Doug, the groom. Determined to learn more, I headed in his direction, thinking: Well, I can at least say hello!

So I did. And he did. Nice smile, warm handshake. Then he asked me, "What is that sculpture up in front of the church?" The sculpture was a free-form artistic interpretation of a cross, not an unusual thing to have in a church. He may not know what a cross is, I thought. Hey, he may not know who God is! Maybe I ought to introduce the two of them. Off I went, describing the cross itself, repentance, baptism, Acts 2:38, regeneration, everything this guy needed to know.

I went on and on, as only I can, while he smiled and nodded and smiled and nodded. Hey, I've got a live one here! I thought to myself. Then, slowing down to catch my breath, I said, "So tell me a little about yourself."

"Well . . . ," he said slowly, "I'm an ordained minister."

I was speechless. (This is rare.) "A minister?" I finally said, as a smile slid up one side of his face. "No kidding!" I stammered. "Did I get everything right?"

"You did well," he assured me, and we both laughed.

One thing Bill found out about me right away was that I cared more about his relationship with God than any potential relationship with me. And that was exactly what attracted him to me. That and my level of self-acceptance. And my laugh!

We stood there and talked in the sanctuary until it was empty, and I realized I didn't have the faintest idea where the wedding reception was. Bill had saved the directions and said, "Why don't you follow me?"

Happy to.

At the reception, we kept an eye on each other as we mingled around the room, finally ending up at the same table. (Imagine that.) More talking, more sharing, then finally we exchanged business cards, and I said, "Call me sometime."

Now came the big wait. Four or five days later (not wanting to appear overanxious, he later said), Bill called. I wasn't home, but my answering machine was. I can still remember coming in and finding the usual "0" replaced with a "1." For a single woman who had not dated in years, any night without a "goose egg" on the machine was a good night!

The message was short and sweet. A warm voice with a Kentucky twang said, "I wondered if you might like to go to dinner with me sometime next week?" I might. "Please give me a call back, Liz," were his final words. Not wanting to appear overanxious, either, I waited four or five seconds before dialing his number.

Our first date came two weeks later; our wedding date was exactly eight months after that. (The only reason we waited that long is that it takes a while to special-order a custom-built size twenty wedding gown.) We'll be forever grateful to Liz and Doug for inviting both of us to their wedding, never dreaming that one ceremony would lead to another.

LIZ CURTIS HIGGS

THE LUCKY PHOTO

My dad was a sophomore at Texas A & I, taking twenty-two hours a semester and working his way through school with a job at a place called the Spudnut Shop. A spudnut is a doughnut, except that it's made with potato flour.

Dad had to be at work at three in the morning, to put fresh newspapers on the floor. The papers were supposed to catch the grease and flour. Dad was on his hands and knees that fall, spreading out pages from the *Kingsville Record*. One night his bleary eyes fell on a photo of a young woman who'd been named the local Farm Bureau beauty queen. To Dad, it was the face of an angel. He carefully ripped the picture out of the paper, folded it, and stuck it in his wallet.

Six months flew by. One April day, a fraternity brother asked my dad, "Hey, Darrell, you goin' to the big Lantana ball?"

It was the biggest social event of the school year. It was also costly for a young man struggling to pay tuition.

"Well," Darrell replied, pulling the photo out of his wallet, "if you can get me a date with this girl, I'll go."

"Epsie? Sure, I've known her all my life. You've got a deal, pal."

The day of the ball was rainy. Darrell, in his haste between classes and work, dropped his billfold in a puddle. The picture of Epsie was ruined. He was sad, but then he remembered he'd see the real young lady behind the smile in just a few hours.

The "blind date" (at least it was a blind date for Epsie) was like the stuff you hear about in fairy tales. They danced all night. Darrell thought Epsie was even prettier than her picture. Epsie was still in high school, and she had to be home at midnight. After walking her to her front porch, Darrell kissed her on the forehead and told her he'd call her soon. He didn't tell her right then, but the moment Epsie smiled at him that night, she went from a picture in his wallet to a place in his heart.

Fourteen months later, when Darrell and Epsie became engaged, the newspaper ran the same photo Darrell had torn out the year before, because it was his favorite.

They married in July on Friday the thirteenth, over objections that they were too young and from different religions and that to wed on such a date was unlucky.

The Spudnut Shop no longer exists, but my parents' union is still standing, more than forty years later. I wish I could tell you I look like my beauty queen mother. However, the legacy of love I've inherited is much more important.

Any Friday the 13th is now celebrated in my family, no matter what month it falls in . . . and my dad still carries a yellowed clipping of a girl with big dimples and the eyes of an angel. Dad says Mom is all the luck he's ever needed.

LORRI VAUGHTER ALLEN

"Whoever lives true life will love true love."
—ELIZABETH BARRETT BROWNING

MERCY STREET

I looked down at the all too familiar handwriting and saw the ink beginning to run, a river of tears and snow. Stillness surrounded me, an endless silence as large, heavy snowflakes continued to drift downward from a wintry New York City sky.

My heart ached with love, with longing, and I thought back to his first letter, the one detailing his arrival in Nicaragua and his forever optimistic nature.

My dearest. They always began the same. *My dearest. I miss you terribly and hope all is well. I have been made to feel very welcome. My "practice" consists of a room about six feet by eight, with a bed and a wooden table and two chairs. Sadly, there is no shortage of patients but all the more reason I'm glad I came. There is one other doctor here, Enrique. He is very skilled and, of even more importance, can make sense of my appalling Spanish! I have been telling him all about you. I can't wait to see you again. Love and kisses, Steven.*

Steven and I met in South Africa. I was there making a documentary on apartheid, and he, fresh out of residency, was volunteering with a group called Doctors Without Borders. I liked him the moment we met. He was tall and lean, and he radiated a calm and unpretentious spirit. I liked his smile too. It came easily and would light up his often troubled eyes, if only for a moment. I used to watch him at the makeshift clinic they had set up in Soweto. He was always there, with a consistency that came straight from the heart. He trusted and believed in people, but most of all, he hoped for them.

It was on a Tuesday that he asked if he could accompany me out to one of the homelands, where I had finally been given permission to film. I agreed, and the next twenty-four hours, shared atop an open truck, bouncing along rough terrain, sealed our friendship. I have often thought of our first meeting and have come to believe that there are some people in this world whom we have an unspoken connection to, in a way that defies explanation.

We continued to write to each other when he returned to New York and I went on to South America, to collect stories on *los desaparecidos,* the "disappeared ones." I found myself waiting for his letters with a gothic anxiety. They were long and intimate, like an ongoing conversation, and through our words we came to know each other and, I suspect, ourselves. When I finally returned to New York, the first thing I did was go to see Steven at the hospital where he worked.

I will never forget the look on his face when a colleague of his tapped him on the shoulder and he turned around to see me standing there. I wish I could capture and bottle that moment like a perfume. He came straight over to me, and without saying a word, put his arms around me and gave me the longest and sweetest kiss of my life. Although I never doubted the sincerity of his letters, with that kiss I knew we belonged to each other.

We went out for dinner to a small café that featured home cooking and was frequented by students who missed Mom's meat loaf. I felt an overwhelming happiness that night, the kind you feel when in the company of good friends.

I think one of the things I loved most about Steven was that he preferred conversation to television. He told me that we would be good together because doctors can heal the body, but artists, they heal the soul. I had never thought of myself as an artist, I was just someone who loved making films, the way he loved being a doctor.

We got an apartment together on Mercy Street. He liked the

name and felt it boded well for our future, believing that I would have to have a forgiving nature to put up with his hours, and he as well to accept my "artistic temperament." Not that he ever complained I was moody, "just a million miles away, someplace I can't go." It was prior to our second Christmas that he made his decision to go to work in a remote village in Nicaragua.

We were walking down the hospital corridor, with its pale-green walls decorated with bits of tinsel and drawings the children had done.

I asked him why he wanted to go.

"For the money," he quipped.

"Right," I said. The job paid sixteen dollars a month. "I thought you were happy here."

"When I leave here, there'll be someone to take my place. Besides, you always tell me that if you can help, you should. Remember?"

He had me there, and I reminded myself that he had never once put up an objection when I was off and running on some project, despite the worry it caused him. So I simply asked, "When do you leave?"

"In February."

"Well," I said, "I guess we better start on your Spanish lessons."

"Kiss me," he said.

"Bésame," I corrected, and kissed him.

We resumed our letter writing.

My dearest. At last I have made a favorable impression on everyone, though not by my medical skill, but rather by restoring a generator with the help of another "medico"—that is what they call us. There was much celebration when several of the houses lit up. The people here are very gentle, shy almost, and it is hard to comprehend how anyone would wish to harm them. I shall be expecting full details of your visit in the next letter. All my love, Steven.

My trip to Nicaragua came eight months later, after a letter from Enrique, telling me that there had been a raid on the village and how many had been killed, including Steven. He had been out in the field, attending a wounded child, when he was shot.

I stood in the silence of the snow and slowly opened the letter Steven had left for me "just in case."

My dearest, for dearest you will always be. I can say of my life that I am resting close to the people I came to help and to love. In a place where I expected to find only sorrow, they brought me friendship and joy. Keep on walking, my love, and know that I am always with you. Steven.

He had enclosed a black-and-white photograph of himself and Enrique, standing in front of their office. He looked a little thinner but in a strong, wiry sort of way, and his hair had grown and was combed back. He looked contented, fulfilled.

I turned the photograph over and read what he had written. *Homo sum: Humani nihil a me alienum puto.* "I am a man: I count nothing human of indifference to me." I sat down on a damp stone bench, and I wept.

Sometimes when I am walking down a familiar haunt of ours in New York, something will trigger a memory of him, so vivid, so sharp it leaves me breathless. I used to think that maybe it wasn't good to love someone so much. That the idea of losing the loved one would be too great to bear. Now I know differently.

A friend said to me, "He was a hero," and I smiled to myself, thinking what he would have thought of that. He was not a hero. Steven was an ordinary man with extraordinary ideas. From him I derived strength and courage. I knew about the frailty of the human soul, but he taught me that the miracle of the human spirit is to give.

HOLLY FITZHARDINGE

> *"Whatever you do to find a relationship,*
> *you must continue doing to keep a relationship."*
> —SUSAN BRADLEY

LOVE IS NOT FOR THE FAINT OF HEART

A walk on a beautiful September night shouldn't have meant an ending. The moon had been full, leaves crunching beneath our feet. The air was crisp and clear. Like us, a neighbor's cat was taking his usual evening stroll, and Mrs. Myrtle had given a friendly wave as she took out her trash.

Now, home alone, I wandered around my apartment, remembering the places that once held his things. The cup on the sink in the bathroom, which used to hold two toothbrushes, now held one. The shaving cream and razor were gone. The chocolate ice cream, still in the freezer, was his favorite. The bed was made with military purpose and hospital corners. The neatness of every room marked his effort.

I opened the closet, knowing I had overlooked nothing when I helped him pack. I searched the floor for a stray tie or sneaker. How I wished that I had not been so thorough. I looked at the empty section of closet space, missing his freshly starched shirts. I stared at the landing, looking hard for his shoes. The tears blurred my eyes, and I wondered if the ache would ever end. I remembered the whole night: it played continuously in my head.

"I don't know what to do," he'd said, with tears in his eyes. The pain seeped into every action and word.

"I love you enough to let you go," I said. My heart ached

with the thought of losing him. We had worked so hard to keep each other. But our families didn't seem to understand our closeness; instead they were deeply upset about our sixteen-year year age difference.

"I can't do it. I can't leave you. We have so many dreams," he responded.

I thought of a few, including buying a house together and finishing my education. We had spent many nights discussing all our dreams until dawn. We shared a deepening love and a growing spirituality. I thought of our dog and cat, each of which had lost a caring friend.

We held each other, knowing that we had fought so long and it was over. The dreams were meant to stay just that, dreams. The tears soaked our faces and clothes. I shuddered with sobs. I did not want to cry. I did not want to make this decision any harder for him. I loved him too much. I never wanted to cause him any pain.

"I'll help you pack. Come on—if we're going to do this, we have to do it now or I won't be able to let you leave."

I got up from the couch and started to gather his toothbrush, comb, and blow dryer from the bathroom, shirts, pants, and ties from the closet, sweats, bathrobe, and other assorted clothes from the bedroom. I swiped at the tears on my face as I packed his things. He just stood there dumbfounded. I had to make him go. It was best for him, for us. I never wanted him to feel as if I had held him back. I couldn't let him regret his decision if he stayed.

I helped him load everything in the car. We shut the door— the perfect punctuation mark for that whole evening.

We caught each other's hands, and we walked away from the car. We held hands and talked softly. It was very late. I couldn't remember the words we spoke. I could only remember his thumb caressing my hand. My eyes blurred as we walked. I wanted to huddle closer to him, but that would only make it harder. Finally, almost by accident, we reached his car again.

We wrapped our arms around each other, holding on frantically.

"I'm so sorry," he choked out.

"I know."

He got in the car and drove away. I stood on the porch, watching his taillights disappear. I stayed there a very long time. I sank to the steps and willed that he turn around and make everything all right. I prayed for him to come home. I needed him.

I had done what was right, yet the pain was extreme. I cried and cried till my head pounded and my eyes burned.

In the days that followed, I would jump at the ringing of the phone or the doorbell. I was so lost. I ached for his arms. I cried constantly, and I thought I saw him everywhere. I took two personal days and stayed in bed. I finished all the chocolate ice cream as I watched a sappy movie that only made me cry harder.

I stayed in the bathtub for hours. I'd let the water get cold and then just refill the tub. Sometimes I didn't realize it had gone cold till I was shaking with chills.

I walked the path that we had walked every day. I didn't talk to anyone about the pain. It was my own. It was all I had left of him, and I didn't want to share that.

Late one Monday night, the doorbell rang. After two weeks, I still jumped at the sound of a ringing phone or a visitor at the door, not knowing, but always hoping, it was him. I put on my old flannel bathrobe and went down the stairs, turning on lights as I went. I opened the door a little and peered out. On the front porch was my sweet honey.

I stood there for a long time, then I pushed the door open and wrapped my arms tightly around him. I cried. He cried.

"I couldn't do it," he said.

"I couldn't, either." I was crying and laughing at the same time.

CHASSIDY A. F. PERSONS

MARRIAGE ENCOUNTER

My sister Bonnie was ecstatic over the new man in her life, convinced he was "the one." Ernie was ruggedly handsome, easy to be with, caring and sensitive, and he made her laugh. And before he even kissed her for the very first time, he told her that he was the kind of guy who dated only one woman at a time. On their fourth date he told Bonnie he would marry her.

So when it happened that a significant amount of time passed with no marriage proposal, Bonnie began to nudge him toward the idea of a bigger commitment. However, with the uneventful passing of their second Valentine's Day together, she decided it was time—time to strengthen her resolve. Bonnie drove over to his place, all the while rehearsing just what she wanted to say to him. She knew she must strike during the time his attention was exclusively hers—before the Bull's game began, during the short commercial breaks, or at halftime. "Brief but to the point," she told herself again. As she entered his condo, Bonnie told him straight out, "Ernie Krause, we need to talk!" Surprising her, he immediately flopped himself down upon his threadbare couch—his bachelor throne. But before she could utter even one of the words she had rehearsed, he asked, "Honey, before you start, would you grab me one of those mints out of that box in the fridge, since you're already up and all."

Bonnie wondered aloud if this man had any limits to his audacity. He just laughed his little dry laugh while she stomped off to the kitchen like an angry, yet obedient, child. She thought her tone had conveyed her urgency in discussing her feelings with him. How, then, had she ended up playing golden retriever, loyally fetching a mint for her bachelor king?

These were no ordinary cheap mints. They were his Marshall Field favorites, which Bonnie had given him on Valentine's Day, a few days before. The same Valentine's Day he showed up forty-five minutes late for their date, the same Valentine's Day he gave her a silly card. And now this!

She recalled the weak explanation he managed to offer for his being so late. Something about having to take care of a matter he could no longer neglect. Bonnie wondered what could be more important than showing up on time for a Valentine date with the girl he'd been claiming to love for the past year and a half.

By the time she reached the refrigerator, anger got the best of her. Bonnie opened the door with such a vengeance that condiments crashed to the floor. She thought about just leaving them where they had come to rest. On second thought, she said to herself, "OK. One of us has to be the adult in this relationship." She returned the jars to their place on the door, then found his prized box of mints on the top shelf of his otherwise almost barren refrigerator. She flipped off the top of the box, to reveal a bold message: It read, very simply: *Bonnie, will you marry me?* Below these words was yet another surprise. There, within the center of a red heart, he had carefully tied the most beautiful engagement ring she had ever seen. Her rage suddenly turned to joy, as tears flooded his kitchen floor!

CHRISTINE D. MAREK

IV
MAXIMUM
EXPOSURE

"At times, all we have to do in life is show up,
be present,
and allow the magic to unfold."

—YITTA HALBERSTAM AND JUDITH LEVENTHAL

SOAP BOX DERBY

*I*t was 1972, the year of Watergate, of Shirley Chisholm's presidential candidacy, of the hits "I Am Woman" and "One Tin Soldier." And it was the first year girls were allowed to race in the Fargo Soap Box Derby.

Good thing, too. My family was in the throes of race fever. My brother had won the local derby the previous summer. Winners cannot compete again.

"Hey, it's my turn! I can do this!" I announced.

And Dad said, "Of course you can."

Was I a women's libber? A tomboy?

No. I was thirteen and had no need of these labels. I learned embroidery and motorcycling with equal attention. My family did not draw such demarcations.

But that summer I would learn all about them.

My first clue should have been that none of my girlfriends spent their evenings in a low-ceilinged basement, pondering wind resistance and wheel-bearing lubricants. Building my car took a year of evenings and weekends. A year of missed TV and teen hangouts. A year of fiberglass shards in my arms and sanding dust in my mouth.

But there was another taste in my mouth—the taste of victory.

And of course I would win. Hadn't my brother won? Wasn't my dad the best car designer there ever was, the best teacher of craftsmanship? Wasn't my mom wonderfully supportive, doing dishes my nights so I could descend the stairs with Dad?

Oh, I didn't always want to descend those stairs. I can still see Dad's face, set firm in answer to my adolescent whines. But the cardinal rule of the Soap Box Derby is that a race car has to be made entirely by its driver's hands.

In early summer, my car came out of the dim basement and into the sunlit backyard. And what a car! All sleek and streamlined, all black and shiny with my name in red letters. I knew every inch of that car. That car and I would cross the finish line together.

July 8: Race Day! There was a parade and celebrities and hullabaloo, but I was in a bubble of calm certainty. Even in the face of the fact there were seventy other challenging racers—five of them girls!

The heats began. My car was fast, and I drove straight. I was winning each race.

Then the trouble began.

And there's always a troublemaker. One of the racers started to taunt me, sitting prominently near the starting gate and shouting, "Cheater! You didn't build that car!"

I ignored him for one race, but after several more he was getting under my skin. Why was he doing this? What had I done?

The field was being narrowed, as the heats eliminated racer after racer. I raced that taunting boy and won, which felt good and right. I thought that would end my troubles.

Little did I know. He was just the herald, the harbinger of the hue and cry to come.

Ah, but the final finish line flashed under me, and I knew I had won. As I had known all along I'd win. I clambered out of my car, and crazy images appeared and disappeared in split seconds, like a frantic dream: race officials grabbing at me, a TV camera zooming in, a woman talking excitedly into a microphone.

And above all, Dad's exultant face. "You did it! You did it, Marci!"

But the frenzy of the win soon turned into a furor of contro-versy. I can still see the apoplectic faces of several of the losing boys' fathers. Accusations flew, terrible and unfounded, as they tried to block me (the girl) from going to the next step, the international race in Akron, Ohio.

"She didn't build that car."

"No way she did. Her father's an architect," the last word spat as if it were an obscenity.

"A cheater shouldn't represent our city at the international race."

The media got wind of the fracas. I was on TV. I was inter-viewed by the newspapers. Radio call-in shows buzzed with callers, both defiling and defending.

Eventually, I sorted it out within myself. I knew I hadn't cheated. I knew they were just sore losers. I knew they would have been sore losers even if a boy had won. But it was plain my being a girl added to their anger.

So I learned that it did matter that I was a girl in a boys' world. And then, standing straight and silent, I unlearned it. Because what did it really matter?

I went to the international race, because I belonged there with the two hundred sixty other contestants from all around the globe who had built cars, raced—and won.

MARCI MADSEN FULLER

THE MIRACLE BUS

*I*t *was a freezing December night. Exhausted from an* intense day of work and the holiday frenzy, I stood at my usual bus stop, on Broadway and Ninth Street in Greenwich Village. Since I hadn't had a spare second to chow down, I was stressed to the max, and my blood sugar level was dropping rapidly. Huddling beneath Woolworth's faceless windows, appreciative of the shelter their awnings provided from the whipping wind, I wondered why every other bus but mine seemed to roll by.

I yearned to go home, curl up under my covers, destress, veg out, but I was on my way to see a new printer, having procrastinated until the final moments before my photography exhibition. I was musing on all this when my bus—the M6—finally pulled in.

"Do you go straight down Broadway, below Canal?" I queried. Last night the bus had randomly decided to turn. So much for the consistency of Manhattan mass transit!

The bus driver, a big black man, smiled reassuringly.

Token in slot, I collapsed into the first single seat—designed for one passenger only, it is the favorite of lone New Yorkers. Across the aisle, two men were seated together, the bus's only passengers besides myself. The first, a tall, lanky African-American, holding a large book, *The Now Bible,* greeted me with a warm "Good evening!" The second man, a dark, mustached Latino, winked a welcome.

I giggled!

Then, without pause, the men and the driver broke into a gleeful, foot-stompin' gospel tune.

"Do you sing together in a choir?" I managed to interject.

"Oh, no, we just met!"

Soon sounds praising the Lord, singing of angels and "The

Good World a-Comin' " reverberated throughout the bus. I found myself tapping my feet, swaying to the beat, and humming along.

Miraculously, the bus never stopped to pick up any other passengers, and I was the grateful recipient of a spontaneous private concert.

I was so blissed out, I missed my stop and had to walk back several blocks.

But when I emerged from that bus, smiling, I was relaxed, peaceful, and ready to embrace the world.

"Thank you, thank you, thank you!" I called as I got off.

Just think, if all the buses in New York City were filled with song, what a different place it would be!

JILL LYNNE

THE POWER OF LOVE

When I turned twenty-four, I thought the world was my oyster. I had a wonderful job with lots of growth opportunity, I had good friends and family nearby, and I had an affordable, brand-new apartment two miles from the beach in Fort Lauderdale. I was perfectly content with my life the way it was.

I have always been a creature of routine. In my early twenties, I knew that I wanted to work slowly toward my Ph.D. and focus on my career. Marriage and family were not even a part of my grand design. Always wanting to be in control of everything, including my emotions, I never mapped out for myself the undeniable power of true love.

The weekend after my twenty-fourth birthday, I went out with my girlfriend Mara. She insisted on taking me to the latest club in Boca Raton, aptly named Heaven. Anyone who is single and living in the South Florida area can tell you how old the club scene becomes once you're past the age of twenty-two. I was sick of flirting with tourists from other places who were only out to "score" with a Florida girl. One-night stands were not my thing. I really didn't want to go to a club; but after much arm twisting from Mara, I finally went.

I remember standing in the club with my friend, my arms folded across my chest. I had a scowl on my face that would've intimidated most any person, and yet there came Andrew, walking toward me. I wonder even today what could have been remotely inviting about me! Nevertheless, he introduced himself, and Andrew and I talked and danced all night. He was everything I was *not* looking for: a tourist from New York who was in Florida visiting his grandmother. I felt I was wasting my time even chatting with this guy. But maybe it was a look he gave me, or the way he laughed. Whatever "it" was, it was starting to happen. I'd never given my number to a guy in a bar before. On this night, I made an exception.

Andrew snuck in a quick kiss as the valet brought our cars around to the front of the club. I expected never to hear from him again; but he began calling at eight A.M. the next morning. Over the course of the day, he invited me to go to the beach and finally to dinner with his entire family. I declined, unable to see getting past the introductions: "Mom, this is Michelle. I picked her up in a bar last night. . . ." We finally agreed to meet again, just the two of us. I couldn't believe myself as I gave what amounted to a total stranger my address and directions to my apartment. All those seminars and workshops I had attended in my college days about how to protect yourself from dangerous situations, and here I was with a neon sign, inviting danger into my home.

I felt breathless when I saw Andrew standing at my door in a suit (I have a weakness for suits!). He had sparkling blue eyes and a generous, loving smile.

At a waterside restaurant, we giggled about meeting in Heaven, and we laughed even harder at the fact that I had been a strict vegetarian for ten years and he was in the wholesale meat business. What a pair we made! There was no topic we couldn't discuss, it seemed, and we felt we had known each other for a lifetime. What clinched it for me was when he asked permission to kiss me good night. I remember saying something like "What took you so long," and as he kissed me, I felt my knees weaken and my heart begin to race. He was different in some inexplicable but wonderful new way.

We went out every night that Andrew was in Florida, and he called me the night he went home to New York. After talking nightly on the phone for several weeks, I went to New York to see him. I wanted to know if there was really anything more than an initial attraction between us. He was so nervous when he picked me up at the airport that we kept getting lost as he attempted to drive us back to his apartment. At the end of the weekend, when we were confirming my flight home with my mother over the phone, Andrew asked me, "Does your mom know I love her daughter?" I didn't "say it back" until two weeks later, when I flew up to attend a wedding with him.

For six months we survived endless plane trips, outrageous phone bills, and frustrations with loneliness and unsupportive friends. We endured chicken pox (he gave them to me, so we had to go through them twelve hundred miles apart!) and self-doubts. But through it all, a powerful love was blossoming between us, distance and all.

Somehow, looking back, I had to have been so totally in love that rational thought was no longer part of my state of mind. Where was my head, to go and quit my great job, give up my free graduate school opportunities, leave my friends, my family, my secure lifestyle, and move to New York to live with a man I had seen only a few days a month for less than a year? And so, with all rational sense tossed aside, I packed up and moved. No friends, no job, just love in my heart. Looking back, we were nuts!

Shortly after I'd made New York my new home, we were driving over the George Washington Bridge. Andrew asked, "Michelle, will you please marry me? I want to spend the rest of my life with my best friend. I love you." Through tears, I said "yes" a hundred times over.

Our honeymoon has never ended. We've built a life together, bought a home, had a child, with another on the way. We always talk about our future. We have discovered that, as much as we have in common, there are many things we feel differently about. But it's those differences that make us fall in love with each other again and again each day.

Now I'm thirty, and as I look back (and ahead), I can say without a doubt that love is a powerful thing. It binds unlikely people together and helps them discover qualities within themselves and others that they never knew they had. To think that I expected to plan out every step of my life! To think that I believed there were no such things as soul mates and deep, passionate love. How was it that I had become so set in my ways at such a young age, determined to live my life according to a self-imposed code that left no room for chance, for magic, for the unpredictable power of love?

How lucky for me that I was given an opportunity to follow either my head or my heart. Thank goodness I went to a higher authority and stepped into Heaven one night for a visit. I pray I never have to leave.

MICHELLE COHEN

THE VIRTUES OF
MR. WRONG!

*F*or most women, there's an unspoken rule that one of our life's missions is to find and capture our "knight in shining armor"—to be diligent and deliberate in our efforts and, once successful, to buy into the American Dream of a home with white picket fence, a family, and, of course, "happily ever after."

It took many years of trial and error in my eternal search for Mr. Right before I would come to discover that there is much to be said for Mr. Wrong too.

Mr. Wrong, for the record, is not someone who is otherwise spoken for—that would be Mr. Stupid.

Mr. Wrong is not a man who is physically or emotionally abusive to women in order to prove his so-called manhood—that would be Mr. On Your Way Out the Door.

Mr. Wrong is not someone doing time behind bars or living the type of lifestyle that would indicate he will be one day—that would be Mr. Some Folks Are Best Left Alone.

But not all Mr. Wrongs are wrong. In your search for your life partner, don't overlook men who could provide moral support, quality time, fun and laughter, and invaluable life experiences. I call men like that Mr. Right for Now.

One of my Mr. Wrongs was handsome, six feet two, intelligent, affectionate, articulate, humorous, and exciting. We met at work. He was clearly not marriage material. And I knew it. He was deemed Mr. Wrong for matrimonial purposes because we were extreme opposites and at different stages in life. I am shy, serious, and ambitious by nature. He is a "people" person, spontaneous and laid back, who takes very little seriously. I'm Catholic, he is nondenominational. I'm into Barry Manilow and Johnny Mathis. He enjoys disco and rap. Not to mention the age difference. But when we came together, he became Mr. Right for Now, and there was not a better time to be had. He taught me to live for today, to plan less, to experience more, and to find something worthy of laughter each day. I taught him the importance of honesty and compassion and the beauty of simple pleasures—like quiet evenings at home.

Years ago, I would not have wasted my time with a man so different from me. I was on a mission back then, consumed with a mental checklist of what Mr. Right would say and do in order to qualify as "the one." Every potential suitor would be scrutinized according to these standards, and the ones who failed the initial screening would be ousted early in the game. But that was yesterday.

Now I know that if we are receptive students, life teaches us very valuable life lessons when it comes to matters of the heart. An incurable romantic by nature, I'm no longer looking for Mr. Right, though I haven't given up hope that he exists and that one day he'll find me! Until that day, I've discovered the temporary but ever-sweet joy derived from experiencing some of life's journey with Mr. Wrong.

JENNIFER BROWN BANKS

"Imagine the best day of your life.
Now imagine living that way 365 days a year."
—AUTHOR UNKNOWN

GINNY'S EXCELLENT ADVENTURE

Ginny was a faithful wife for forty-two years when her husband, Norman, died of cancer. She had spent two years nursing him through his illness. Throughout his career, Norman worked for the railroad, so the last thing he wanted to do when he wasn't working was travel. Ginny, on the other hand, had an unfulfilled passion for travel. They did drive to Florida once, but as soon as they got there Norman wanted to drive home. To hear Ginny tell it, she barely had time to use a Florida rest room.

After his death, with no one to care for at home, Ginny declared, "I'm hittin' the road." And hit the road she did. Using her retirement money, she traveled to the Galápagos Islands, Africa, China, South America, Fiji, England, Australia, and New Zealand. "Not too bad for an ol' gal who has barely ever been out of St. Louis," Ginny used to say.

When Ginny's son invited her to join him, his wife, and their friends on an eight-day rafting trip down the Grand Canyon, her response was predictable: "Let's go!" Never mind that she had never been rafting and couldn't even swim.

It was on that rafting trip that I met Ginny: a vivacious seventy-year-old who held on to the ropes till her knuckles were white and laughed the entire way at the sheer thrill of living.

The Canyon is a spiritual place, and for eight days the only song I could remember was the first verse of "Amazing Grace." Ginny didn't mind. She'd ask me to sing it over and over. Once back home, she mailed me the words to verses two through six: "Just for a change," she said.

Two years later, Ginny got a stomachache. She thought it was just too much travel food. By the time she got around to seeing a doctor between trips, he said there was no point in operating. She had six months to live.

"Mom, what do you want to do with your remaining time?" asked her son. "I want to travel, silly, just as long as I can. And I want to go to Paris."

They came to visit us in North Carolina for Thanksgiving, and we all danced the macarena in the living room. They went to a Texas beach for the warmth, but they never made it to Paris. Ginny knew she was winding down and wanted to go home to St. Louis, back to the house she and Norman had shared.

On my way to Chicago to give a talk, I had a premonition that I needed to stop off in St. Louis to visit Ginny. I called her son to ask if I could come the next day. His reply left me chilled to the bone. "You'd better hurry. Mom just announced she has picked tomorrow to die." The next day was April 15, and Ginny liked the thought of "going out" on the day taxes were due.

I put on my angel earrings for the trip. gold hoops with angels sitting inside, swinging on my shoulders. I wanted all the angels I could gather with me for this journey.

During the flight, I realized that one of my angel earrings was missing. The flight attendants and I practically ripped the airplane seat apart, but one angel earring had simply vanished. As I took off my lone earring, I couldn't understand why this was happening. Even if it was only symbolic, it felt like my angels had deserted me.

By the time I arrived in St. Louis, Ginny was alert but weak. The hospice nurse came, and we gave Ginny a bath, changed her sheets, and clothed her in new pajamas. As I held her fragile body in my arms, I realized we were preparing her for her shroud. But Ginny was not sad. She made her last day an event.

Laughing and teasing about her lime-green sheets, she told me, "Citrus is the hottest fashion color, and I intend to leave in style."

After the nurse left, Ginny asked me to sing to her. I held her close to me once again and sang the only verse I could remember of "Amazing Grace." Her last words to me were, "Now you go to Chicago and give a *really* good speech!" It suddenly struck me that when I'm old and I look back on my life, I don't want any regrets. I want to have packed as much into life as Ginny did in her last years.

When I left her room, her daughter handed me a small box. "Several days ago, even before she knew you were coming, Mom said she wanted you to have these."

Inside the box was a pair of her favorite gold hoop earrings. I understood immediately why my earring had disappeared. Ginny is now the angel swinging from those gold hoops. She is constantly reminding me to live life as she did—to the fullest. Together we're having one excellent adventure!

BAILEY ALLARD

MY TRUCKER

*T*he wind roared all night, and the rain fell hard. Quietly I leaned over Joshua, stared at his face, and knew he was sleeping peacefully. As I slyly took one giant step over him, onto the front seat, I felt his hand grab my ankle, and I could feel the smile spread across my face.

"How'd you know I made a movement?" I asked. "I was so quiet."

He responded with a grin. "You can't sneak out! I know every motion of this truck, and you know by now you can't put anything over on me."

I'd been so sure he was sound asleep! Six weeks on the road, and it was Thanksgiving morning. We were on the last leg of our cross-country trip in Joshua's eighteen-wheeler moving van, on our way to Florida from Texas. The schedule was to unload in northern Florida and drive to the south and stay in a condo on the beach for a few days of relaxation. Then he would be off west again, and I would fly back to New York. This spur-of-the-moment trip for me—a fifty-year-old grandmother and "prima donna"—had been wonderful, and I was going to miss him.

But today I missed home. Living in a truck, not being able to jog my familiar road every morning, contact with only one person—it was all beginning to get to me. One part of me loved being alone with my trucker, but something in me was off today.

As we traveled down the highway, I listened to the soft swish of the windshield wipers. I thought of Mom. She was probably making her homemade cranberry sauce right now, then she'd start her special pumpkin pie with heavy cream and brandy, to take to my sister's house this afternoon. My sister Kathy would be setting the table with beautiful family china about now, for our traditional Thanksgiving. I should be in my kitchen, making corn pudding and the cream cheese brownies everyone said were a "must." Of course, my father would stop by. He always drove around the morning of the holiday, stopping in to see each of his three daughters. Daydreaming, I could actually hear his car pulling into the driveway and coming to a halt—when I realized we had actually stopped! Josh had pulled up to a service station. I ran to the pay phone and called my oldest sister.

"Happy Thanksgiving!" I said, about to cry.

"Hi!" Barb answered. "You know, I keep thinking it's so cool and exciting you're on the road. Its not like hopping on a plane and missing everything along the way. Not too much going on here—we're just doing the same old Thanksgiving."

"Yeah," I answered. "It's raining and cold, and it's Florida! We'll be eating Thanksgiving dinner in a truck stop."

"Hey, the food is the best in the truck stops, and your gravy will be better than we could ever make. You've said so all along, and besides, what a great story to tell your grandchildren! Gotta run—I hear Daddy's car in the driveway!"

And that was the end of the conversation. Was she just trying to make me feel good?

We drove the rest of the morning and had lunch about two-thirty.

"We'll get a sandwich now and stop about seven tonight and get a turkey dinner then. How is that with you?" he contentedly asked.

Josh came from a family of boys. They had a flower shop, so holidays were mingled with working and delivering flowers, and dinner was squeezed in along the way. A family of girls makes a bigger fuss over holidays.

We entered the diner and ordered, and I asked the waitress for a piece of pumpkin pie.

"No, wait," Josh said. "Have it tonight with our dinner."

"I want it now."

"Nah, wait," he said affably. "We'll have pumpkin pie with our Thanksgiving dinner later."

"I want it now," I said like a stubborn kid.

He smiled at the waitress, baffled.

I wanted that pie now just because everyone at home was together. I looked at him, I looked at the waitress, and I walked out of the restaurant, leaving my sandwich and soda untouched. I went over to the truck and started to cry.

He came out and said, "Let's go." He didn't understand, didn't understand my tears. Well, neither did I. I didn't know what to say. We rode in silence. I felt the tears rolling down my face, and I couldn't explain it to him.

"I'm sorry if I did anything wrong," he said sincerely.

Him? I was the one who did something wrong! I reached for him across the seat, but I wanted to be even closer, so I climbed behind him and put my arms around his neck.

"It's not you, Josh. It's just that I'm not home for the holiday. Yet I want to be with you."

We drove until dark and pulled up at a truck stop. It was packed; I was surprised by how many people were not home for the holiday. We ordered our turkey dinner, and Josh reached for the phone on the table and said, "Why don't you call home."

Trying to be nonchalant, I said, "No, I'm with you." But he insisted, and I hesitated no longer.

I called Kathy's house, and the whole family passed the phone around, wishing us Happy Thanksgiving. Kathy's mother-in-law said, "I bet Josh is just thrilled to have you with him—he's usually alone on a holiday." I hadn't looked at it that way. I'd thought he was so self-reliant.

We got back in the truck, and he expertly maneuvered it out of a tight spot. I looked over at him and really noticed him— not just the muscled chest, the physical man I was attracted to, but *him*. I realized he understood me and brought me serenity like no one else. His hand reached over and rubbed the nape of my neck. I could have purred as the knotted muscles of the day relaxed, and I finally knew this was where I wanted to be.

CONSTANCE CONACE

V
PATHFINDERS

*"Hell would be if God were to show me things
I could have accomplished
if only I had believed in myself."*

—AUTHOR UNKNOWN

PRAY TO GOD AND READ THE PAPER

I have always had a special view of love. Even as a ten-year-old, I remember, I believed in a kind of love that was eternal and powerful and unlike any of the relationships I had observed around me. Throughout my life, every fountain coin and birthday wish remained the same: "I pray that one day I will find true love and that it will last forever." There were times when I had almost given up, but even as I approached thirty, the wish remained fundamentally the same. I had been burned enough to be discouraged, but was hopeful enough to know in my heart that if I was patient and faithful, God would find me a husband to fulfill all my adolescent dreams. My mother always told me to stop trying so hard: love would come when I was not expecting it. Mom was right.

Before I was ready to be married, I knew I needed to clean up the stray ends of my life. The first step involved moving out of an apartment that was subject to seasonal flooding. The desire to move and be free of the worry of high tide was in my head, but I had not actually put thoughts into action. In fact, I ran around so much with work and friends and insignificant errands that I couldn't seem to find the time to buy a paper to look for a new place to live. Until one day I ran out of my apartment in the usual rush, only to trip over the morning paper. Not that odd, except for the fact that I don't subscribe to any morning paper. That day I picked it up and decided that if God was delivering a paper, maybe I was supposed to read it. I found three ads for promising apartments and one for sharing a house. I got two bizarre answering machine messages and hung up. I called the other two. One person, Paul, called back, and I arranged to meet him and possibly share his house. I don't know what I expected, but he was sweet and funny and didn't mind that I had a cat. He offered me a glass of orange juice, and we sat and got acquainted. I spoke longingly of my alma mater and found out that he had graduated from the same school. I suddenly flashed back to freshman orientation, when the speaker told us that 85 percent of Bucknell alumni married Bucknell graduates. I'd never forgotten that statistic. I looked at the house, I looked at the man, and I arranged to move in the next month. There was something in my heart that knew, and I was afraid to mention it to anyone for fear of breaking the spell. I moved in and made myself at home. We soon developed a breakfast routine and shared morning conversation. Sometimes we would watch television and talk until late at night. He teased me about my penchant for eating Ben & Jerry's ice cream for breakfast. I laughed at his ability to imitate Jimmy Stewart and Scooby-Doo. Eventually, I broke up with my current boyfriend, and he ended his relationship of the moment. I've been in his house for a year now, and we're engaged. Now we read the morning paper together.

SUSAN LaMAIRE

"Dream passionate dreams. Design their reality."
—CANDIS FANCHER

FLIGHT OF DESTINY

"Whatever do you think you're doing?" my mind screamed at me. "Who the hell do you think you are?"

I was in the middle of a flying lesson—one that was going so badly I burst into tears. The harder I tried to learn to fly the tiny single-engine airplane, the worse I got. I couldn't seem to do anything right!

It didn't help that my instructor was young and gorgeous and I had a crush on him. Not only did I want to succeed for me; I wanted to look brilliant, for him. But it was going so poorly that even he lost it and began yelling at me! After his first couple of words, I couldn't hear him anymore. All I could think of was: You're a fool to try to fly airplanes. After all, you're just a girl. You'll never get it!

As I drove home, all my doubts and self-loathing flooded to the surface. All the stupid things I'd done and said throughout my life now came to mind, and there seemed an overwhelming lot of them. My mind told me I was stupid, dumb, and ugly. What's more, I couldn't believe my arrogance at even *trying* to learn to fly! As if I had a hope of *ever* getting it! I cried bitter tears all the way home.

Amazingly enough, the next day at the appointed time, I got back into my car and drove to the airport. Convinced as I was of not being capable, I kept going. For you see, the passion in

my soul was a runaway fire, and nothing—not even my negative self-talk—was going to stop me from becoming a flight
instructor.

On my second lesson, when my instructor reviewed the basic
maneuvers, I laughed in joy as I soared, wheeled, and wobbled all
over the sky. Learning to talk on the radio was another chal-
lenge. In this world of male radio voices, I wanted to sound
calm, cool, and professional. I worried about it so much that I
stumbled all over myself trying to get the words out! But learning to land was the most important. When my instructor did it,
it looked so easy. My turn came, and I floated and bumped.
That night, I even dreamed, over and over, of awful landings. I
was completely convinced that I was a lost cause, yet the following day, I planned to practice more landings. I flew in, and as
we rolled down the runway, I realized that I had just made a
landing so smooth that we hadn't even *felt* the touchdown.
Success!

In hindsight, it all happened in baby steps. Almost before I
knew it, I soloed. It was the most triumphant moment of my
life. Not only did I do it all by myself, but I did it well. Even my
mind chatter couldn't find fault. On every takeoff, I felt the
freedom of my spirit disconnecting from the earth and becoming part of the universe.

That was twenty-one years ago—that mystical time when I
began to learn to trust myself. In my earlier years, I used to
fight the part of me that wasn't sweet, soft, and obedient. Now
I appreciate every feisty quality about myself. And remember
my self-talk about being stupid, dumb, and ugly? Well, I don't
think so! My confidence is sky-high, and I've come to know the
truth: I'm wonderful, special, talented, and perfect just the way
I am. This discovery has given me compassion and respect, as I
honor the beauty and perfection in other unique individuals
everywhere. My inner peace and serenity pulsates so strongly
that I know others sense it. Thank God I reached out for what
I wanted.

As for my goal of becoming a flight instructor . . . I flew
through that goal and beyond. I am now an international pilot

for United Airlines. Weekly, I fly to Paris, London, and other magical places.

I am passionately living my dream!

ROBIN RYAN

FERN CAVE

ach year my sister and I take a weekend trip to-
gether to pursue our strong interest in birds and nature.
This time she had talked me into going with her to the
annual Bald Eagle Conference.

The weekend was an informative and entertaining mix of
birding, lectures, and field trips. On the last day of the conference, we carpooled to a site called Fern Cave. The name made
my skin crawl. All my life, I had suffered from claustrophobia
so intense that at times I would not use elevators.

Our guide pulled up in the open desert and stopped his car.
We all moved out into the frigid February air, then walked a
short distance. I kept looking around my flat, barren surroundings, wondering where a cave might be. The high desert
stretched for miles, covered with sagebrush and dusted by an
icy, arid wind. The ranger stopped walking. As we approached
him, I saw a yawning hole in the desert floor, covered by a wide
steel grate.

The ranger bent down, picked a sprig of sage and poked it
through his buttonhole, then removed a small leather medicine
bag from his pocket and placed it around his neck. What was
going on?

Our guide unlocked the grate and we descended into another
world. As I crawled carefully down the ladder, the ranger's
words echoed in my ears: "This was an ancient Modoc Indian
holy place, used until 1873, when the Modoc people were sent
to an Oklahoma reservation. Only recently did several Modoc
medicine people return to Fern Cave."

We entered one end of a lava tube, where the roof had fallen
in long ago. Below the opening was indeed a fern grotto,
greenly lush and starkly out of place. The air had become heavy,
humid, and warm. The ferns were beautiful and healthy, fed by

the light from above, the nutrients from hapless rabbits, rodents, and snakes that had fallen in, and the water dripping from the cave roof. It was an amazing ecosystem: a full-size terrarium.

But even more amazing were the layer upon layer of pictographs that covered the walls near the opening in the cave. These were not secular drawings. This had been a cave for spirit quests and ceremonies of importance to the native people. The ranger told us that when the Modoc medicine people entered Fern Cave in the early nineties, they fell to their knees in awe and respect. The spirit images descended from the quarter-mile section of the lava tube beyond the chamber and moved gently into two circles. The grandmother spirits formed the inner circle. The outer circle was formed by warrior spirits.

We were given time to wander the cave on our own. Feeling like a voyeur, I self-consciously flashed my light on the mysterious pictographs around me. Shutting the light off, I moved into a large chamber where the roof of the cave grew to at least thirty feet in height. A peaceful, loving feeling enveloped me. It was dark and dense, like heavy, warm bedcovers on a cold winter's night. I stood in silent wonder at how I could feel so welcome in a place like this—a cave! Yet I felt surrounded by love, and the feeling of spiritual presence was unmistakable. I wanted nothing more than to sit and drink in this thick, pungent, loving air.

Gradually, people began making their way back up the ladder, as I stood silently in the bowels of the cave, in tears. My heart ached with longing. I didn't want to leave, wanted to spend the rest of my life here. Finally, it became apparent that I was the last one left, and our group leader motioned to me. I struggled to pull myself back up the ladder. As I reached the surface, I required assistance to avoid falling backward.

I stood on the edge of the cave opening and attempted to adjust to the desert world. The bitter February wind whipped by as the sagebrush rustled all around. Solemnly and silently, we walked back to our vehicles.

I have never completely returned from Fern Cave. On several occasions since then, visitors to my home have told me they sensed others in the room with us. As the familiar feeling of overwhelming love surrounds me, I know the grandmother spirits are present.

SHARON KINDER

LETTER TO TIM

I *knew Tim by sight. Or rather by sound. Everybody in* Central School did. Not that he was loud—although even when he was eleven, his voice had that ringing, penetrating quality. He was an outrageous joker-punster even then. As far as I knew, he wasn't aware of me.

One afternoon, though, we ended up in a classroom together with my friend Sue. Tim chatted with us, all the while lifting used staples off the chalk tray and plunking them into an old Band-Aid box. I watched him do this for a few seconds, then blurted, "Why are you doing that?"

He shrugged. "Same reason you were keeping that notebook of animal names last year."

I stared at him, forgetting the Band-Aid box. The previous year, I'd started jotting down my various pets' names—a more ambitious undertaking than it sounds, since my brother Gary and I were always dragging cats home from my grandparents' farm. Probably fifty or sixty of them had passed through our lives by that time. I'd been afraid of forgetting even the littlest kittens, who'd been with us maybe a few weeks before distemper picked them off. Then other kids had begun giving me pets' names, and I'd written those down too. Why, I don't know, except that even then I was caught up in the poetry of names and naming, just as now the names of herbs and quilt patterns create a vivid magic for me. But that afternoon in the darkened classroom, waiting for the bus, I was just floored that a strange boy had noticed my oddball scribbling.

In high school, we met up again and became good friends while he chased after one of the girls I hung out with and a couple of the others chased after him. We talked on the phone some and in our sophomore English classroom a lot. We acted in a couple of one-act plays together. And once he gave me a poem he'd clipped out of the newspaper—a simple, moving piece that I kept among my papers for years. I don't remember all the words, but it was about having "wise eyes."

We drifted apart, then happened across each other after our freshman year of college and started dating. Eventually, we married and had Marissa, a child with all her dad's quick restlessness and imaginativeness. We were never a picture-perfect couple. I used to joke that we'd be arguing with each other about dentures and walkers when Marissa finally shipped us off to a convalescent home. But we'd both get teary-eyed and sniffly over the dumbest scenes in movies and laugh when we caught each other doing it. And there were those moments when soul met soul and we saw with each other's eyes. "We're more alike than you realize," he once said to me; and he was right. We were friends, fellow questers, and part of each other's childhood, with more memories than we could ever shake free of. Staples in a Band-Aid box. And he believed in my dream of being a writer, even on days when I couldn't quite make myself believe in it.

"If I've done nothing else in my life," he'd say, "I've tried to be supportive of your writing. . . . I believe you have what it takes to be a great writer."

That early Tuesday in July was one of those "the wall looked at me wrong" kind of days. Nothing seemed to be going right. Then I had a call from an editor, who bubbled over with enthusiasm about a piece I'd put a lot of myself into. I was glowing when I put down the phone. "Wait until Tim hears about this!" I exulted.

He never did. His van skidded on a slick all too familiar road on his way home and flipped over, hitting a pole and killing him instantly.

A few days later, we buried him in the wooded little cemetery behind the house that overlooked the mountain he'd loved. In what seemed a parody of our wedding, nine years earlier, the brother who'd walked me down the aisle guided me to my husband's graveside. The sun touched the cherry coffin, bringing out the red glints in the wood, and I thought: What a beautiful coffin! And the thought, odd as it was, stayed with me throughout the service. When it was over, I stooped down and kissed the lid—I'd been unable to look at what was left of him.

I could not let him go into the ground without some sign and held out my hand for the spade. The funeral director shook his head gently and made a motion with his hand: You don't have to do this. But I did. And afterward, I bent down and kissed the lid one last time, dirt and all.

"Let me watch you go with the sun in my eyes," Diana Ross sings in "Touch Me in the Morning." I remember listening to that line with a good friend back in high school; we'd turned to look at each other, moved out of our adolescent egocentrism by the pain and the poetry of the words. Well, I had watched my love and friend go with the sun in my eyes, all right. But the love wasn't dead: It was as close as my heart and stronger than death.

For weeks afterward, I could not write. Nor could I let all the tears out. Finally, one night a poem appeared, brought into being out of my pain. And it told me that somewhere in the battered, darkened house of my being was a person who could still flame into feeling. I kept a journal. It helped, though the words still came haltingly, as though I were recovering from a stroke. But they came back to me, and that was all I cared.

"You must do that thing you think you cannot do," insisted Eleanor Roosevelt, who overcame great shyness and personal pain to do great things for other people. The one thing that I knew I had to do for my soul to heal—the one thing I couldn't quite bring myself to do—was to write about Tim's death. Then my counselor said to me, "Maybe you could write a good-bye letter to Tim."

So this is my goodbye letter to the smart-mouthed kid with a Band-Aid box, the boy who surprised me with the poem about wise eyes, the blunt, sensitive, playful man who gave me Marissa, laughter, and his belief in me. And as I've sat here writing, the tears have finally found me and freed the words and feelings trapped under the rubble. I have a voice again. It's a different voice. I don't know if it—or my eyes, for that matter

—are any wiser. But it is capable of greater depth, openness, and, I hope, compassion. Out of great pain, a new voice has been born.

T. J. BANKS

AND BABY MAKES THREE

I *step from the shower, wrap the towel around me, and* stare down at my big Himalayan cat, Sheba. Her wise sapphire eyes contemplate the tears streaming down my cheeks, onto her luxuriant white fur. I sense her telling me, "Mom, I know what you really want is a kid with two feet, but what you got was a kitty with four paws. If you do a good job with me, the word is you'll get your kid."

I prayed that night and every night that my cat was right. Coming as I had from a violent, dysfunctional family lacking real love, it was just not enough that I'd become a successful entrepreneur and traveled the world. After passing the fortieth year of my unmarried existence, I craved what was missing in my life: someone I could love and someone to love me back.

A tenacious inner voice prodding me along, I began the adoption process. Seven years dragged by. Finally, I got the heart-stopping phone call that told me that I qualified for a baby girl soon to be born in Las Vegas, Nevada. I would turn forty-eight one week after her birth. *You have to be nuts, Donna,* a part of me was thinking. *It takes herculean energy to raise a child, and you're too damned old to go through sleepless nights and the financial burden of a college education. And if something happens to you, what then?*

Even friends familiar with my struggle to adopt warned me of the downside and seemed reluctant to offer encouragement. And yet I refused to be discouraged. I passionately wanted a child. Then Sheba snuggled up beside me, and her big blues seemed to say, "Go for it. I love ya, and so will What's-her-name."

When I brought Mariah Chelsea Hartley home, my world turned upside down, but I was ecstatic. It had really happened. My baby girl was home in my arms. Yes, there were sleepless nights, gallons of formula, dozens of dirty diapers, and the haunting insecurity of motherhood. Mariah's smiles blossomed forth, and the unconditional love shining in her eyes became my happiness.

The months flew by, and I struggled against my tight work schedule to spend every moment I could observing Mariah's baby miracles: a hand brushing my cheek, gurgles of delight, chubby miniature arms wrapping around my neck, and the utter joy of hearing "Mama" from rosebud lips crinkled up in a smile. As a new mother, I've learned that each day unleashes new experiences and a reason to show patience and tolerance for the tiny being you love.

And what does my furry cat princess feel about this invasion of her territory by cries in the night and curious poking fingers? I can tell you, we really are a family. At least that's the way I understood it after I returned from the grocery store, pulled into the garage, and saw Mariah asleep in the back seat. Since she was in eye view of my kitchen, I left the car door open and didn't disturb her. Sheba gave me her "Where's the kid?" meow and proceeded to search the house. A while later, I found Sheba curled up next to my sleeping daughter. I knew I had made the right choice. Even Sheba knew. There was no doubt as to what my feline friend was saying this time: "Hey, Mom, and baby makes three."

DONNA HARTLEY

"Taking care of yourself does not require a lot of time—
just meticulous timing."
—AUTHOR UNKNOWN

IT'S ABOUT TIME

As children, we're instinctively aware of the simple, natural rhythms of the earth. Growing up without electricity or TV, I would often watch the drama of a thunderstorm rolling across the South Dakota prairie instead. Excitedly I'd wait for the ominous-looking clouds and the electrifying bolts of light in the night sky. My father would say, "After you see the lightning, listen for the thunder and count—you'll know how far away the storm is."

Country life was full of cycles and rhythms. Knowing the right time for plowing, planting, and harvesting was critical to a dry-land farmer. Understanding the breeding of cows at a particular time ensured calves' coming into a world of spring grass and not winter snow. It all made sense and seemed like part of a master plan.

When the time came for me to leave the farm and attend the big-city university, I found that people woke up to alarms instead of the breaking morning light. Appointments and schedules were not in harmony with one's body clock but made to suit someone else's convenience and efficiency. The weather, the seasons, and the true time of day were virtually ignored. I felt disoriented and out of sync.

Struggling for balance, I took some classes in chronobiology (the study of time and the body), which was a relatively new science in the sixties. I learned about a symphony of rhythms in nature, including those in my own body. It was amazing to find that there was a "best time" to do almost everything: there's an ebb and flow, a waxing and waning of our alertness, our strength, and our energy. A familiarity I had felt with the "master plan" of my childhood returned. I managed my schedule to optimize my performance at school.

On one spring break, I was enthusiastically telling my father about the research being done at chronobiological labs on the timing of cancer treatments. My father listened patiently and replied, "Cancer cells are like weeds. Every farmer knows that weed killer sprayed on crops at one time of day will kill the weeds and the plants will be resistant. At another time of day, they'll both die."

After college, the corporate life promised me money, travel, and a career; my interest in things like chronobiology faded. I took a job in computer sales and became progressively detached from my emotions and feelings as I focused on quotas and achievements. My boss would say, "Whatever it takes," and I would do whatever it took, at any personal cost. I came to find later that the cost was greater than I'd imagined.

After several years of success, I had a growing bank account and a failed marriage, and my father had passed away. I had no one to perform for or impress. I could feel nothing: pain, anger, love, or happiness. I was out of balance, out of sync, off kilter, and alone.

And then I was diagnosed with breast cancer. Dealing with this crisis knocked me off the corporate gerbil wheel and put me in touch with deeper feelings once again. I longed for the synchronicity and balance I'd enjoyed as a child.

It had been twenty-five years since I paid attention to the research on cancer treatments at school. Now I was desperate to know what the researchers had learned while I was absent from "life." My first call for information was not to the cancer hot line but to my former university professor. He told me that top researchers had found that the time of the month a biopsy is performed, and the time of day the treatment is given, are significant to long-term survival. Specifically, he said:

- Breast cancer surgery may be 30–40 percent more effective if performed midway in the menstrual cycle.
- Treatments given at the right time of day are more potent and may cause fewer side effects.

My diagnosis was a wake-up call. It tuned me in and reminded me that when we get intimate with our bodies' internal timing, we can sense what's coming—like the thunder before the storm.

Now I exercise at the best time for my body, eat at the right time, even make love and schedule business meetings at the optimal time. My doctor says my prognosis for long-term survival is great.

Country wisdom tells us that there's a right and a wrong time for most everything we do.

I have a friend who's been happily married for thirty-five years. She gets up at five A.M. He goes to bed at four A.M. She laughingly says, "Our love is always hot, and the bed is never cold." Another friend writes songs or vacuums nude at two A.M. Early-morning people hit the ground running, breathe in the fresh air of dawn, and wonder what's wrong with the rest of us. I found that my best time of day was often wasted in traffic on the way home from work.

"Making hay while the sun shines" makes sense whether you're on the farm or in the city. We must find the opportunity to live in balance by matching our efforts with the flow of our natural rhythms. It's about time for you too!

NANCY KIERNAN

VI
FREE
AT LAST

*"The soul should always stand ajar,
ready to welcome the ecstatic experience."*

—EMILY DICKINSON

> *"A workable measure of your progress*
> *is how fast you can get free when you are stuck*
> *and how many ways you know to get free."*
> —KATHLYN HENDRICKS

A WALK ON THE WILD SIDE

At last, a few days all to myself, away from the stress of the city.

"Watch out for hanta virus," had warned my husband, the noncamper.

"Remember the forest belongs to the wild things that live there," had chided my son, who respects wild things.

"Be r-e-a-l-l-y careful of the Big Bad Wolf," had chirped my five-year-old granddaughter.

"Zip-a-dee-doo-dah, zip-a-dee-ay!" In a closed car, going fifty-eight miles an hour up Route 5 away from Los Angeles, my fifty-eight-year-old voice sounded pretty good.

Through the Grapevine and on to Bakersfield. No rush. No worries.

At Giant Forest Lodge, a friendly woman handed me directions to my cabin. A sign behind her caught my eye: DO NOT FEED THE BEARS. "Who would want to feed a bear?" I said.

At seven A.M., I awoke to the gentle sounds of birds. No lunches to pack, no meetings to plan.

I pulled on my sweatsuit, brushed my teeth, put on sunscreen and mosquito repellent. With a water bottle in my backpack, I was ready to experience the tranquillity of the forest.

MORROW ROCK, a sign read. I stood tall, looked up the trail, and accepted the invitation.

I reached down to pick up two walking sticks. Waving them over my head like a warrioress, I called out to the ghost of my childhood. "I am Jane, you are Tarzan." My brothers and I spent most of our spare time in the woods near our house, imitating childhood heroes.

"We are marching to Pretoria, Pretoria, Pretoria!"

The sky is a great audience. Swinging my sticks back and forth made me feel powerful.

As I walked on, the branches of a sequoia ahead of me began shaking. Its cones fell like hail on the forest floor. The barrage didn't make sense. It wasn't windy. I couldn't see anything. Yet it shook violently. I put my walking sticks over my head and ran through.

The cones continued to fall behind me as I sat down on a fallen log. I had been walking more than two hours and felt hot and tired. It was about nine-thirty. I opened my backpack and took out my water.

I noticed a bluebird, a meandering butterfly, and some half-eaten red berries on a thorny bush nearby. I heard what seemed like the intrusive sound of a passing car in the distance and what I assumed were park rangers building something. About five minutes went by; I was thinking of taking a nap.

Suddenly a loud thump ripped away my serenity and catapulted me into life-threatening danger. A black bear dropped out of the tree I'd just passed and began walking toward me on all fours. I felt so dumb. No wonder the tree was shaking and the berries were half eaten!

My insides started screaming. But my mouth wouldn't move. My body wanted to run, yet I couldn't outrun a bear.

I thought I was having a heart attack. A bad childhood case of rheumatic fever had left me with an irregular heartbeat. "Nothing to worry about," my doctor said. "Just leaky valves." Wrong! I definitely had something to worry about.

Terrified, I turned my back on the bear and staggered in the direction of where I thought I had heard the passing car.

My thoughts raced back and forth, up and down, like a television picture on the fritz. I knew everyone would be mad at me if I got eaten by a bear.

I walked with fierce determination. Waved my sticks over my head. And sang.

"Whenever I feel afraid, I hold my head erect, and whistle a happy tune . . ."

Off the path, weaving in and out of obstacles, I sloshed into marshland. Frantically I looked over my shoulder, hoping the bear was gone. No luck! He was twenty feet away, slowly closing in. Shock waves rolled through my body. My knees felt weak.

A fallen tree appeared out of nowhere, to create a forty-foot bridge over the marsh. Could I balance on it? I'd been a dancer . . . thirty years ago. Could I cross and get beyond the marsh to where I was hoping against hope there was a road and people . . . and escape? I stepped up and prayed Mr. Bear would be too big for this small balance beam.

Knees shaking, I teetered across the tree . . . slipped and fell . . . scrambled back up and shakily went on. The bear's footfalls competed with my pounding heart. He was on the tree. Perfectly balanced. Fifteen feet away. Barnum & Bailey would have hired him in a flash.

African drums began to beat wildly inside my heart. I wondered why a search-and-rescue party didn't carry me out of this morning nightmare. Where was Tarzan of the jungle when I needed him?

Suddenly I heard a deep, booming voice inside my head. *"Do you want to live?"* It was jarring. I wondered if, indeed, I really had a choice. I reached the end of the log and jumped off.

"Do you want to live?" continued to reverberate inside me. The voice helped me put the brakes on fear and terror and take an angel's flight into determination.

"Yes, yes, yes!" I answered. I turned around and angrily stared the bear straight in the eye. I pounded my walking sticks over my head and shouted: "I will not miss my daughter's acting debut. I will not miss my son's cooking at his new restaurant. I will not miss my husband's new musical show. I will not miss my granddaughter's next birthday. Now, *go away.*"

I turned, tore through undergrowth, bushes scratching, snagging my clothes. I went on as if the bear were still behind me, climbed a twenty-foot embankment, and, too numb to move, watched a car drive by. I looked back. I couldn't see the bear, but I could feel him in the brush, his eyes still following me.

Frantically, I flagged down another car and scrambled into the metal womb, grateful to be alive. Feeling a growing surge of new strength and joy—born out of having had a close call and been given a precious gift—I started humming under my breath: "Zip-a-dee-doo-dah, zip-a-dee-ay."

JUDITH MORTON FRASER

*"You and I can live in a world of enchantment,
but only when we feed
and care for our soul."*
—DEBORAH OLIVE

THE WARM FUZZY
HOSTILE GROUP

"**T**wo hundred people will be attending, and you need to know that they all hate each other, hate their work, and don't want to hear what you have to say. And by the way, we are a nonprofit organization, and we don't have a lot of money to pay you."

I stood in shock as I heard myself say, "I would be honored to speak at your regional conference."

I hung up the phone and proceeded to have a complete temper tantrum.

"I didn't volunteer for this," I yelled to God, as I stomped around my kitchen.

"Oh, yes you did, Jody," I clearly heard. "When you left your corporate job, you said you would teach the world Soul Purpose Principles if I would support you. Well, I am supporting you, and I need you to teach *my* truths to these folks."

"OK, God," I mumbled. "Who am I to argue with you? I will do it, but I don't like it."

"You don't have to like it; you just have to be willing to serve," I was gently reminded.

The invitation to speak came in January for an April event. For three months I jokingly referred to this opportunity as the "hostile group." For three months I stewed over the fear of speaking to an angry, unwilling group. For three months I visualized dodging the raw eggs and rotten tomatoes I was sure they were going to throw at me. For three months I kept trying to rewrite my keynote speech, to sound more corporate than spiritual. Finally, the day had arrived.

"Even though we have not met, and even though some of you may not want to be here," I started out tentatively, "and even though some of you may not want to hear what I am about to say, I know four things about you that you will agree with."

Smiling faces beamed back at me. Hmm. Silently I laughed at myself, thinking this was not the response I had prepared myself for.

"Every one of you here wants four things," I continued. "And if you had these four things, you would tell me you were living a soulful and purposeful life. *One:* one hundred percent harmonious relationships. *Two:* a vibrant, healthy body. *Three:* an expanding sense of prosperity. *Four:* to be living your soul purpose and making a difference."

Enthusiastically, they nodded. "In order to create these experiences, you need to know a few things about your Soul," I suggested, my confidence having returned.

- *The Soul demands to be free.* Freedom, by definition, means: Not being dependent on others. Being self-reliant. Not being determined by anything beyond the Soul's own nature or being.

  Americans are not feeling free. According to the Center for Disease Control, 750,000 Americans will die of heart disease in 1997. What is even more interesting is that more heart attacks happen between the hours of seven and nine A.M. Monday morning.
- *The Soul yearns for the silent pause.* We each have 1,440 minutes in a twenty-four-hour period. After years of helping people discover their Soul's purpose, the most common statement I hear is: "I don't know." In order to discover why we exist and what to do with our creative

energies, we *must* sit quietly and listen. Just two minutes a day, or more. Great wisdom emerges out of a silent moment.

- *The Soul delights in the tribal pulse.* We all need and want to belong. Living a soulful life requires us to take ruthless inventory of the people we hang around with. Are they positive, supportive, and nurturing? Are they willing to tell us the truth, even when we don't want to hear it? Are they willing to let us tell them the truth, even when they don't want to hear it? Are the people in our lives spiritually focused, and if not, why would we choose to hang out in a negative, degrading tribe?

- *The destiny of every Soul is to present its finest creative expression to humanity.* Our Soul, that quiet, shy, powerful, unique part of us, holds our physical temple, our body, so that we may express our own set of talents and skills. It is our very destiny to say *yes* to our greatness and boldly step out into the world, sharing and serving humanity in our own unique way. We simply will not be happy until we do.

As I concluded my presentation, I received roaring applause, many accolades, and thanks. Riding the elevator up to the lobby allowed me a precious moment of quiet.

"OK, God, you win. I surrender my will to you. Show me where and with whom you want me to serve next. I will speak, teach, and write about *your* Soul-purpose principles. And thank you for the opportunity to speak with the fabulous warm fuzzy 'hostile group.'"

Things are not always what they seem. I now know that what we resist in life is often our biggest opportunity to learn and grow!

JODY STEVENSON

CREATE YOUR OWN
HEAVEN TODAY

When I learned that my favorite aunt had died, I was horror-struck. Her death came as a shock because my mother had just written to say she was doing much better. To make matters worse, my family didn't tell me about her death for a week, because I was away and they "didn't want to worry me." That compounded the grief. When I finally found out, I shed powerful tears for days, as if to send my aunt Bea higher and higher into heaven.

One night during that period of grief, I had a dream. The feeling was so strong and the picture so vivid that I can still see and feel it today. In the dream, I was standing in heaven, in front of a beautiful English cottage. Set back in a gorgeous garden, with a stone path leading to the front door, the cottage itself was covered with roses. A white picket fence surrounded it.

There I was, standing in front of the fence. The setting was very tranquil. I had a deep sense of inner peace such as I had never experienced before. It was all-embracing. I didn't want it to go away.

Out of nowhere, a figure stood in front of me.

He radiated the same incredible peace. I asked him, "What's this all about?"

The answer I got back really surprised me. "Welcome," He said. "You can stay here too if you would like, but you have to follow one rule."

"What's that?" I asked.

"You can use only positive words and positive thoughts about everyone and everything," he said. "If you don't, you'll drop right out of here."

He didn't say where I would go, but I had a feeling I knew.

I wondered if I could discipline my mind to stay that positive.

One thing I knew for sure was that I wanted that tranquillity more than anything. I wanted to stay.

I was about to say yes when I woke up.

The impact of that experience was so strong that I remember it as if it were yesterday. I tell audiences I speak to: "Think what life could be like if we used only positive words and positive thoughts."

Here's the real question: Do we have the power to create heaven on earth? I *know* we do. We can do it together—thought by thought.

CHRISTINE HARVEY

YOU ARE MY BROTHER

an love dispel evil? *Can peace overcome* war? I had always argued so, taking the moral high road. "Love and forgiveness is all well and good," some friends would argue, "but what place do they have if *you're* the one under attack?" Still I persisted in believing love has a place and a power of which we may not always be aware.

Not long ago, while attending a medical conference in Philadelphia, I returned to my hotel room to freshen up before a late-night committee meeting. Locking the door behind me, I entered the bathroom. I quickly combed my hair and bent over the sink to wash my face. As I closed my eyes and splashed cold water over my skin, I instinctively knew I was not alone. Jerking my body up, I watched in the mirror's reflection as a hand reached out and ripped back the shower curtain behind me. Reeling, I barely had time to react before a man dressed in army fatigues leapt from the shower and pinned me against the sink. I screamed as he clasped my arms with one hand and started to shut the bathroom door with the other.

He grabbed me, and we were suddenly face-to-face. As I looked at him full on, I realized I would never win a war of strength against him. In that moment, my mind and my body seemed to go in different directions. With my heart beating wildly, I continued to scream. Yet another part of me felt a strange peacefulness and began speaking to him in my mind. Locking eyes with him, I started repeating over and over in my head the phrase: "This must be a mistake. You are my brother. There can be nothing but love between us. You cannot hurt me. This is a mistake. You are my brother. There can be nothing but love between us. This is a mistake. . . ."

"This is a mistake," he said suddenly, and he released me

and slowly backed away. Shaking his head, as if dazed, he repeated, "This is a mistake," and he turned and fled out the door.

KATHI J. KEMPER

THE JOURNEY HOME

Our destination is Troyes, a city in the Champagne region, about ninety minutes from Paris. I stare out the window of the train, hands clenched tightly over the package on my lap. My husband, Tom, and I are bringing my mother's ashes home.

Last June, eleven months ago, I drove Mom to the doctor for her monthly exam. As always, she was pronounced in excellent health. Took her diabetes medications, her blood pressure pills. Didn't smoke or drink. Followed a careful diet. At age seventy-seven, she seemed likely to live for another ten or twenty years. So why, after lunch, did our conversation turn to death?

I was standing at the kitchen sink, washing dishes. Heaven only knows how the subject came up, but I mentioned that when I died, I wanted to be cremated. Mom, drying dishes, cocked her head, considering this.

"Maybe I do too," she said suddenly.

"Really? How come?" I was interested. It occurred to me that we had never discussed this part of living before. Mom's answer was typically French: realistic, sensible.

"Well, at first it sounds yucky"—*yuqui*—"but so is being buried, when you think about it. Being cremated is sanitary. And it's cheap! I saw on *20/20* that funeral directors rip you off"—*reep you uff*—"and I don't want you wasting money on me after I croak." We laughed. At that moment, the prospect of her croaking seemed very far away.

"And where do you want your ashes to go?" I asked her, already knowing the answer.

"France!" she exclaimed. "In my own backyard." Mom arrived in the U.S. as a war bride fifty years ago, admired her adopted homeland, was a proud naturalized citizen—but Gallic blood flowed in her veins, and she remained French to her toes.

Then she looked doubtful. "Can you bring ashes to France? Is it legal?"

"Oh, sure," I promised casually, not really knowing, but who cared? If it was what Mom wanted, it was what I would do— someday, a long time from now.

But how could we know that a month later a tumor would show up in her liver? And that soon she'd be too weak to care for herself, chemotherapy shrinking her already tiny frame to eighty pounds?

Six months later, she was gone.

I'm a therapist by profession. I thought I understood bereavement. But now I learned firsthand about the mother-daughter connection. No matter how much other love you have in your life, when your mother dies, your world is cut out from under you. For weeks I lived in a daze: lost, rootless, terrifyingly alone. This despite a loving husband, despite my loving friends. I found I contained an inexhaustible supply of tears. I wondered if I would ever feel all right again.

On the train, I am edgy, short-tempered. I hold the box containing her ashes, wrapped in a silk scarf she brought from France fifty years ago. Next to me is a city map of Troyes, my camera and extra film, and Kleenex. Lots of Kleenex.

I keep remembering my last trip here, to visit Mom's sisters, and how wonderful it was. I feel the tears welling up behind my eyes, as I imagine myself scattering the ashes. I keep my eyes fixed on the passing scenery, determined not to think about it. No need to feel this awful more than once.

Rue Lachat is a thin, dusty alley, ending in a cul-de-sac. We walk to the very end. There is the stone cottage owned by Mom's family for over one hundred years. There is the green-painted gatepost, paint flaking now. The gate is wired shut.

My aunts sold the house to the city over twenty years ago. It has sat vacant ever since. The last time we were here, we didn't dare do more than study the property from the outside.

Tom undoes the wire easily, and we step through a gate. To our left, a stone fence, at least six meters high, surrounds the property. A long path trails along the fence. We follow it to the end. A wooden gate, leading to the garden, is at the end of the path. Lifting the crossbar, we push the gate open and step inside to Mom's backyard.

It's an oasis, dazzling in the sun. Everything is pale green, the new springtime leaves tender and glossy—overgrown now, a jumble of ivy, of weeds, of buttercups, of fruit trees gone wild.

I have heard about this yard my entire life. I walk slowly through the greenery, touching plants, caressing the tiny apples forming on the trees. Silent, except for birdcalls, the drowsy hum of a bee.

My head is humming, filled with my mother. In my mind's eye, I see her little hands gesturing, watch her eyes gleam, see her wide, guileless smile. Her voice, her dainty accent, is so clear in my ears.

"Your grandfather loved birds. He used to sit on his chair in the yard, with his wooden leg propped on a stool—and sparrows would come and perch on it! . . .

"Your grandmother could grow anything. All the vegetables we ate she grew. During the war, all we had was rutabagas. The Nazis confiscated everything else. Lucky for us they didn't like rutabagas!"

So now here I am. Here on the site of a lifetime's worth of stories. My ancestral home. I'm the fourth generation, the last of my mother's line.

Finally, I kneel down, unzip my tote bag, lift out my precious burden.

"Welcome home, Mom," Tom says quietly.

"I promised I'd bring you back," I whisper, weeping. Just a little.

I poke a hole in the bag of ashes, shake a little dust onto the ground. It scatters lightly, lands on the pale-green leaves. I watch, fascinated. So quickly, it becomes part of the landscape, part of the yard. And then my leaden mood evaporates. I've been dreading this moment for months, and now it's here, and it's not awful. In fact, it's wonderful. She's here, she's home. I can feel Mom over my shoulder, encouraging me. *Let's geet theese show on ze road!*

Suddenly lighthearted, I rise to my feet, move out of the yard, hurry down the path to the main gate. Sprinkle some ash on the doorpost. Sprinkle a little in the mailbox. Sprinkle some over the path as I return to the garden. A forty-two-year-old Tinker Bell, scattering fairy dust.

"Ma, that's you all over," I say cheerfully.

Filled with joyous contentment, I feel her smiling behind me, feel my aunts, my grandparents, my great-grandmother, laughing at my performance. Death isn't forever, they're saying. We are. So are you.

In the middle of the garden, I hold the bag straight out in front of me, and I begin to spin, a slow circle. A sudden breeze touches the bag, catches the ashes, pulls them out, swirls them around me in a silver mist.

"Au revoir, Maman!" I shout.

"Bon voyage!"

"Je t'aime!" I scream. *I love you!*

The ashes dance in the breeze. The sun blazes overhead. I am laughing. Inside, I am lighter than air.

MARIE HEGEMAN

ME, MYSELF, AND I

If you've never truly discovered your own personal strength and worth as an independent woman, try traveling to an unfamiliar city alone.

I visited Minneapolis recently on business—I, a nearly native Texan, who's never experienced subzero temperatures. Several friends and family members had warned me how cold it is up there in the middle of January, how dangerous it is to be outside, and how my ears would fall off if I spent more than one minute in the cold. Sure, I listened—I'm always ready to take advice from those more knowledgeable than I am.

On the other hand, if I spent all my free time in the hotel, I'd never get to experience this beautiful city. So on my second day in the Twin Cities, I drove out to a suburb about twenty minutes from my hotel, to visit my former pastor's new church. Yep, I got lost, just as tourists do in a strange city when they get the wrong directions. But I discovered Hopkins, Minnesota—one of the quaintest cities I've ever seen. Hopkins is really a mixture of suburb and small town. Better yet, it snowed the entire hour I spent looking for the church. I've always wanted to live in a place where it snowed for Christmas, and even though Christmas was over, I pretended I was traveling to my family's home to spend the holiday in a snow-covered house with a snow-covered yard.

That afternoon, after finally finding the church and going to lunch with the pastor and his family, I checked out the Mall of America. Since I'm from Dallas, I'm used to seeing huge malls, but this was the Galleria times three and then some. It was possibly one of the most enjoyable adventures I've ever had. Being alone, I could walk as quickly or as slowly as I wanted. I could stop in any store I wanted and stay there for as long as I liked. I ended up spending three fun-filled hours in the mall, and then I decided to leave without having to ask if that was OK with my companion.

Don't get me wrong. I love spending time shopping and frolicking with friends and family. But this was a chance for me just to get away by myself and discover how much fun *I* am to be with.

You see, if I had been too afraid of the snow and the ice and the subzero temperatures, I'd never have discovered the warmth and beauty of this wonderful city, or how capable I am of getting around without anyone's help. Next time I go, though, I'll try to book the trip for June.

STEPHANIE LAURIDSEN

MODELING FOR LIFE

One late-summer day during my eleventh year, Mother and I spent a morning on a whirlwind shopping spree for back-to-school clothes. This was a rare event. Mom had a chronic illness and didn't often feel well enough to spend a day shopping. But on this particular day she seemed energized, as was I.

Mom treated me to lunch in the department store's restaurant. As we entered the dining area, I noticed elegant models sauntering from table to table, wearing the latest fall fashions. Since this was the prime buying season for school clothes, I wondered aloud why there were no preteen and teen models.

Impressed with my idea, Mother encouraged me to talk with someone. By the time dessert was served, she convinced me not only that my idea was great but that I should be one of those models!

I felt excited and scared. Her encouragement gave me confidence, and I actually began to believe in my idea and in myself. Mom's enthusiasm did not stop there; she persuaded me to talk to the store manager. Even though my stomach was churning, I was ready to apply for my first job!

Now, I should tell you I wasn't a willowy preteen version of Brooke Shields. No, I was short, a little chubby, bespectacled, and freckled—maybe cute but definitely not classic model material. Yet Mom's reassurance had convinced me I was beautiful and capable in that moment.

As the elevator doors closed, sending us up to the manager's office, I hesitated again. "Do you really think this is a good idea?" I asked.

In that moment, my mother spoke words that come back to me often—words that have changed the course of my life more than once. "What have you got to lose? You'll be no worse off if he says no. And maybe, just maybe, he'll say yes!"

So, refocused and inspired, I proceeded. When the elevator doors opened, I marched straight up to the secretary's desk and asked to see the store manager. The secretary hesitated, then let the manager know I wanted to see him. Before long, we were ushered into his office. As I sat across from him at his desk, I confidently explained that he had an opportunity to create more sales by showcasing back-to-school preteen and teen fashions this time of year. He listened politely and with interest. When I said I wanted to model, he gave me a job application, saying he would consider my suggestion.

While he never did call me, the next summer the department store ran a search for teens to model in the restaurant for a back-to-school fashion showing! In truth, I didn't really care that I was not selected. I had my reward. Mom gave me a gift that has endured a lifetime. Although she died a few years later, when I was fifteen, Mom's spirit is always with me when I face scary life situations.

Mom taught me it was safe to take risks, to believe in myself, and most important—to ask for what I want!

JOEANN FOSSLAND

VII
MOMENTS
OF TRUTH

"Truth is the only safe ground to stand upon."

—Elizabeth Cady Stanton

WE ARE ALL CONNECTED

While a junior at the University of Minnesota, I took a much-needed vacation to Mexico. I was tired. Tired in the way that only bartending full time at night while taking seventeen credits a quarter can make you. I went by myself, leaving my boyfriend and my books behind with the snowdrifts. I didn't want to meet anyone. I didn't want to party. I didn't even want to talk. I just wanted to stare. Sit on a beach and stare at the waves. Maybe poke around some ruins and stare at them too.

So when I kept bumping into the same gringo all over the Yucatán peninsula, I ignored it. I took the ferry to Isla Mujeres to stare at the phosphorescent fish, and he happened to be with the group waiting for the boat back to the mainland. I caught sight of him among the market tables at Mérida, where serapes and silver bangles were sold. I knew he wasn't following me, and I knew he must have noticed me, just as I couldn't help but notice him. Still, in need of rest and separation from people, I avoided eye contact with the ever-present gringo.

After climbing around the temples of Tulum, I climbed aboard a crowded bus for my return trip. I squeezed through the aisles toward the back and spied a perch on the edge of a seat that already had two people. The bus lurched onward, and I found myself sinking deep into thought. Even though I'd been surrounded for days by unfamiliar people, I realized we are all connected in some form. At that point, I looked up, to see seated next to me none other than the gringo!

We gave up trying to ignore each other. This was obviously kismet. The conversation came easily as we decided to become instant friends. We reached Cancún in a festive mood and headed for a lively little cantina with colored lights and palm trees.

After a satisfying dinner, a shared flan, and two cups of coffee, the gringo suddenly said, "Hey, what's your name?" We didn't even know each other's names! "Jean Wenzel," I said. A strange expression crossed his face. "What?" he asked, even though I was sure he'd heard me. "Jean Wenzel," I said again, enunciating very clearly.

He just looked at me. I looked at him. Finally, to break the odd spell that seemed to have come over him, I prompted, "What's yours?" He didn't reply, but he reached into his bag and pulled out his wallet and flipped it open to his driver's license. Yes, we really are all connected—his name was Gene Wensel.

JEAN WENZEL

THE "WRITE" MATCH

This had not been an ordinary day for me. I looked at the lighted clock as it tick-tocked its way to an ungodly three A.M. My husband, Harold, was oblivious to my tossing and turning. He couldn't possibly imagine my anxiety.

Normally, I have no concerns on the cruises I take. My handwriting expertise becomes entertainment, and the lectures I deliver are usually fun and informative. I take on the role of a stand-up comedienne.

That particular day, we had had over two hundred people jamming the auditorium. Typically, we choose a half-dozen couples at random and have a little fun with them. This day I was in rare form, and the audience was with me.

If I see something ominous through my handwriting analysis, I play it down. I have always believed that you should make the deposit before the withdrawal.

Amanda and Paul were engaged to be married shortly. They were traveling with their parents on this cruise, and they happened to be one of the couples I had selected for handwriting analyses.

Their future, they told me, depended on my input—not only for their lifetime commitment but for a "dream" house they were preparing to build, which would accentuate their individual lifestyle.

I immediately spotted something wrong. Amanda's writing was very large and covered the whole page. The way you fill your piece of paper is the way you fill your space in life. Her *t* bars were high, way past her *t*'s and flying across the page. She was a romantic—a dreamer with castles floating in the clouds. There weren't enough hours in the day for Amanda. She had a tremendous amount of scattered energy.

Paul's writing, on the other hand, was tiny, clear, and to the point, which indicated to me that he was very focused, detail-oriented, and meticulous. Every *i* dot was placed directly over the *i* and every *t* bar was in the center of the *t*.

It was obvious that Amanda needed people and Paul needed his private space, even though he enjoyed being with close friends.

Should I indicate that they may not be compatible, or should I turn romantic and tell them never mind the differences—that opposites in most cases attract each other?

Did I do the right thing? Handwriting analysis is not the answer to all problems. It is merely another technique for assessing whether there are problems. I took the side of the romanticist. I told them that they were made for each other: to go for it and build their dream house together.

They could be a good balance for each other, I felt. Amanda would bring excitement and spontaneity to Paul. Paul would keep Amanda well grounded and maintain the necessary stability.

I have had the opportunity of analyzing thousands of handwritings over a period of twenty years, but when I met Paul and Amanda, I felt a closeness and believed our paths would cross again one day.

The months flew by, and I was very curious as to how that love match turned out. I needn't have been concerned. My turning and tossing proved to be for naught. I received a letter (would you believe it was postmarked Sugar Notch, Pennsylvania?) from Amanda and Paul with a picture of their dream house. They looked extremely happy, and so did their newest addition, a baby girl they named Alice Stefanie Wilson—A.S.W. happen to be my initials.

ALICE STERN WEISER

LEADING FROM THE HEART

*A*s a new businesswoman, with a fresh M.B.A. at the age of twenty-eight, I thought I knew it all! I moved up quickly in my first position with a major corporation and soon found myself managing six hundred–plus women.

I had learned well how to manage the numbers, increasing our profits and finding new market niches. What I had not learned in business school was the human element—how to be a leader of people, not just a "manager."

A key aspect of my role was to give speeches to our staff at our semiannual meetings. Public speaking terrified me, as I had no idea what I could say that would be of interest to anyone. And some four hundred associates attended at these meetings—a daunting number.

My boss, a middle-aged gentleman, coached me to give updates on the business. To lessen the damage to my psyche, I would prepare and rehearse my speeches. I mastered the numbers—our profitability, our business direction, our venturing into new markets.

At one of these meetings, I had prepared my speech, done the requisite rehearsal in front of my mirror, and perfected my index cards for prompting. I was ready—or so I thought.

I stepped up to the podium and began my speech. People began to drift away. I heard an inner voice tell me, "They hate this! They're all wondering when it will be over and lunch will be served! Why do you always give these speeches, when you know they don't work?"

I looked up from my notes to check on the women in the first few rows. Sure enough, they seemed pulseless! I stopped and really looked at them (at least the few I dared to establish eye contact with). I made a quick decision. Loudly crumpling my speech into a big wad, I threw it over my shoulder. "Aw, the heck with this!" I stunned the audience and myself.

Having done that—quite dramatically, I might add—I looked out at the audience again. What was I going to say now? I still had fifteen minutes left for my presentation! After a few anxious moments, I said, "Let's talk about how we are doing and what's next. We are having a fantastic year, and we should be celebrating!"

I went on to talk about all our achievements, what I dreamed of for our organization, and how, together, we could do anything! The "speech" was a big hit! Instead of talking at them, I talked with them.

That day was most memorable for me. I learned that to succeed with people—especially women—you have to relate on a human level. What you *know* isn't as important as establishing trust and letting others know who you are. I needed to give them insight into who *I* was, what *I* valued, and how much *I* cared before I could gain their commitment and enthusiasm. I now call it "leading from the heart."

A few years later, I spoke again to this same group. Having grown significantly on the job, I had decided to move on to new challenges. The person I had been grooming was ready to take over my position, and I was to introduce her.

As I finished my remarks, the group stood up, one by one. I received my first standing ovation! I realized then how much my associates had taught me about leadership. A true leader communicates with people. A true leader allows others to lead, empowers others for success, and leads from the heart.

I also learned how amazing it is when people are truly on "speaking terms" with one another—whether with an audience of four hundred or with a single friend.

HOLLY ESPARZA

"The naked truth is always better than the best-dressed lie."
—ANN LANDERS

MY SAILOR MAN

Both of us between husbands and feeling carefree, a friend and I ventured to a dance club playing sixties rock 'n' roll music one night in the early eighties.

We stood in the back, watching the theatrics of both dancers and band. Absorbed in the atmosphere, I hadn't noticed the young man standing next to me until he asked for a dance.

His name was Terry, and he served as a first mate on a dredge ship currently in dry dock on the banks of the Columbia River. A merchant marine, he enjoyed the luxury of working one week on and one week off. As we talked, I recognized a spiritual kinship. On his reading list were *The Road Less Traveled* by M. Scott Peck and *Illusions* by Richard Bach. All evening we discussed the power of positive thought, the creative potential everyone possesses, the oneness of humanity—not the usual bar conversation. But we both communicated that neither of us wanted a committed relationship, just companionship. We both lied.

I admired his appearance—tall, six feet three, great physique, dark, thick hair, dark-brown almond-shaped eyes, and an exotic aura, the result of his Indonesian and Dutch heritage. I imagined him posing for the pages of some studly magazine, instead of holding me in his arms on the dance floor. That evening, I left the club enamored.

The following day he met my three children. I warmed at his instant rapport with them. His potential as a partner increased moment by moment. Already I'd formed a list of positive attributes beyond the obvious physical ones—like the mutual fondness between him and my children, and his embrace of a similar spiritual philosophy. Over the years, I came to discover a deeply compassionate soul, an attentive listener, a wise human being. The measure of his thoughtfulness and kindness caught me off guard. When my children's birthdays came around, he offered gifts to both them and me. "It's a big day for you too," Terry said. "This is the anniversary of the day you labored them into life." I throve on his unconditional love of me.

In the four years we dated, I kept watching for the emergence of his dark side. The only annoying thing I ever came up with was that he held his face too close to his plate when he ate—a ship-born habit. Without a good handle on his "grub," his plate might end up in shipmate's lap, especially on the open seas. Wasn't much of a defect, but it was all that surfaced.

We harbored a dinosaur in the living room, however, an irreconcilable difference, which we both ignored. Terry was eleven years younger than I. At his age, I'd married, borne three children, owned a home, and struggled through a divorce. I'd already lived a life he had yet to experience. Terry never kept his love of children a secret, or his desire for parenthood. He became a volunteer in the Children's Celebration at our church, joined a Big Brother program, and visited his home in North Carolina, as much to play with his nieces and nephews as to see the rest of his family. I'd made it perfectly clear that there'd be no more babies for me. The years of raising three children alone convinced me.

Neither of us wanted to address the dinosaur; we tiptoed around the monster. After all, we fit together, were comfortable, happy, and in love. But always, in the back of my mind, I couldn't bear the thought of his relinquishing parenthood to remain with me. On Saint Patrick's Day, 1985, while both of us sat crying into green beers at Paddy's Bar, I said goodbye. We agreed to continue supporting each other emotionally until we discovered our perfect mates. His arrived sooner than mine. Within a year, he met Rita, a young Irish student majoring in early childhood education. A suitable match. Too distraught to attend the wedding, I sent my love and then hopped on a plane for San Francisco to visit my daughter.

After he married, I stumbled in and out of meaningless relationships. Occasionally, I'd see him and Rita at church, but I tried to avoid them. One look at my face, and Rita would know that I still loved her husband. I'd spare them that. True relationships are eternal, I told myself. I'll keep his memory close to my heart. Maybe we'll meet again in the afterlife.

Sundays, it was my job at church to attempt to regulate the noise during the minister's meditation time by bouncing noisy children with their parents into the family room. One Sunday, hearing a whimpering child in front of me, I placed my hand on the father's shoulder. Terry's eyes looked up. Neither of us spoke. Slowly he rose to face me, then he held out his arms, offering me his baby girl. Except for her blond hair, she epitomized Terry. I held her close to my heart, cradling and comforting her. "You could have been mine," I whispered in her ear. "You could have been mine." Tears streamed from my eyes, dampening her blanket. When Terry and Rita rose for the group song, I returned their child. In the darkened church, I felt certain my tear-smudged makeup wouldn't give me away. Terry's soft eyes held mine for a long moment. We remained silent. Then he turned his attention back to his family and to the service. Quietly I slipped out of the room to weep over this final chapter in our love story.

Within a few more years, I'd meet and marry my life partner. But that day, the radiance in Terry's face as he offered me his child assured me that I'd made the right choice. I could only thank God for teaching me the truth about unconditional love. Sometimes it's best to love from a distance. . . . Other times, it means letting go.

LINDA ROSS SWANSON

> *"To love what you do and feel that it matters—*
> *how could anything be more fun?"*
> —KATHARINE GRAHAM

FEEDBACK IS A GIFT

My training work takes me into a wide range of corporate settings, from old-line financial institutions to funky communications firms. And I observe in my workshops a wide range of ways in which we make our professional lives harder on ourselves than we need to.

One technology company I consulted with operated in a highly competitive market where speed and product integrity were the keys to success. They were under tremendous pressure, both internally and from clients; and the employees needed each other's help and feedback in order to produce. Unfortunately, the prevailing atmosphere of fear, anger, and general paranoia made it hard to give and harder to get.

And now ten participants were gathered around the conference table for a session on "Giving and Receiving Feedback."

I had prepared my usual snappy two hours' worth of exercises, ideas, small-group breakout sessions, flip-chart lists, etc. My professional style is to be highly prepared, "buttoned up," and firmly in control.

We started with eliciting people's feelings about how feedback was or was not working in their environment. The bottom line was it wasn't working. People were upset and bitter about it; and even though each person wanted to be treated better, they had a hard time translating that into how to treat others.

I introduced an exercise I'd read about. Each participant

wrote his or her name at the top of a piece of paper, then the papers were passed around the table, until everyone had written a positive piece of feedback ("Something I like or admire or appreciate or respect or value about what you do") on everyone else's paper.

So far, so good. Papers were returned. And ten people now sat with a piece of paper in front of them, listing nine statements of positive feedback from their colleagues.

I took a deep breath. "Who would like to volunteer to have your paper passed around again? Only this time, the writers will read aloud to you what they wrote—and they can expand on their comment, if they wish. All you need to do is sit, listen, and say thank you. In fact, 'Thank you' is all you may say. Any takers?"

Silence. Chairs tilted back from the table. Eyes were averted. Doodling got intense. Nervous giggling. "Not me." "Nope." "I'm not going first." Blank looks into the mid-distance. The room was stuffed so thickly with tension, it seemed to cut off our air supply.

"Wait a minute, folks," I commented, "This is the good stuff. This is positive feedback, remember? This is what you want to hear."

Finally, a reluctant volunteer tossed her paper into the ring. "OK, let's go." She grimaced, crossing her arms protectively in front of her.

It started haltingly, awkwardly, and gradually it built upon itself. People heard from their peers words of thanks and encouragement and praise, everything from "I appreciate that you always say good morning when I come in" to "I'm amazed at how you manage to come up with off-the-cuff ideas when we're in client meetings."

They began to look at one another, making real eye contact. Readers began to elaborate on their written comments, expanding into longer and longer heartfelt comments. People couldn't wait to volunteer next. A huge void in the room, an emptiness that we had hardly perceived earlier and had barely realized needed filling, slowly began to fill with goodwill. And as that emptiness that we hadn't even recognized (it was just "corporate culture," "the way things were") began to change, body language changed. Breathing got deeper. The energy in the room shifted. It got slower, broader, more inclusive, and flowed generously out to others instead of being hoarded tightly inside.

I watched, spellbound, the faces of the givers of this feedback and those receiving it. People were glowing. And I, too, was moved by the immense shift in energy. I left center stage and sat down, quietly, to the side. I stopped directing. I put away my watch. I lowered my voice. I understood I was witnessing something extraordinary, and the rest of the planned workshop certainly wasn't going to continue according to my schedule— what was happening in front of me was far too important.

This day had created its own rhythm. The tremendous collective need we all have to be recognized and appreciated for our work had taken hold, and the participants were basking in words of acceptance.

What a powerful lesson we learned! Our personal needs as individuals can be honored in professional settings in a way that will make us that much more empowered to do the job. I've never met anyone yet who didn't work better when she or he felt better.

Or as Ray, one of the participants, said to me a few days later: "I always thought feedback was something to fear—no one ever seems to have anything good to say around here. So I guess I made it pretty hard on anyone who tried to talk to me. I sort of shut myself off from that stuff, and I probably wasn't the easiest guy to work with. But I can't tell you how surprised I was to hear my co-workers had noticed my work and really respected my contributions. That just blew me away. In fact, I'm taking a whole new approach—now I think feedback is a gift."

I couldn't have said it any better myself.

DIANE RIPSTEIN

RHYMES AND REASONS

As I sang to my newborn son, I contemplated my decision. The tune soothed my baby and me.

When I think about Patrick, my firstborn, I remember how difficult those first few months were. Whenever he got restless, I'd draw from my teaching days and sing a rhyme or two.

Patrick's first cry had been in late August—and so was the first day of school for my former students. I missed the cheerful faces of the schoolchildren and the musty smell of a closed-up classroom. Had I made the right decision? Should I have continued teaching after having a baby? Would I lose contact with my teaching peers and fade into lost volumes of aging yearbooks?

As conflicted as I was, I knew seeing my young baby mature into a toddler and a little boy was something I did not want to miss. On snowy mornings past, I'd be scraping my windshield before work. Now I was cuddling my son under warm blankets and watching the snow fall. An afternoon at the museum, a visit to the library story hour, or a walk around the block was very special for both of us.

While most of my focus was on mother-child activities, I also found time to sew and read, luxuries that were virtually nonexistent before. I enjoyed making Patrick's pumpkin costume for Halloween and felt proud of his Christmas stocking, with the sequins I had worked so hard to apply, hanging on the fireplace mantel.

Unfortunately, we at-home moms are many times misunderstood. I am asked, "Why are you wasting your life and career staying at home?"

My reply is simple. "I can always go back to teaching, but never to those wonderful days of motherhood." What a sad commentary on society when the most important job in the world must be defended.

It has been six years since I made this decision. It is just as special to see two more stockings above our fireplace (yes, with sequins too!) and the costume gallery I have created since that first October.

I walked near my sons' room last night and listened to Anthony corral his imaginary puppies and Dominic wail for attention. I started to enter and comfort my little one, only to be pleasantly surprised by my oldest son singing those same rhymes from my teaching days to calm his littlest brother.

As I leaned against the door, a new song filled my heart. It was then I realized I hadn't given up teaching at all!

ANTIONETTE VIGLIATURO ISHMAEL

> *"In search of my mother's garden,*
> *I found my own."*
> —ALICE WALKER

IT'S ALL IN THE FRIJOLES

The last six weeks of my mother's life became an opportunity for me to seek wisdom, to give thanks for all she had given me, and to rectify old hurts.

I was adamant about not leaving any unfinished business between us. I wanted to end our time together on good terms. Why else was I given a warning about Mom's limited time on this planet just days before her terminal diagnosis?

The warning had come in the middle of the night while I was in a twilight dream state. "It's time for me to go . . . it's time for me to go," she told me. I immediately got up, dressed, and drove to her home, twenty minutes away.

I half expected her to be gone when I arrived, but when I walked quietly into her bedroom, she woke up and asked, "What are you doing here?"

"I dreamed you told me it was time for you to go, and I didn't want you to leave until I told you I love you."

"I love you too, but not at four o'clock in the morning," she replied. That was the first glimpse I got of Mom's wry sense of humor.

Four days later, she collapsed. The doctor told me she was suffering from kidney disease and gave her six weeks to live.

My mother was a physically small woman, five feet tall. Born in Mexico, she had only an eighth-grade education and had made her living as a seamstress. But she was a woman of tremendous character and discipline.

To set a good example, Mom went back to school to achieve her own high school diploma when I was in high school. She worked to improve her English by daily reading the newspaper out loud, and helped friends and relatives as they went through their struggles with the language.

She read biographies and autobiographies written by famous and often self-made men and women, along with fine literature and poetry. She loved to read lessons from the Bible and from *Science and Health with Key to the Scriptures* each morning before going to work. Mom was strong and tough-minded, wise and practical, elegant, refined, and gracious.

One day as she lay in bed a few weeks after the grim medical diagnosis, I asked her what made her so strong. The sun streamed through the French windows of her bedroom as I leaned forward in anticipation of the wisdom I was about to receive, sure it would transform my life.

I had expected to hear her draw from the teachings of Mary Baker Eddy, discoverer and founder of Christian Science, and one of her role models. Or to draw upon an inspirational quote from the Bible.

"Beans! Beans have made me strong." I laughed, but was somewhat disappointed that she didn't leave me with a stronger message.

It wasn't until months after her death, as I was preparing *frijoles de la olla,* and recalled Mom's instructions on how to cook the perfect beans, that I realized the power of her deathbed message to me.

Mom took great care in washing and sorting her beans. After running water over them several times, she would spread them out on a tray or a large dish and then pick out and discard any imperfectly shaped, shriveled, or dark-colored beans. She always eyed them carefully. Each bean for her pot had to be a perfectly flawless pinto. "A bad bean can sour the pot," she would say.

Mom also cautioned me against adding cold water to the cooking pot if the water evaporated below a certain point, or the beans would turn dark and not appear fresh when served. Her beans were not only delicious but pretty to look at.

While I was cooking, I realized what Mom had meant months earlier.

Not only are beans the staple of the Mexican diet and filled with strength-giving iron, but the rigor she applied to eliminating any undesirable beans was the same exacting attention she paid to eliminating character flaws and weaknesses in herself and those around her. The beans were a vivid example of what she had tried to teach me as a young girl.

And so I finally got it. What all that tough love was about. The emphasis upon developing character and self-control. Taking in only the good and rejecting the bad. That day, in the kitchen, I understood why beans made my mother so strong.

YOLANDA NAVA

"Surround yourself with people who respect you and treat you well."
—CLAUDIA BLACK

SOMETHING TO CHEW ON

Confidence in yourself is like money in the bank. I've heard that eighty-five percent of your success comes from having confidence in yourself. This is one of the key points I teach in success seminars, and one I learned the hard way.

Several years ago, I had a boss who got belligerent every time he had a few drinks at lunch. When he returned to the office from one of those two- or three-hour "business lunches," he'd always pick on somebody. We all dodged when we saw him coming. But one day I didn't duck fast enough, and I became his victim.

He chewed me out loud and long in front of several of my co-workers. (He obviously hadn't heard that it's important to praise in public and criticize in private.) By the time he was through yelling at me, my confidence was down the tubes. And the worst part was that I still had to tape a TV show that afternoon and give a lecture to hundreds of people that night. I had a tough time making it through my appearances. I choked up a few times, remembering the devastating things my boss had said to me earlier.

I'm a tenderhearted person who cries easily, and I cried all night long, humiliated by the verbal lashing that afternoon.

Once the tears dried up, I knew I had to take action to get my confidence back. Lying in bed the next morning, I thought of everything I'd learned about building confidence and self-esteem. Silently I listed all my good qualities, before slipping out of bed to retrieve my "Treasure Box." This special box is filled with notes of appreciation I've received, newspaper clippings about me, honors, and love notes from my husband and my sons. My spirits were buoyed after reading several pieces. Then I developed a plan to turn around the situation with my boss. I noticed my confidence rising already just by my thinking of taking positive action.

"I need to talk with you, please," I said as I walked into my boss's office next day. He looked apprehensive as he motioned me toward the chair in front of his massive desk. The chair was low, to intimidate others. I smiled warmly at him while making a point of sitting as tall and proud as I could.

"I'm sorry I upset you yesterday," I told him, "and there are some facts you haven't heard." Calmly I pointed out the information he was missing, and then I asked, "Now, could you tell me something good about me? After all," I added in jest, "you're the one who hired me, and I wouldn't want you to jeopardize your credibility with the staff!"

He stared at me hard for a few moments, then released his arms from their grip across his chest. He started listing positive things about me—many more than I had expected. I walked out of his office feeling more validated than I had expected. My being proactive was definitely working.

A couple of weeks later, though—right after lunch—the boss's secretary called me on the intercom. "Rita," she said, "he's *really* upset and on his way to chew you out. I know how he demoralizes everyone. Get ready."

My heart sank only momentarily, then I stood up, chuckled to myself, and stepped out into the hallway to wait for him. I had his number! There he came, his temples pulsating, his fists clenched, and his teeth all but bared. He was primed for me with both barrels. I smiled widely and waved real friendly-like, as if to say, *Come on down!* He hesitated as it dawned on him: When he got through chewing me out, I was going to say, "Okay, now say something good about me!" Instantly, he wheeled around and stalked back to his office.

Do we hang around and just let someone chew on us at will? Never. If we can't make a significant difference with that person, it's time to make plans to move on. In my case, however, once I dealt with my emotions, the solution was simple. I asked for what I needed! By doing so, I was able to make a large deposit into my "bank of confidence."

RITA DAVENPORT

VIII
THE ANIMAL CONNECTION

"No animal should ever jump up on the dining room furniture
unless absolutely certain
that [she] can hold [her] own in the conversation."

—FRAN LEBOWITZ

> *"To keep something you must care for it;*
> *more, you must understand what kind of care it requires."*
> —Dorothy Parker

ONE SOUL, TWO HALVES

My husband grew up on a farm where his family raised horses and dogs, so he has spent much of his life in the presence of animals. Yet he remarks in reference to Cali and me, "I have never known an animal and a human who were more like two halves of the same soul."

I was a young teacher working in a foreign country and she a two-month-old ball of matted fur when we met. I decided a German shepherd dog would be a good companion for a single female living alone in a remote village. Big and robust by four and a half months, Cali stepped on a scorpion ambling across the porch one night and was quickly reduced to an immobile, lethargic pup. How she managed to live through the incident I do not know; a friend's puppy, two weeks younger, had died from such a bite within two hours.

Cali lived, but she was completely paralyzed. She could not even move her mouth to eat, so I fed her by dripping raw egg down the back of her throat. Her body deteriorated so much so that her coarse hair turned curly from coiling around the bones protruding through her coat. As if that wasn't bad enough, she developed a blood infection and high fever from the wound, so I carried her across the country on rattletrap buses and in my arms to an American vet, who put her on IV fluids for a week and then sent us home, saying there was nothing more to be done. Nonetheless, I collected water at night and submerged her in it during the day to control her fever. And so we lived for over a month: I, at five feet three and one hundred pounds, carrying a forty-pound paralyzed dog across my shoulders everywhere I went, and she defying death.

Having spent so much time carrying her around with me to monitor her health, I felt it was silly to leave her home once she recovered and was able to get around on her own. She hiked with me through the mountains and curled up under a child's desk each day in the rural schools where I taught. She ate her dinner next to me on the dirt floor each night, and when I went to use the "bathroom" behind a tree, she would squat next to me. We were constant companions and best friends, and to this day I can think of nothing we would not do for each other.

Not that I needed proof of this loyalty, but she demonstrated it one night after I'd moved to a house with a bedroom that opened directly onto an enclosed courtyard. The outer double doors were made of two pieces of wood, which were attached to the adobe walls with rusty nails and supported inside by a two-by-four. A strong wind could have knocked down that door; but I was due to return to the States in just a few months and had become somewhat complacent. Besides, I arrogantly assumed I was young and strong and could take care of myself in an emergency.

Cali's growls woke me in the middle of the night as she stood guard over me on top of the bed, facing the door with her teeth bared. I heard footsteps on the concrete patio outside, advancing slowly toward the bedroom door. Never in my twenty-four years had the implications of a sound been clearer to me; never had I been more terrified. While I had rehearsed such a scenario in my head countless times—how I would defend myself with quick kicks to the shin and groin and blows to the bridge of the nose—when the moment to act presented itself, I was immobilized by fear. My body was like lead; I could not even move my arm to reach for the knife I kept hidden under my pillow. I just lay there, unable to breathe, sure I would suffocate before the man outside had a chance to kill me. "Breathe!" I said to myself, and finally managed to suck in a gulp of air. The footsteps echoed closer, and still I could not move.

As he threw his body against the door to break through, Cali leapt from the bed, and their bodies hit those two wooden boards at exactly the same time. Through the cracks in the wood, she clawed at him with her paws and slashed at him with her teeth. Still he persisted. Yet every time he stepped back and flung his body at the door to break it down from the outside, she flung her body at it from the inside and held up that rickety old door. After what seemed like an eternity but could not have been more than twenty seconds, he ran off—as scared of my dog as I had been of him. This time it was she who saved me.

The more time we spent together, the closer we became, until the similarities seemed almost eerie to those who do not trust in the bonds between animals and the humans they love. Whenever I got a cold, so did Cali. When my allergies got bad after I'd returned to the States, Cali developed allergies too, and after a series of tests, it was determined that we are actually allergic to the same foods and pollens. When my allergies improved, so did hers. At my wedding, a large outdoor affair, a friend held Cali on a leash throughout the ceremony. Just as the minister asked, "Do you take this man?" and right before I responded "I do," a long, loud howl echoed from the back of the crowd. It was Cali, most surely saying, "I do too."

Unfortunately, the similarities did not end there. Six months after I was diagnosed with a benign heart murmur, Cali was also diagnosed with a heart murmur. We were driving cross-country on our honeymoon, with Cali in the back seat. She had developed a weepy eye, and I was concerned some road dust was irritating it, so we stopped at a veterinary hospital in Salt Lake City to have it checked. The vet looked at her eyes, then as part of the routine exam put the stethoscope to Cali's chest. His forehead furrowed and he bit his lip as he moved the stethoscope across her body for a full five minutes. Finally, he straightened up and addressed us. "Her eyes are fine," he said, "but she has a serious heart condition." As I held her and cried, we did an immediate ultrasound to confirm his diagnosis: subaortic stenosis. There really was not anything to be done; the cardiac specialist we took her to said he had never heard a worse heart. "If you treat her normally, she has two months to live," he said. "But if you keep her inside at all times, prevent her from running around or exerting any energy, she may have a life span of up to two years."

"I can't do that," I said. "She plays outside every day; we run together all the time. She'd be absolutely miserable locked up inside."

"Then you'll kill her," the vet said.

"But she'll die happy," I retorted. "I know she'd prefer a short, happy life to a long, miserable one." Though devastated at her prognosis, I relished the opportunity to ensure that the end of her life would be as much fun as the beginning had been.

That was well over three years ago. Cali and I walk or jog a couple of miles to the park every day—depending on my level of stamina!—where she plays with a pack of dog friends and swims in the river. She has since traveled back and forth across the country twice more, has hiked the redwood forest, and is so healthy that the only reason we go to the vet anymore is to update her vaccines. Oh, her heart is still in terrible condition. In fact, whenever we do go to the vet, the staff always asks politely if everyone in the office can listen to it. "You'll never hear a heart like this again," they say to one another. The vet admits he has never seen a healthier-looking dog with a worse heart, and adds that there is no medical explanation for her longevity.

I can explain it, though. Cali teaches me every day that there are forces greater than medicine and technology. From the minute she recovered from that scorpion bite, she has repaid my nurturing with unwavering loyalty and friendship. She has been the guardian of not only my physical body but also my soul. In times of loneliness and fear, she has again and again offered herself wholeheartedly and unselfishly to me. Out of love for me, she continues to live.

I am no fool; I know that eventually Cali will die. Nonetheless, I have had the opportunity to share my soul with a wise and generous teacher. When I needed it most, God sent me an angel disguised in fur to remind me of the power of love.

ELLEN URBANI HILTEBRAND

KEEPING THE HIGH WATCH

Almost home, *fifteen minutes ahead of schedule*. I had just enough time to change clothes before jumping back into the car for a forty-five-mile commute to meet a real estate agent who was showing me a property in my soon-to-be "new neighborhood." A stoplight! Damn it—the longest light in the area.

While waiting for the light to change, I caught a glimpse of a rather large bird, flying low. A very small bird appeared to be nipping at the large bird's tail, as if in attack. But after watching awhile, I realized that the larger bird was the mother, that the small bird must be taking its fledgling flight. Suddenly the baby bird lost altitude and fluttered erratically, obviously unable to stay aloft. The mother swooped down and lifted the baby on her back into the still, clear-blue sky, and then pulled away again. Unsteadily, the baby regained its flying ability, and the mother remained only inches away. Slowly the mother moved a few feet to the side, and then a few feet below. Baby was doing fine.

Tooting horns at the signal change reminded me that others needed to move their cars for destinations unknown. I drove slowly, observing my birds. Watching this momentous occasion for baby and the loving, protective measures by mom had become more important than any scheduled appointment. So I would delay my meeting fifteen more minutes. This was life!

I thought back to when my baby took her first steps. First I held her hand and then, ever so gently, I released it, but keeping my hands close enough to catch her if necessary. My eyes swelled with tears. I felt such love for a mother who nurtured and was now helping to release her young to follow the path of life. My own daughter had had a baby nine months earlier and was experiencing motherhood for the first time.

We release our young so many times, in so many ways. Their first steps, their first days at school, their first dates, going away to college, and of course marriage. But we never release them from our hearts.

Mom and baby bird were soaring freely as I approached my garage. No time to spare now—I raced to the door. The phone began to ring. Oh, let the machine answer it, was my first thought, but I felt compelled to answer. Another five minutes down the drain, I thought.

My daughter was calling from her home, fifteen hundred miles away, with news that her son, my grandson, had taken his first steps minutes before. I began to cry. I believed that I had been there in some beautiful, unexplainable way. God had shared the moment with me.

I called my real estate agent and had her rearrange the appointment for a few hours later that day. I went for a walk on the beach and sat awhile, just looking out over this beautiful world. Taking a deep breath, I looked up. Birds soared overhead. And my grandson had started his own journey through life. Carefully, I hope—one baby step at a time.

EILEEN DAVIS

"Dogs' lives are too short. Their only fault, really."
—AGNES SLIGH TURNBULL

DAZY JOY

She had been failing for almost a year when she stopped eating. The next day, she took no water. Being human, I wanted her to live. Using the turkey baster, I tried to drip liquids down her throat, but she turned her head away. "Enough," she seemed to say with her eyes. "It's time for me to die."

With that she crawled into my lap and allowed me to rock her slowly back and forth. Hours we spent together that day, her thin shepherd body draped over my arms, my face against her neck, memories swirling in my head.

I thought about the day we first met. Apparently the school stray, a beggar and a botherer of students and faculty alike, she was tied to a bench, awaiting the arrival of the dogcatcher, when I breezed into the university office. We looked into each other's eyes, and our souls met. I untied her, carried her to my office, and fed the starving young animal. In no time, she was in the back seat of my car, heading to her new home.

My husband and I named her Dazy Joy, and she became our constant companion and most devoted friend. She went everywhere with us: vacations, day trips, family dinners, and holidays. She became the matriarch of the family, frequently barking out instructions as if she could talk.

Over the next many years, Dazy Joy served as overseer to the dozens of rescued animals who came and went at our home. A firm disciplinarian, she was also tolerant of the newcomers. Yet in spite of the many pets and people who occupied her space over the years, she never relinquished her role as guardian over us, the animals, and the house.

She could always read my mind.

So on that final day, sensing I'd reached a restful place in my mindful reverie, she slipped out of my arms and stood solidly on the floor. In tears, I watched Dazy Joy amble her tired, weak body from room to room in the house. No door was left unnudged as she entered and paused in each space to look around. Her purpose seemed twofold. Using every bit of the strength she had left, she was saying goodbye. And before letting go of her role as guardian over me, Dazy Joy needed to check one last time to make sure all would be well in my world. Satisfied, she walked to the front door and beckoned for me to follow her.

That day, sixteen and a half years after our first meeting, we made the journey back to the fate from which I had once saved her. I held her close as she willingly accepted the medicine. Eight years later, I still hold her close. A framed picture of her on my nightstand is my constant reminder.

CINDY POTTER

> *"Dogs will come when called.*
> *Cats will take a message and get back to you."*
> —Missy Dizick and Mary Bly

OSCAR

We first met Sylvester when he emerged from the shrubbery in our front yard. He was timid but hungry, and his plaintive "meoooww" was obviously a request for food. My husband, Rocky, and I began to bring him scraps of food each afternoon, and he came to expect them, showing up at the same time each day. He was a stray one—a tomcat who lived in the woods, and we began to feel responsible for this independent little spirit. But we weren't ready to call him "our cat" just yet. We named him Sylvester because he looked just like the cartoon character, with the same markings and tufts of fur on his cheeks. You could almost hear him say, "Thufferin' thuccotath!"

I realized it was high time for inoculations and neutering after he'd had a run-in with a family of raccoons. They beat him up good and tore big patches of fur off his hide. So I made the appointment with the veterinarian for the following week. We decided he had "adopted" us and he was now ours. But it wasn't to be. A couple of days later, I found Sylvester on the back porch, lying very still. I rushed him to the vet, where he died that night.

It was a sad day for Rocky and me.

"If only we'd gotten his shots sooner, if only we'd taken better care of him," we lamented. In the next few days, for some reason the name Oscar kept popping up in my head. I mentioned it to my husband, and we agreed to name our next cat Oscar—but only when we were ready for one.

A week or so later, my mother called and said she had a cat for me. I told her I wasn't over Sylvester yet, and besides, I thought I'd wait awhile. But my mother was unusually insistent.

"This cat needs a home or he'll be taken to the Humane Society!"

She said her friend Bernie was feeding the cat. It had been abandoned at her apartment, where she could not have a pet.

"I really appreciate your intentions, Mom, but no, thanks. Does the cat have a name?"

"Yes," she said. "Bernie calls him Oscar."

Chills traveled down my spine. I knew this was my cat! When I went to pick him up, I fell in love immediately. This little fellow had a big gray splotch on his nose. He looked me in the eye and came right up to me, as if to say, "It's about time you got here."

Oscar is still with us. He must have been a very successful stray, because when we first got him, he was a little chubby. We put him on low-fat cat food, got his shots, and had him "fixed."

He is, as Bernie put it, "A very fine kitty indeed." We call him a dozen different variations of his original name—Osca-furball, Oscalario, Oscabidilly-oskies—to fit his moods.

I feel as though this cat came my way for a reason. Oscar has given me the gift of a second chance at "motherhood." The fact that I knew his name before I even knew of him confirms my belief in what many other cat lovers know—that I didn't find my cat; he found me.

CINDY HANSON

LOOK-ALIKE LUCYS

*S*oft and fuzzy, with slightly worn light-brown fur, the little bear looks as though she has been hugged a lot. Her eyes are shiny black and her nose is an upside-down triangle made of yarn. I am constantly brushing the fur out of her eyes, so she can see better.

When I first saw my Lucy, she was sitting in a store window, tucked in with a hundred other teddy bears. But she stood out like she was the only one. She looked just like my daughter's bear. As we stared at each other through the window, my eyes filled with tears. Knowing she would be coming home with me, and that she represented much more than a stuffed bear, I took a few moments to compose myself before going into the store to purchase her.

"Bears don't like bags," I said as the clerk handed me the change. "I'll carry her." Lucy felt comfortable under my arm, as if she belonged there. A gentle stirring in my heart, and a measure of the peace I had been seeking settled in.

My soft bear lay snuggled under the covers between us that night as my husband and I talked quietly about the other Lucy. Our daughter Janice had loved the life into her Lucy, until even we thought it was real. Jan would tell us about the bear's daily adventures, weaving elaborate tales of mischief and fun. Laughing, she blamed Lucy for the crumbs on her sheets, saying the little bear sneaked cookies into her bed. In later years, Lucy took rides in Janice's car, secure in a seat belt until a cute guy pulled up next to them. Then the two of them would wave madly, getting the boy's attention and a big smile.

Janice often moved bears from my collection to her room down the hall. Baby Bear was her favorite. Investigating, I would find the two bears, Baby Bear and Lucy, keeping company in the old wooden rocker, "sharing stories and waiting for tea," Janice would tell me with a straight face.

Lucy became her confidante, listening attentively to endless chatter about school and horses and boyfriends. Once in a while, tears of a young girl's frustration and disappointment matted the fluffy fur. The little bear gave quiet, unconditional love, and Jan loved her back.

The games we played with the bears added humor and lightness to the sometimes difficult teenage years, when independence was important to her and guidance was important to me.

We were the best of friends and still playing bear games when Janice died suddenly, at the age of twenty-two. Her Lucy rests with her, and I picture the two of them laughing and scheming as they continue their adventures together.

I slept with my Lucy for several years after Janice's death. The wise little bear seemed to listen with all her heart when I talked of happy memories, or whispered how much I missed the fun and laughter Janice and I shared. Sometimes, when the grief was overwhelming, she caught the tears of sadness. Always, she felt warm and comforting to hold. She gave me unconditional love, and I loved her back.

Healing comes with time, and I no longer need to sleep with my soft brown confidante. These days, Lucy nestles close to Baby Bear in the old rocking chair and listens to my morning chatter.

I tell her about our four beautiful grandsons and the funny things they say and do. I talk about dinners and hikes with old friends, and describe the new friends I have made. I tell her that I love my art classes and that I will graduate from college soon. Her little mouth is buried in matted fur, but I know she is smiling. I know that Janice and her Lucy are smiling too. And I know that our Lucys are connected to each other, just as Janice and I are connected—through pure love.

SUSAN MILES

A FLUTTER OF
BUTTERFLY WINGS

Mom always told me, *"You will try to deny it and you will try to resist it, but you cannot help what you feel."*

This thought was going through my head the first time I met Nick. It was not a clap of thunder or an explosion of any sort, but rather like a whispering flutter of butterfly wings in my stomach, a loud beating of my heart . . . bup-bup, bup-bup, bup-bup . . . and my pulse throbbing in my ears.

I waited for the alarm bells to go off in my head. I wanted Nick to grab hold of me and kiss me hard so that those bells would go off, stopping me in my tracks. When the warning bells finally came, I told myself, "Look at your finger! You're practically married to another man!" But every time those bells sounded, I ignored them, because it hurt too much to think that I wasn't in love with the man I was supposed to marry.

I waited for the feelings I had for Nick to go away. I wanted them to go away. It wasn't right to feel this way about another man. But as the days turned into weeks, the weeks into months, I found myself drawn deeper into his world.

The light, male musky scent of him touched my nostrils before he was even in sight. His laughter, deep and thorough, made me smile in response. The feel of his eyes on my back caused me to turn automatically to find him watching me, waiting for me. I could not help wanting him. It was a force I had no control over. Like gravity, it pulled me in.

One day he was sitting at his desk, concentrating—hand in his hair, a frown creasing his brow. I noticed the straight lines of his back and the veins that ran down his arm as he worked. I felt a strange sense of something . . . something akin to pride. Then, before my eyes, I saw him as he would be in fifty years.

His dark hair now gray, the lines of laughter embedded in the skin around his eyes, and the once-straight back slightly stooped with age. The stirring sensation of butterfly wings in my stomach returned with force. That was when I was certain I loved him. I took a deep breath and smiled, finally at peace with myself.

I left my boyfriend and followed my heart. It led me straight into Nick's arms, where I have been ever since. We are married now, and it has been five years since I first felt those butterfly wings fluttering. They are not there every day, nor every time I look at him. But I have found that when I feel I love him the least, they flutter the hardest, and in the times when I love him most, I don't feel or hear them at all. They are simply there as a reminder—from my heart—telling me that I made the right choice.

LON MY LAM

*"When you feel really lousy,
puppy therapy is indicated."*
—SARA PARETSKY

A GIFT OF LOVE

*L*ove came bounding into my life on four legs just
when I needed it most. Auric—the Latin name for gold
—was a golden retriever, with a special capacity for
love. He looked and acted like a normal pup, but as he grew,
his special qualities became more apparent.

His first year with me was the hardest I've ever known. Not
only did my marriage end with a sad betrayal, but I was being
stalked by a mentally unstable man. I work as a morning radio
personality, and this fan had become obsessed with me after
hearing my voice. A restraining order, routine police patrols by
my house, and a special alarm system did little to ease my fears.
Auric became what little security I had. He stood by me as I
peeked out the windows, checking for any signs of my unwanted suitor. At times, he'd check out the house for me, running from room to room as if to show me that nobody was
there.

Many nights I'd curl up on the rug in front of the fireplace
and fall into a restless sleep. I'd wake up to find Auric lying
nearby, watching over me. Some nights, when sleep never came
at all, I'd sit alone, crying, trying to rid myself of the pain and
fear aching in my heart. Auric never left my side. He'd sit with
his head on my knee for hours, offering what comfort he could.
And, like any good friend, he knew when I'd wallowed long
enough in self-pity. He'd growl and bark—rear end wagging in

the air, chin on the floor, a favorite toy stuffed in his mouth—urging me to snap out of it and play. The silliness of his mood would build until I'd agree to a game of fetch or keep-away. He'd have me tearing through the house after him in fits of laughter.

Fortunately, things improved dramatically in our second year together. The "stalker" had been placed on probation, under strictly monitored supervision, and I finally felt free to return to the world of the living.

Auric and I ran the wooded trails near our home, played games in the park, and spent hours fly fishing along a mountain river. He instinctively knew not to bother the wildlife we encountered there. Considering the retriever blood that pulsed through his veins, I regarded this behavior as not only unusual but remarkable.

One bleak winter day near the beginning of his third year, I lost him. I'd lain down for a nap, and I woke to find him gone. He normally sat in the front yard each afternoon, to watch the kids walk home from school. I checked there first, finding no sign of him. Frantic trips around the neighborhood failed to reveal his whereabouts.

I spent weeks tacking up flyers, knocking on doors, and making trips to the shelter. Finally, a worker there took me aside to gently help me face reality. My special dog would not likely be coming home. This kind man explained that someone had probably found or taken Auric and decided to keep him. Privately, I pored through old photos, remembering him. Family and friends listened sympathetically as I choked out my favorite Auric stories. Some of them even shared their own stories with me.

Several months passed, and one Sunday morning I spotted an ad in the newspaper. A family needed to find a home for their two-and-a-half-year-old golden retriever. I drove to the address, secretly expecting to see my long-lost friend bound toward me in fond remembrance. Soul pals, together again! Sad, silly me. Instead I found a shy, sweet lad with quiet manners and an insatiable appetite for a game of fetch. I sank into a lawn chair, elbows on my knees, chin in my hands, and watched.

This dog didn't have the stocky good looks of my old friend. No sign of any uncanny perception visible in his brown eyes, either. The only thing he seemed interested in was a stick being tossed back and forth across the yard. Depression settled over me like a chilly fog. After a few minutes, my sadness gave way to feelings of guilt and worry. What would become of this unwanted dog if I didn't offer him a place to live?

I drove back home with Sam riding in the back of the car, all his worldly possessions in tow; a chipped plastic bowl and a tattered leash. I glanced at him in the rearview mirror. His eyes darted furtively from the back of my head to the rapidly passing landscape beyond the car window. He looked insecure and in desperate need of a friend. Someone with enough time for taking walks and trips to the river and playing games of fetch. I suddenly remembered Auric, and I smiled at the lesson he had taught me about the magic of unconditional love. As I caught another glimpse of Sam, I decided right then and there to open up my heart and give my new pup a chance.

DEBB JANES

IX
ACTS OF KINDNESS

"Too much of a good thing is wonderful."

<small>Mae West</small>

THE MEMORY JAR

As Mother's Day approached, I asked myself, "What does Mom *really* want for a gift?" She didn't need another knickknack, I don't know her style or size in clothes anymore, and I used up all my good gift ideas last year (I gave her a fruitcake). I was stumped.

Then it hit me. What she really wants to know is that she made a difference in my life. For many of us, our parents worked hard and sacrificed. Some even gave up their dreams so we could have ours. All they really want is some feedback that their efforts worked! So to say thanks, I made my mother a Memory Jar.

I bought a cut-glass jar with a lid. Then, on one hundred little pieces of paper, I wrote down memories like:

- *I remember our talk the night before I got married.*
- *I remember calling you from the hospital and telling you your first grandchild had been born.*

I set the wrapped cut-glass jar on Mom's coffee table. She edged her way along to the center of the sofa, sat down, and pulled the gift to her lap.

Mom wasn't sure what it was when she saw the label: "The Memory Jar." Noticing her inquisitive look and the arch in her eyebrow, I instructed Mom to take the lid off the jar, reach in, and select a memory.

"Oh," she said. "This is like that old TV show *This Is Your Life!*"

"Kind of," I replied, my voice already trembling. "Except it's really about your life and mine together."

Tears sprang up immediately in her eyes as she read her first memory:

- *I remember you giving me my first bicycle—shiny blue and just my size.*

Mom reached for another slip of paper, and I said, "Wait! You only want to pull one memory out each day and savor it." Finding the memories too irresistible, she laughed, waved me off, and reached into the jar. Mom wanted more memories now!

- *I remember how scared I was (at age nine) when you went to the hospital for surgery.*
- *I remember how I loved to watch you get ready to go out dancing on Saturday night. I knew my mom was the most beautiful mother in the world!*
- *I remember how smart you were raising six kids.*
- *I remember waking up Christmas morning and unwrapping the doll I'd prayed would be under the tree.*
- *I remember saving half the money to buy go-go boots, and the other half you added.*

Mom looked up at me, laughing and crying at once. She whispered, "You've just created a new memory for me. I will always remember this Mother's Day."

I became excited, thinking about the possibility of adding precious memories to the jar from now on. I even felt a twinge of sweet pressure to be sure and create more momentous times to share—especially when Mom read the last memory some time later, looked up at me half-jokingly, and said, "Got any more?"

MARY LOVERDE

ROAD WARRIORS

My mother always told me, "Never judge a book by its cover," and as a young girl growing up in the sixties, I tried very hard to follow that sage advice. It was easy back then; I lacked the wisdom and experience to understand that sometimes the cover of a book spoke volumes, that it would tell you everything you needed to know without your ever having to crack the binding. As an adult, I learned that one must trust first impressions, for often they are far more accurate than studied opinion.

One dark night about ten years ago, after a long day of frustrating meetings during which every design I showed my client was critically shredded on the spot, I was driving home on the Massachusetts Turnpike, making the two-hour trip from Springfield to Boston. I was tired and cranky, eager to get home to the comfort of my family. I had stomped out of my last meeting without even bothering to make a pit stop before the drive, and my full bladder was terrorizing me. I comforted myself with the thought that at that late hour there wouldn't be any waiting lines outside the ladies' room at the rest area. It always makes me crazy to see the men waltz right in, while I stand outside fidgeting and twitching, trying to stall off the inevitable.

Pulling off the highway and into the rest area parking lot, I found myself in a forest of huge trucks, grimy gray giants in never-ending rows. I got out of the car and locked it and made my way to the head of the row. As I walked, I saw a man emerging from between two trucks a few rows down. I strained to see him through the darkness, and my first impression was that he blended into the velvety night; in black pants and T-shirt, boots and a cowboy hat, he was just another form of darkness. I began to feel a bit nervous.

He roughly paralleled me as we both made our way through the parking lot, and as he edged closer to me, I could see a greasy blond ponytail hanging down, bouncing off his back as he quickened his pace. I wondered why he was quickening; maybe he had to pee too. But he was looking at me, his expression far too interested for my liking. I saw a cigarette pack rolled into one of his sleeves, a tattoo on his upper arm.

I hurried, leaning into the cool evening breeze. The sound of cars and trucks whizzing by on the turnpike could not overshadow his footsteps, which were faster than my own. He appeared to be younger than I, and for the first time in my life, I felt the fear of a woman growing older, the vulnerability of knowing without doubt that I was slower, weaker, and more frightened than my unwanted "traveling companion."

We drew steadily closer to the building that housed the rest rooms, my salvation, but every time I stepped up my pace, he did so as well. Feeling my heart pound, I looked quickly through the lobby window to see if there was anyone nearby, anyone who would notice and respond if I hurled my purse through the glass door, as I was now contemplating doing. But no one was there; where, I wondered, were the owners of all those trucks? Not where I needed them to be, obviously.

It was ten feet to the door, then five, then three, and then a hand reached out, and I saw it in front of me, and the acid remnants of my last cup of coffee spilled into my gorge. Speech deserted me; I wanted to scream, but nothing would come out. I was completely spitless, dry and pitiable and, I was certain, about to be ravished.

And then the hand settled on the door handle and pulled outward, and the door opened before me as if I were royalty. I stopped and turned slowly, and I stared in shocked relief at my unlikely knight. He stood there, a man I had taken to be a menace, with a cherubic smile on his face. With his other hand, he reached up and removed his hat and in a gentlemanly gesture, swept it down to his chest. "Evenin', ma'am," he said through a gap in his front teeth.

He was so young, just a boy, but oh, what a good boy! A

blossoming man, out on one of his first jobs, pleased with himself and liking the world. I wanted nothing other than to call his mother and tell her what a good job she'd done raising her son. But somehow I think she already knew.

ANN BENSON

> *"What would you do
> if you knew you could not fail?"*
> —AUTHOR UNKNOWN

FOR THE LOVE OF STUDENTS

*I*t was never quiet at our house. I was born to a college professor father. No student escaped either his compassion when appropriate or his fury at a mediocre performance. His classes were always jammed to overflowing with students of all descriptions and mind-sets. His teaching load exceeded that of any other faculty member, even though his subject was neither particularly popular nor "easy."

And when the students were not in his classroom, they were at our home. Talking and laughing in the house, playing badminton and croquet in our large yard, cooking hamburgers on our backyard grill, sharing—hesitantly and shyly at first, but then with the growing confidence that comes with acceptance and respect—their dreams, their plans for the future, their growing awareness of who they were, what they had to offer, and how they planned to pursue it all.

My dad fed them in the classrooms, and my mother fed them around our table with her own brand of love—bountiful Southern cooking. She had a keen sense of when to be spartan and when to pour out lavishness on others from her own alabaster jar.

We didn't have much money, so my mother had carefully saved all the unspoken-for coins she could stash away. I remember the day when we got the coins out, counted them, and went all the way to Raleigh to buy her dream tablecloth. It was white, beautiful, and pure linen.

From that day on, the Tablecloth was always on our big dining room table. At the end of every day, with good smells filling our house, my mom would make her way through our house and yard, inviting those students who had never had dinner with us before to join our family around the table: a special place where we laughed, poked fun, examined issues, made resolves, and set goals.

At the end of the meal, Mother would hand each student a pencil with a very dull point, and she would say, "Sign your name to our tablecloth, and sometime tomorrow I will take my white linen thread and embroider your name on our cloth."

I remember my dad looking each student directly in the eye and saying, "We want your name on the cloth because the day is going to come when we will be able to say that *you* ate dinner with us when you were just a student."

Every time I look at the Tablecloth, which is now mine, I see the embroidered names of governors, I see Arnold Palmer's name and the names of people who have made a strong mark in our world in medicine, law, and the ministry. I wonder how many of those students whose names cover the cloth succeeded simply because an old professor and his love-filled wife gave them the gift of encouragement.

EMORY AUSTIN

LOVE NOTES

*O*ne sunny afternoon in May, when pink azalea,
purple wisteria, and white dogwood painted our
backyard in vibrant colors any child would love, my
husband, Allen, called to tell me that finally a baby might be
available for us to adopt.

We wasted no time in contacting the attorney handling the
case. We quickly discovered the deadline was *now.* The birth
mother would collect the applications that afternoon. With the
clock ticking, I answered the questions about why we would
make good parents.

Several weeks went by, with no word.

One rainy afternoon, I saw Cindy, who worked with the
attorney, at the post office. I asked, "Have you heard anything?"

With downcast eyes, she answered, "I'm sorry. The birth
mother picked up the applications, but she has disappeared."

Disappointed, I relayed the news to Allen.

Over the months ahead, I pondered on what might have been
and wondered about the birth mother.

In December, I received an unexpected phone call from
Cindy. She exclaimed, "The girl is back in town, and she selected you and Allen!"

Our lives had never been more chaotic. We both had full-time
careers, and Allen had added the extra duties of becoming
mayor of our town. Still we were thrilled about the "possibility,"
even though we were warned over and over not to get our
hopes up. But how could we not?

So the countdown began.

At once I wanted to order nursery wallpaper, until Allen
pleaded, "Please, Debbie, no decorating and no baby showers.
You'll be too disappointed if it doesn't work out." Instead we
took care of the financial and medical arrangements. A social

worker inspected our home—and us. There were mandatory physicals, including checkups for venereal diseases.

This last experience led me to ask our attorney to obtain a family health history from the birth mother. The request resulted in a series of notes that bounced back and forth on index cards between the mother and me. Eventually, our correspondence shifted away from discussions of health. She asked, "What do you consider a *happy* home? A *good* education? *Appropriate discipline?*"

Little by little, I began to think like a mother. Together we were preparing for the birth of the baby—hers and mine.

And oddly enough, this stranger turned into a friend.

Though neither of us wanted to meet, our notes revealed that we shared similar interests, such as the theater, walking on the beach, and reading. Even our printing looked identical. I also discovered that she was articulate, humorous, mature, and selfless in her desire to provide a loving family for her baby.

One cold February day, I received a jubilant call from Cindy. She said, "Congratulations! You have a baby girl!"

"Is she OK? How is the mother?" I was ecstatic.

"They are both fine—just fine," Cindy said, laughing.

Tears streaming down my face, I called Allen. I could barely get the words out. "We have a baby girl!"

Within hours, everyone in our small town knew about the birth of our baby. Friends loaned us a car seat and a cradle. Onlookers watched as we raced from store to store, piling our buggy high with pink diapers, tiny smocked dresses, sleepers, and soft pastel blankets.

Meanwhile, the birth mother held the baby, making sure she was healthy. She was adamant that no one adopt her but us.

In less than twenty-four hours, bouquets of flowers arrived by the dozen and pink balloons floated above our mailbox. Best of all, our baby daughter came home with us.

Meredith gripped her daddy's finger as I slipped off her socks to count her ten tiny toes. "This little piggy went to market," I cooed, as Allen laughed. "And her nose looks like yours," I said. In fact, Meredith did look like him!

As I dug into the hospital's gift bag, I saw the final letter from my friend, tucked beneath the baby wipes and the lotion. I wasn't able to open it just yet.

Falling in love with Meredith came naturally, but I did not expect to feel love for a stranger when Allen and I decided to adopt; and I did—I came to love the birth mother. Thankfully, Meredith would always be our bond.

So with tears flowing, I read her love-filled note, which ended, "I gave her life, now you give her love." My note back would have said, "We always will!"

DEBRA AYERS BROWN

SURROGATE DREAMER

I was annoyed when the phone rang, as I was trying to get dinner going and finish a research paper due the following day. It was the long-awaited finals week of my graduate program. I considered letting the call go to the message machine but changed my mind. It was my best friend, Janice, telling me that Stephen, her husband, was dead; he had died a few hours earlier in her arms of heart failure while they were out dancing.

The night before, I had invited Janice and Stephen for dinner. Since weekends were my main study times, it was rare for me to plan even a small dinner party—especially the week before finals—but I felt a strong need to see them. I reasoned that it was just an informal get-together with longtime friends. Besides, my husband and I were eager to hear about their recent trip to the Caribbean—a celebratory cruise that marked their tenth wedding anniversary. They were deeply in love, like teenagers, really, and they cherished each other.

Instinctively, I had prepared Stephen's favorite meal: grilled fillets, salad, mashed potatoes, and key lime pie. Lingering unusually late, we ventured into long and deep conversation after dinner. Upon reflection, there was a sense of completion and deeper bonding that evening with these two special people; we also made plans to all go to the Caribbean on a mutual vacation the following spring. Stephen was a large bear of a man and gave the warmest of hugs. I wish I'd known when they left, just past midnight, that the good-bye hugs were to be our last from him.

Instead of taking finals, I devoted the next few days to assisting Janice with the details that surround an unexpected death. Stephen was only forty-four. Amid shock and emotional waves of coping, there were multitudes of decisions and logistics

of living to consider. The intensity of the experience was overwhelming, but the spiritual beliefs we shared were a luminous
glow in the darkness of our grief. Stephen was beloved by all
who knew him, and the outpouring of love, caring, and help to
Janice allowed me to shift my attention back to school.

Janice hoped to reach Stephen through her dreams—to connect with him as a vital and vibrant form—but she couldn't.
Knowing that emotions can block dreams, I reassured her that
they would return when she was stronger.

Three days after the funeral, Stephen came to me in a vivid
dream, wearing the tuxedo—complete with cummerbund—he
had taken on the cruise with Janice. I saw him perfectly; radiant, smiling, and robust. I noticed his shoes especially—highly
polished and very formal. I thought this odd, as Stephen had
been a very casual person, who rarely wore a tie, much less a
suit.

Janice was quiet when I told her about the dream. Unknown
to me, she had decided to have Stephen cremated the day before
and had dressed him in the clothes he was wearing in my
dream. The shoes were one of several pairs he had just purchased. It was as if this detail underlined the authenticity of the
dream experience. It was the first of many.

In another dream, Stephen, walking on the beach, delivered
a specific message for Janice to listen to John Denver's "Annie's
Song." He handed over the cassette.

I told Janice about the dream the next morning. We shed
sweet tears as we listened to the lyrics of the song together.
"Let me drown in your laughter, let me die in your arms . . ."
I'm convinced Janice was able to heal more easily knowing
Stephen was watching over her in a personal way.

Until Janice was able to dream of him on her own, I became
the "surrogate dreamer." Our close friendship ties and love for
each other provided fertile links for dream communication that
were not available to Janice in her swollen emotional state. As
her grief lessened, her dreams and images of Stephen returned.
Mine began to diminish, and they came to a remarkable culmi-
nation a few years later during my trip with my husband to the

Caribbean in the spring. We toasted him—"Bon voyage"—as we traveled the itinerary that we had planned together the night before he died.

MARLENE L. KING

SPECIAL DELIVERY

I had been seeing Josh for over a year and a half. He was my first love, tall and handsome, with a boyish smile. He had an uncanny way of making everyone around him laugh, especially me. I adored him.

Josh was a master of surprises. He had a unique and wonderful way of expressing his feelings. I would often find roses at my door or notes on my car windshield. On one occasion, he dropped by my apartment in a new four-door brown sedan. As we walked toward the car, he explained to me that its best feature was a large trunk. How could he be so excited about a trunk, when the car had so many other interesting gadgets? As he lifted the back hatch, I realized why the trunk was so special. In it lay a dozen red roses for me.

Needless to say, when Josh said he was planning a surprise for my twenty-fourth birthday, my imagination ran wild. At this point, we were carrying on a long-distance relationship, he in Connecticut and I in Wisconsin.

Three days before my birthday, Josh called to find out where I was going to be on the eve of my birthday.

"On the eve of my birthday?" I asked. "What's so important about the eve of my birthday?"

He explained to me that his present would arrive at approximately 12:01 A.M. on October 14, my birthday. He wanted his present to be the first one I received that day.

I told him he would never find a service that delivered packages twenty-four hours a day.

"On the contrary," he said. "I deal with many companies that deliver twenty-four hours a day, seven days a week." He told me to expect a package from Russell's Expedite Service on October 14 at 12:01 A.M.

I think I counted the hours, maybe the minutes, to the eve of my birthday. What could possibly top the airplane ticket and homemade videos of Boston's beautiful fall foliage from last year's birthday?

Josh checked in with me the morning of the thirteenth. I told him I would call him as soon as the package was dropped off.

I worked late that evening and arrived home at nine. My roommate and I decided to relax and watch television until the package arrived. Finally, though, tired after a long day, we both decided to head to bed. It was about eleven-thirty.

"I can't imagine that he found a place that would deliver twenty-four hours a day," I told her, not for the first time. "It'll be here tomorrow morning."

Just as we were about to turn off the lights, the door buzzer rang. My heart jumped. We ran to the front of our building, pajamas and all, and flung the door open.

"Are you Lisa?" asked the delivery woman who stood before us. "Yes," I said.

She said, "I have a package for you."

And with those words, from around the corner came my "special delivery" from Russell's Expedite Service. It was Josh! Josh, the master of surprise and champion of making a woman feel special. He was truly my first present of the day!

Josh and I both have new loves in our lives now, but his memory lingers on. Because of Josh and his great efforts to please me, I now pay attention to the surprises I can create for the special people I love. Josh was a teacher to me. He taught me at an early age that when it comes to matters of the heart, *little things are big things.*

LISA JUSCIK

RITUALS THAT TOUCH
THE HEART

Recently, I spoke at a conference with Mary Lo-
Verde. She focuses on how family rituals touch our
lives. Knowing that we are all teachers to one another, we asked the women in the audience to share rituals they
have in their families.

To set the tone, I described a family ritual that has had a
lasting impact on my life from the time I was a young girl. My
father began writing poems to us with each Christmas present
he gave. The whole family writes poems now, and each year
our Christmas experience lasts all morning as the extended
family—our sons, their wives, cousins, aunts and uncles—take
turns reading a poem they've been given as a gift.

As our kids grew up, they started with simple poems like
"Roses are red, violets are blue . . ." Often the poems give hints
of what's inside the wrapping. It's been fascinating to watch the
young poets develop. Last year our twenty-three-year-old son,
Rick, got a round of applause for this one: "Stuck with yourself
in stormy bad weather, / outside your house with cotton, not
leather. / Thinking of old times as the rain wets your head, /
you remember last Christmas—all the loot, all the bread. /
One gift stands out from Xmas '96, / it's that nice gift from me,
old Ricky-Pix. . . ." And on it went. . . .

Over the years, the poems collected have become a lifetime
treasury. While the actual gift may well be forgotten as time has
passed, the poems are not. These gems are carefully stored in a
small chest. If a fire were to ever break out in our home, that
chest, with its special contents, would be one of the first things
I would attempt to save.

Ten years ago, my husband placed an unopened pouch of
Sweet Dreams brand tea in my jacket pocket. It was a way for

him to say, "I'm thinking of you" whether he's home or traveling. Without a word, we continue to take turns exchanging that now rumpled tea bag in each other's clothes hanging in our closet. When I find it in one of my jacket pockets, I wait awhile, then return it to one of his. I never know when that "sweet" message will make me smile again!

Recently I gave my daughter-in-law a decorative wheelbarrow to put on her front porch. I have one too. We are creating a tradition of getting together to fill our wheelbarrows with seasonal delights, like pumpkins near Halloween and holly at Christmastime.

After I told my stories, the women began describing to us a number of their cherished rituals. One gives each of her children a back rub each night when she tucks them into bed. Another woman takes a bite out of the sandwich she packs in her husband's daily lunch! Even when they're not together during the day, they are connected.

Another woman moved me deeply when she stood up and shared with all of us how difficult it had been for her to be a long distance away from her young granddaughter. She wanted to feel close to her but didn't know how. This grandmother waited until the perfect solution revealed itself. She called her granddaughter with an idea that has since become a ritual between the two of them. "I love you so much," she told the young child, "and I have a way that we can feel close to each other all the time! Each night at bedtime, look out your window up at the sky and find the moon. Whenever you see the moon, think of me. And when I go to bed at night, I'll look out my window, find the moon, and think of you."

I've learned to pay attention to the meaningful ways we can get close to the people we love through rituals. From simple deeds to grand gestures, the richness of our lives is proportionate to the gifts we give from our hearts.

KAY ALLENBAUGH

LESSON FOR A LIFETIME

"*If they steal it, they steal it,*" Tim, my trusting husband, said as he went off to shower and get ready for dinner.

Our moving van was locked tight under a security light in the motel parking lot. I attributed my anxiety to exhaustion after hours of driving, punctuated with children's questions and my tears. We were leaving Cincinnati, where we'd had lots of friends and a church that meant much to our family. Bittersweet emotions accompanied us as Tim drove the van and we followed in the car.

When we stopped in Corbin, Kentucky, for gas, Tim and the girls decided we should celebrate our anniversary, an occasion we had barely noticed. We had fourteen years of marriage to celebrate, plus we were moving home to Georgia, to our family and an exciting ministry on the campus of the university.

The next morning Tim dressed early and went to check on the truck. As I was braiding J. J.'s hair, he burst back in the room, saying he couldn't find the van.

"What do you mean, you can't find it?" I said. "How can you lose a twenty-four-foot moving van?" The words tumbled out of my mouth, and I wanted to recall them immediately as I saw color drain from his face. Missy began to cry. She knew from his tone that Daddy wasn't teasing. The seriousness of the situation began to sink in.

The hours followed in a blur. The police came and asked a lot of questions. We telephoned the van company, our family, and various insurance companies. We returned to our room after a valiant effort to eat breakfast and make a list of the moving truck's contents. All the while, a giant cold fist grew larger and larger in the pit of my stomach. Reality was settling in. When my brain began functioning, the panic started. What would we do? How could we survive? We had no savings—so how could we replace anything?

Tim suggested that we pray. I didn't feel like praying, and I suspect he really didn't, either. Nevertheless, we joined hands and prayed humbly and simply. Amid sniffles and sobs, we asked for our things to be returned. We praised God that no one was injured and that we had each other—our real treasure. Only the passing traffic broke the morning silence as we waited.

That afternoon, we received a call from the police: they had recovered our truck on a back road. Our hopes soared! When we arrived at the abandoned van, we found only Tim's desk and a few cartons of books. Only later did we realize that Tim had just what he needed to get started in his new ministry. More resources would follow.

I couldn't contain my tears as I picked up love letters strewn over the truck bed. This violation of my privacy was more than I could bear. I searched through the boxes of books and papers for our daughters' baby books and my wedding album, but they weren't there. Who would do something like this? Who would want to take things that had no real value other than sentiment?

It's been fifteen years, and each time I recount this story, I marvel at the response of friends, acquaintances, family, and strangers. In an outpouring of love, we received more than $16,000 in cash, plus clothes, household goods, pantry items, toys, bicycles, appliances, and tons of cards and letters.

The theft of our moving van is a benchmark for us. We speak of events as "before the theft" or "after the theft." It is and will always be a significant event in our family's history, but it isn't a negative one. In many ways, it was a "blessed theft," for in the removal of the weight of worldly possessions, we learned the lesson of a lifetime—forgiveness.

SHEILA S. HUDSON

X

A DEEPER REFLECTION

"Some days there won't be a song in your heart.
Sing anyway."

—Emory Austin

FOUR WEDDINGS
AND A MIRACLE

Children do not learn the alphabet in one lesson. It takes time and repetition. So why should we have expected my husband's young children to grasp the meaning of their daddy's marriage to a woman other than their mother with just one ceremony?

Justine and Tyler were seven and five when Doug and I became engaged. After a year of dating, I felt blessed that they welcomed me into their little worlds so openly and lovingly. And yet behind every smile lived a shadow of apprehension. While Justine asked me why storybook step-mothers were always evil and Tyler asked me why his dad and I couldn't just be friends, Doug and I were asking our-selves and each other how to create a wedding ceremony that would help build a new family group. A couple of starry-eyed "I dos" with Pachelbel's Canon playing in the back-ground wasn't enough. That's when we decided to have a series of ceremonies, one at each season of our first year to-gether.

Our first wedding ceremony took place in our living room, in front of a few friends and a raging fire, on the winter sol-stice of 1994. After the exchange of rings, the minister invited Justine and Tyler to join us at the hearth. It was an oppor-tunity for me to express my love and declare my commit-ment to them as their stepmother. "Always remember," I said, "you have a mom to mother you and a dad to father you. And now, as your stepmother, my job is to angel you." As a token of my love, I presented them with little glass an-gels. They went to bed that night, saturated with cake and candy, each clutching a little angel. Before drifting off to sleep,

Justine smiled and whispered to a family friend, "Just think, when I wake up tomorrow morning, Kate will be my step-mom."

So began my life as a stepmother. No one knows except another stepparent how double-edged that (s)word is. The books say to just be a friend. Yet as the first months of step-family life unfolded, I found myself taking on more and more parental duties. On the surface, I enjoyed a good re-lationship with Doug and his kids. But underneath my pol-ished and ever-so-well-read veneer, I began to seethe with the first waves of resentment. I did everything Doug and his ex-wife did, sometimes more, but I never got the rewards. Every time I'd hear Justine declare to her dad, in a lit-tle singsongy voice, "I love you, Dad-dee," feelings of irrita-tion would well up until I was dangerously close to shouting, Hey, what about me? I sadly learned at a stepmoms sup-port group meeting that I should get used to those feelings. Words like "I love you" are reserved for the real mom and the real dad. "Nothing short of a miracle will make a child say that to a stepmom, no matter how well liked she is," I was told.

Energized by the first signs of spring, I approached our sec-ond wedding ceremony with a renewed sense of confidence and joy. Doug and I repeated our vows to each other in front of a group of two hundred family members and friends. I repeated my vows to Justine and Tyler, honoring their mom and dad, and reminding them about my commitment to angel them. This time I presented them with animal totems—a little wooden fox for Justine and a tiny furry mouse for Tyler. They were so excited they practically snatched the little critters out of my hand.

Summer rolled around and so did ceremony number three, this one with my family in Iowa. For a third time, I repeated my vows to Doug and his children. I presented Justine and Tyler with small dreamcatchers, Native American art pieces, explaining that as I angeled them, I'd help them catch their dreams. They proudly hung them above their beds in the tiny

motel room, then began to reminisce about the series of ceremonies and symbols I had given them.

Overwhelmed by the weariness of traveling with kids and
sharing my purse, pockets, and pup tent of a motel room with
them, I felt myself growing a little distant. I was spending an
enormous amount of energy trying to resist the temptation to
wallow in self-pity.

We took the kids for a twilight walk near a cornfield for
their first glimpse of fireflies, or lightning bugs, as we used
to call them. It was a Disney moment, the field aglitter
with little beings of light performing an ancient aerial ballet.
If you listened closely, you could hear the soft strains of a
cricket sonata. The air was heavy with humidity and the aroma
of summer grasses. Suddenly, without warning, Justine came
up and took my hand. We walked along the dusty country
road, silently sharing the splendor of this real-life field of
dreams. And then she said it—quietly and sweetly, in that
singsongy voice reserved for her dad: "I love you, Kate." A
million fireflies flew out of my heart as I responded, "I love
you too, Justine." She was quiet for a moment and visibly
nervous. Finally, she confessed, "I've always wanted to say that
to you, but I was afraid if I loved you it meant I wouldn't
love my mom." I asked her if she understood the difference
now. She said yes, and that she understood the similarities as
well.

That fall, the fourth and final ceremony took place, back in
our living room, with the same people from the first wedding.
We celebrated the autumn equinox by honoring the harvest and
restating our personal vows. This time I gave the kids bigger
animals, in honor of the bigger love we now shared—a unicorn
for Justine and a big mouse for Tyler.

Just like learning the alphabet, I believe it took the time and
repetition of our four wedding ceremonies for the kids to become familiar with our new family group. And not just the kids,
but Doug and me as well. Now when the hard times hit, instead
of letting my feelings run from A to Z, I can reflect on the
rhythms of the seasons and remember that special summer

night in Iowa. There will be no more wedding ceremonies, but the summer fireflies that live in my heart all year round are already preparing for more miracles.

KATE McKERN VERIGIN

DOES THE BREAST
HAVE A SOUL?

*I*t had been three weeks since I heard the dreaded news: I had extensive breast cancer. The doctors estimated I'd had it for at least two years. The tumor was large, and based on my consultation with many doctors, my options were limited. My breast would have to be removed. It didn't take long for me to think of my children and husband and decide to go ahead with surgery. But the thought of losing a part of my body would not penetrate into my psyche. For days before the surgery, I would stand in front of the mirror, looking at both my breasts, trying to picture what it would be like to have only one. I would cover one up and turn this way and that, as if I were trying on a new dress.

This cancer did not come at a convenient time—not that anything of this nature ever does. My international sales company was in the process of launching a major new product in the Pacific Rim. We would be meeting with fifteen distributors in Thailand in only five days. As I sat at my desk, knee deep in brochures, manuals, and travel arrangements, it was amazing how fast the Bangkok meeting, the urgent crises in the office, the constant demands of the outside world, all disappeared. All that mattered now was my survival and spending time with my family. I dropped everything, suddenly saying no to those tasks and people I simply did not want to spend time on. For the first time in my career, I did not tell my family I had too much work to do, that I couldn't cook dinner for them or take my children to a movie or go out for dinner with my husband. For the first time, I said, "Work will wait, my family won't."

On the morning before surgery, I went out to breakfast with one of my good friends. I sat there watching him eat his bacon and eggs, and I said again and again, "I don't want to do this. I want to be someplace else. I don't want to lose my breast." As I cried, he stroked my head like a parent comforting a small child. "It's only skin," he said. "It's not important." But the tears continued, not out of fear of the surgery but from fear of losing a part of myself. "How do you know I'll be the same person when this is over? What if I lose part of who I am?"

My friend comforted me until it was time to go to the hospital. My parents had flown across the country to be with me, and my husband was going to come from work to join us. We all gathered in my room, but in the hour before the surgery, I was very restless. I asked everyone to leave. My mind was not settled. The nurses tried to give me a tranquilizer, but I refused. "No, I have to sort this out in my mind."

Then it occurred to me: "Does the breast have a soul? Am I killing off something that is as much a living thing as I am?" I knew what I must do. I must say thank you and goodbye to my breast.

I searched the hospital room, found an old envelope, and asked the nurse for a pencil. Again she tried to get a tranquilizer down me, but I knew that it would cloud my brain. I was determined to write down what was going through my mind. Almost everyone had told me, "It's only skin—it's not necessary." But that's not what I felt. I felt it was part of me and I was part of it. I asked myself, "Where are my feelings? Are they only in my heart?"

I kept thinking: How do these people know my soul is not in my breast? Before they took it away, I wanted to move the part of who I was that was in there somewhere else.

I wanted to thank my breast for what it had given me. It had helped me to know that I was passing from girlhood to womanhood. It had nursed my babies and fed them well. It had given me shape. It had pleased my husband and it had pleased me. Could I be whole without it? Or was I still angry at it for betraying me? It was as if my breast had plotted against me: me, who had taken care of it all these years . . . me, who had taken such pride in it. How could my breast turn on me like this? Many years ago, when I was out of college and moving into the world on my own, I told my parents they must let go of me. It was time. Was I ready to say good-bye to my breast in the same way? Could I say, "It's time"?

Now I began visualizing the part of me that resided in my breast moving into my arms, my legs, my stomach, and my heart. Just as I finished, I heard the gurney at the door. They had come to separate me from my breast. I looked at the nurse peacefully and said, "It's OK, it's time. I've mourned my breast. I've said thank you. I've moved the part of my soul that's in my breast to other places in my body. They can take it away. After all, it's only skin."

LYNNE MASSIE

"A successful marriage requires falling in love many times,
always with the same person."
—MIGNON McLUGHLIN

ALL THAT GLITTERS

*O*h, yeah, I remember him. Mom didn't approve,
but I did—Sam Elliott in a tux, silver mane of hair
slicked back into a ponytail, mustachioed and smell-
ing of Brut. He was the embodiment of cool. I'm not sure if he
was cooler in his Christmas tux or strung long-legged over the
seat of his Harley shovelhead. I slipped in behind him and
dreamed *bad-boy* dreams, my arms wrapped around his waist
like a brand-new belt. He was everything my mother never
wanted for me.

Now, Mom loved the CEO I dated. In Armani and toting a
six-figure income strapped to his side like a modern-day cowboy,
he had a ponytail too, but clipped and très chic, just enough to
keep him young. A real boardroom Brad Pitt. I walked the
manufacturing line with him once, and when I saw how far
away he stood when he talked to the welders and grinders
and women in the finishing room, I found myself slipping out.
Again.

Find a nice man! Settle down! My girlfriends and I ran from
the persistent pleas of our mothers, and spending time in local
singles bars and restaurants, trying to look nonchalant, we
swept eager eyes over clenched crowds of suited, sweet-smelling
men. Hey, is that him? Tossing hands through carefully casual
hair and checking our butts with a back glance in the mirror,
we pretended it didn't matter. It was 1992, and a woman didn't
need a man to feel complete. So why'd we keep on looking?

Because somewhere the threads of the fairy tale still sweep off the spindle, and we keep hoping there's more out there for us than Rumpelstiltskins and dwarfs. Where did that prince get to anyway?

So the day I lifted my head up from a bucket of parts in my own factory job and fell in love from across the room, it was with more than just a little surprise. I mean, for a girl raised on magnolias, white gloves, Southern sun, and Scarlett tales, who'd have thought love would come in the form of a broad-shouldered Vermonter with the conversational skills of Gary Cooper. It took a while to realize that "yep" meant "I love you too."

But sweeter than maple sap, he is as solid as Vermont granite, solemnly funny, and heartbreakingly New England practical. He can fix anything with a motor, builds killer science projects for kids he loves unswervingly, and possesses a reverence for nature as timeless as the Green Mountains that bore him. Most at home in silence, he maneuvers through a loud Southern family with quiet grace, smiling where others would guffaw, and speaking only when he has something to say.

Sometimes I trace the smattering of freckles across his chest, connecting the dots until they form the Big Dipper, and in the secure blanket of his stillness, the miracle of love burns my throat with tears. Intricate in its simplicity. No flash. Just pure sweet honest substance.

He could have been a gas station attendant, a tax accountant, a landscaper. But what if I'd kept looking for Sam Elliott? I might have looked right past my man. I watch him while he's sleeping, the tired deep sleep of a man who works hard to care for his family. And sometimes I try to picture what he'd look like on a Harley. But then again, why mess with perfection?

MARY CARROLL-HACKETT

A NEW DEAL

Three years ago, I wrote the following journal entry: *There is only silence. Silence, once my most desirable ally, is now the thing I dread most. I have isolated myself into paralysis. I sort wash, collect groceries, answer phone calls, love the children and my husband, but something is missing.*

I have tried counseling, God, meditation, and even with all this I am still depressed. Turning myself into a highway fatality is not the answer, but the temptation is strong. I've exhausted all options to cure my depression except for one: drugs. Today is the day I am going to ask for professional help, for a reference to a psychiatrist.

A month later, the psychiatrist sat me in a cloth-covered peach chair with a good five feet of pond-green carpet between us. She sat, legs crossed at the knee, in an upright mahogany desk chair, with a clipboard in her lap, and she spent eighty minutes asking me questions and jotting copious notes.

I would have walked out if she had not been my last resort. Throughout the "evaluation," I searched for some sign that she had a life as well. There were no pictures of children, no wall-mounted plaques of achievement, only her doctorate diploma, its printing too small for me to read from where I sat. The plants in the room were silk, the vertical blinds were drawn against the afternoon sun. It was a room nothing could die in, because there wasn't enough life to make a decent death.

At the end of the interview, she took my $175, wrote me a receipt, and gave me the good news: I was clinically depressed, and "in view of the diagnosis, help is available." She unlocked an upright cream file cabinet and handed me a psychic Band-Aid of marsh-green-and-cream capsules suspended in shrink-wrapped cellophane, together with a leaflet explaining side effects and benefits. I stuffed it all in the bottom of my purse.

The next day I combed the library for articles and books on

Prozac. The only book I found was *Listening to Prozac*. *Time* and *Newsweek* articles were abundant. The only article with any meat to it was a thirteen-pager in *Psychology Today*, titled "The Transformation of Personality."

I copied the article and wondered whether I wanted my personality altered. I knew I didn't want to be depressed anymore: my husband was reading up on life insurance policies, and my kids prefaced every conversation with, "I don't want you to cry, but . . ." Yet fractured as it was, it was my personality. Did I want to trade it in on someone nobody knew, even though what little energy I had went into dragging one foot in front of the other? I imagined the scene: "Let's make a deal," the psychiatrist says. "I'll trade you your depression for what's behind door number two." The audience screams conflicting advice, and in the end I have to make up my own mind. "The door," I say. And with that the curtain is whisked back to reveal Vanna White draped against a pedestal of Prozac. "These pills won't change your personality," the grinning psychiatrist says. "They'll change your life."

So I went to counseling, meditated, prayed, and took Prozac. I still felt some resistance: I'm used to doing for myself. Drugs were for people who were too weak to do it on their own. From teenhood, I'd known depression's rhythms and cycles. I was always on guard for that initial downslide, which still came as a surprise. A month into taking Prozac, I wasn't sure, but I thought I felt better.

Six months into life with Prozac, I searched less often for the signs of downslide, almost trusting myself to make long-term plans. Plans for a job, for a sailing vacation in the Caribbean, for old age—which I might even see.

A year down the road, I was hired for a job as a teacher's assistant in my kids' primary school. I worked half-time, cooked, played, ate, wrote, and loved. It was as if someone had taken the plastic wrap off my serving bowl and for the first time in my life I had a clear shot at the food.

Two years later, I was working full time, with enjoyable people, health benefits, and good pay. But a nattering at the back of my mind turned into a din as weeks flew by. I wanted to quit my job and write. I knew it was possible. Possible because the bottom no longer fell out from under me. Possible because at a time when I was at my lowest, I asked for help. Taking Prozac or any drug to help clear away depression's fog is as essential for some people as setting a broken arm. It has not been a substitute for asking myself the hard questions and acting on the answers; it has not transformed my personality; but it has placed solid ground where there once was none.

It took me a week to confide in my family my dream to write. They supported me fully. I quit my job the next day. I was ready to make a new deal. Ready to step out of silence and write my way home.

BURKY ACHILLES

"Time will outweigh the moment."
—DEMI MOORE

ENTRANCES AND EXITS

When I became pregnant with Nicole, friends kept telling me the pain of childbirth would be easily forgotten in the joy and love of parenting. They were right. Our lives were forever changed for the better the day Nicole entered the world. The moments surrounding her birth are forever etched clearly in my mind, minus the pain.

Nearly eighteen years later, when she chose to end her own life suddenly on a dreary day in February, other grieving parents gathered my husband, Scott, and me within their embrace. They looked into our eyes and said the pain would get better with time, even though our lives would now forever be divided into "before" and "after." Again we found the words of friends to be correct, though the pain of parting was so much more intense and enduring than any labor contraction.

Having worked in public schools as a speech/language clinician for sixteen years, I suddenly found myself with a communication disorder of epic proportions—a development that I could attribute only to my grief and ever-present anxiety. I now panicked at my thickened tongue, my scattered thought processing, and my slurred speech. Even my nonwaking moments were haunted. I had always enjoyed frequent and vivid dreams. I was now afraid to go to sleep, in fear of what I might dream.

Nicole's presence in our lives had brought such joy that we'd tried to have other children, but we were not successful. After her death, approaching the middle years of our lives, we found ourselves shocked, numb, devastated, and dreadfully alone.

We lacked energy to do even the most normal of tasks, and our ability to concentrate vanished, except when it came to books. We read voraciously, eager to learn all we could about suicide in our search to answer "why?" Scott and I clung together, defying the grim statistics of marriage splits following the death of a child. We also joined suicide survivor support groups, driving great distances to attend meetings. From these I slowly regained the ability to verbalize thoughts, and we began to unravel small threads of the mysterious tapestry surrounding our daughter's death. We asked the usual "what if"'s and pieced facts together, never really finding an answer. Nicole had given precious few clues to us or any of her friends of any existing depression. Up until the time of her death, she had been happy, loving, caring, kind, and active in school and church. Maybe if she *had* been a bit more of a rebel . . . but "what if"'s are useless. We have come to accept that perhaps the suicidal mind needs medication just as the diabetic needs insulin.

We were fortunate to be surrounded by family, friends, colleagues, and a community that let us share our grief openly. Their hugs restored our energy, their gifts of food restored our appetites, and their calls broke deafening silences.

And when my dreams resumed, I found them to be comforting also. In my very first dream, Nicole's favorite color—sea green—enveloped me. Not too long afterward, she was giving me a hug. Once, she strolled with me along an ethereal garden path lined with fresh flowers.

As our energy levels returned, Scott and I found that traveling over major holidays and significant dates helped us survive better. We discovered we could even laugh again, but we agreed that life was now like a tree without tinsel.

Grief is different for everyone. Finding reasons to go on can be difficult but is necessary. If you are fortunate enough, a point may be reached in the grieving and healing process when you no longer would trade the future to change the past. This began for us three Februarys following Nicole's death, when we adopted two remarkable babies—our son, Tony, and our daughter, Gina. The four of us have begun anew.

We don't have time to worry that we are old enough to be their grandparents, and a day never passes that we aren't thankful for the entrance of all three children into our lives.

Will these beloved babies ever keep us from missing Nicole? No, never. But we look back at our time of deepest pain, and that makes this new delight so much more appreciated. To enter the highest joys, we have found you sometimes have to walk through and exit the deepest of sorrows.

LINDA G. ENGEL

FOR BETTY

"**G**ood things come to those who wait," he had lectured on too many occasions. It was his favorite saying, and even as I backed the car away from the house and the life we had built together, he stood silent in the driveway, just waiting.

It was his nature to wait, as he did throughout the troubled moments of our marriage. He said nothing and did nothing as he waited out the storms. Living with me was like being a passenger on a runaway train, and we traveled different paths at different paces. In my youth and impatience, I had yet to discover myself, and soon it became clearly inevitable that we should part.

In the months of separation before the divorce, I shuttled back and forth, searching for confirmation of what I already knew. I wore out the skies from the state I had moved to and back home again, in search of an answer. We had been through counseling, we had been through it all, yet our differences were basic and beyond repair. We both knew it, but neither of us could make the final move, so our lives lingered unfairly in purgatory for several years, as time drifted slowly away.

On one of my frequent flights back home, I sat next to Betty, a vivacious woman of sixty-five. I soon learned that Betty was traveling first class because the airplane had upgraded her following her son's death. Her only child had been a pilot for the airline, until he called her one day to report a "strange sensation," which turned out to be a brain tumor. Sadly, he died soon after. Not only that, said Betty, but her husband had worked and saved his entire life so that they could travel the world together when he retired. He did retire, but he died unexpectedly just weeks later, and the plans they had made would never be realized.

Betty and I talked for the duration of the flight. "I don't know how there could be a God," she said bitterly. "Everything I ever loved is gone. I have no children, I have no husband, I have nothing at all. If there is any advice I can give you, it's to do it now. Don't wait until it's too late to do the things you want to do in life."

Weeks later, I found myself thinking about Betty and the advice she had given. I also found the strength to move on, away from the relationship that wasn't right and into the next phase of my life. It is years later, and I still think of Betty and thank her for that morning we spent together on the airplane. I know I will live a fuller life because of it, and I know that I'll never delay the things I want to achieve. Good things might come to those who wait, but great things happen to those who refuse to.

TAMMY KLING

UNITED STATES OF
MOTHERHOOD

*T*he *luminous numbers clicked as the time moved* from 1:59 A.M. to 2:00. I shifted the weight on my lap and moved my son from one breast to the other.

Quickly Michael made it clear that he was no longer interested in nursing. I shifted him to my shoulder and patted his warm little back, waiting for that satisfying burp that would signal his stomach's acceptance of my late-night offerings. Beneath me, I felt my legs growing numb and tingly. Even with a cushion, this wooden rocker was painful to sit in for long periods, night after night.

From the light of the streetlamp, I could see shadows in my son's room. The quiet of the evening settled around us, but still Michael wouldn't sleep.

"Colic," said the pediatrician. "We don't know why it happens. He'll grow out of it at about three months. We suspect their digestive system starts to mature by then. You're home free the day he passes gas. Sorry."

Sorry! Sorry? My patience and my body were worn thin. All the baby books had profiled an infant who would spend most of his early first year snoozing.

With my southern hemisphere sporting more stitches than a Quaker's sampler and my hair coming out in chunks, I was a poster child for postpartum distress. My sanity began to unravel as I hallucinated that I was part of an ancient Mayan culture where babies were gourds. The next day, when I dragged myself, baby and car seat in tow, into the pediatrician's office, I had been up forty-eight hours straight. Michael had slept a mere forty-five minutes during that two-day eternity. Thirty of those forty-five minutes had been on the car ride to the clinic. If I could only stay awake long

enough, I might be able to drive to Alaska and back in three
months.

The drugs to ease Michael's system began, thank goodness,
to take effect. His naps fell into a general pattern, though it was
far, far shorter than that presented by the experts. But nighttime
was party time for Mr. Mike. I read books about letting him
scream. I listened to tapes by experts on walking away. I tried
gizmos and gadgets that shook me and his bed like a blender
on whirl. But I couldn't walk away or relegate him to machinery.
He was obviously in distress. The least I could do, I reasoned,
was sit with him through the long and painful nights while he
squirmed and struggled to fall asleep.

So we rocked. We rocked the circumference of the earth.
Then we rocked our way to the moon. Tonight we had been
rocking toward Pluto. I brushed the velvety crown of his head.
So dear, so soft, like chick down. I curled and uncurled his tiny
fingers. I struggled with my anger. I sat there alone with him as
my husband slept. Why wasn't the baby sleeping? How long
could I go without rest? A wave of shame broke over me. Wasn't
I blessed to have him? Wouldn't a million women give anything
to be holding a child?

Then, as I glimpsed the moon moving behind a cloud, a
thought came to me. A million women. A million mothers. A
million babies.

Suddenly I realized that I was not alone. All over the globe,
women were holding their babies. Some were lucky enough to
sit in rockers. Some crouched on the ground. Some had a roof
over their heads, as I did. Many more were exposed to the
elements, shielding their babies from the rain, the snow, the
sun.

We were all alike. We held our children and prayed. Some
would not live to see their children grown. Some children
would not live out the year. Some would die of hunger. Some
from bullets or sickness.

But for a moment, under the same pale moon, we were all
together. Rocking our babies and praying. Loving them and
hoping.

From that night on, I viewed my time with Michael differently. The fatigue never left me. The seat never seemed any softer. But as I sat with him, I felt the company of a million, a billion mothers—all holding our babies in our arms.

JOANNA SLAN

XI
SERIOUSLY FUNNY

"If someone makes me laugh,
I'm [her] slave for life."

—BETTE MIDLER

A STREAK OF LOVE

*O*ne warm spring night on Iraklion Air Station in Crete, I left my dorm with a girlfriend and decided to check out an impromptu party in progress between the two dorms. Boyfriendless at the time, I kind of automatically swept the crowd with my eyes in search of a "potential"—and stopped on Frank.

I'd seen him around the base before, and I'd always thought he was cute. Tall and thin. Curly black hair. Mustache. Kind of Jim Croce–looking. I parked myself next to him and immediately engaged him in conversation.

I found he had a sweet smile and a sexy New York accent. (Terribly exotic for a girl who'd grown up among the cornfields of Indiana.) But it wasn't just his good looks and accent that charmed me. He was a genuinely nice guy, easy to talk to—and best of all, he made me laugh.

I was so engrossed in Frank and his lively conversation that at first I didn't notice the commotion around us. Too late, I looked up in time to see a flash of bare skin disappear around the corner of the building. Everyone laughed hysterically and pointed in that direction. Suddenly I realized what I'd missed.

"My first streakers!" I gasped. Then I turned to Frank accusingly. "And I missed them because of you!"

Frank looked properly contrite. "Sorry. I'll get them to do it again."

I didn't think Frank was serious, but before I could say a word, he scrambled up from the ground and disappeared around the corner of the dorm. A few minutes later, I heard a peal of shrill laughter. I whipped my head around, and there they were—the two streakers, as naked as babes, running like mad demons down the span of lawn between the dorms. The laughter intensified and my eyes widened. A third streaker had joined the other two. He was tall and thin, with curly black hair and a mustache. Kind of Jim Croce–looking.

Oddly enough, Frank missed the whole thing, or so he said. He reappeared at my side a few minutes later as if nothing had happened.

"Thanks," I said dryly. "You didn't have to go to so much trouble to impress me."

He shrugged. "Well, I couldn't let you miss your first streakers."

What could I say? He'd done it for me.

That was the beginning of our relationship. It's been twenty-three years now, and we have two wonderful grown children. Frank doesn't streak anymore. He feels it no longer fits into his lifestyle—him being a respected computer programmer and all. Oh, he still gets naked—just not for the general public.

Everyone who knows the story of our first meeting thinks I saw something I liked that night when Frank streaked past me in the buff. I did.

His personality.

CAROLE BELLACERA

VENUS RISING

When I was seventeen, I spent a few weeks of summer vacation visiting a cousin who lived in the country. It was a far cry from the big city, and every little thing in nature excited me. A barn filled with horses, trails meandering through a dense wooded area, deer, fancy birds, and fish jumping in a nearby lake all created an enchanting environment.

My cousin Jeannie was a tomboy, yet we got along well. She could do all the things the boys on the next farm could do— she shot rabbits, hunted for pheasants, chased wild turkeys, and helped out with farm chores.

Jeannie also played tricks on the boys next door, like the time they went horseback riding. While the guys were in the lake, she rode off with their horses, and they didn't get back to the farmhouse till dinner was over.

One steamy summer morning, I went to the lake by myself. Since no one was around, I took off my clothes and jumped in. I floated on my back just looking up at the clouds through overhanging trees, appreciating wildflowers along the bank. My gosh, it was so beautiful. The birds never sounded more musical, and for a little while I thought this surely was Heaven. I was happy and totally carefree. It felt as though I were swimming in warm velvet.

Suddenly I heard the crackle of branches on the ground and the movement of grass. I ducked down in the water up to my chin and peered into the nearby trees. Out of the green, I recognized Dusty, one of the boys from the neighboring farm. Coming toward the lake, he began to laugh when he saw my look of total surprise. He plopped down on the ground and made himself comfortable My eyes shot to the spot where my clothes were. I said *were!* They were, of course, gone!

"What have you done with my clothes?" I hollered. Dusty just sat there and said, "They ain't far. All you has to do is c'mon out and fetch 'em."

"If you don't give me my clothes, I'll tell my uncle when I get back, and then you'll be in real trouble!"

"Oh, yeah. I reckon so—that is, when you *git* back. See, unless you c'mon out, they ain't no way you'a gon' git back."

This went on for several minutes, and I realized my frustration won out. I couldn't help but cry. Now I hated the lake. Nothing seemed beautiful anymore. Frantically, I looked around for something to hold up in front of me so I could get onto dry ground. But what? A broken bough of branches perhaps . . . something . . . *anything!* I felt a slow surge of panic creep into my throat. I had no idea just how far this charade would go, as Dusty laughed even louder. Should I stay in the water that now felt cold and slimy, or should I make a run for it?

I waded to a nearby marshy area in the lake, hoping to find something. My foot struck a hard yet round object. I reached down to pick it up. It was a rusty enamel pan—just large enough to cover up the lower part of my body. Thank heaven! The pan appeared to be caked with rust and mud, but so what? I put it in front of me and crossing one arm over my chest, I tossed back my head and proceeded to walk out of the water to gather my clothes. I'll show *him,* I thought.

As I walked toward the shore, I snapped, "I'll bet you thought I couldn't get out of this lake!"

Dusty squinted his eyes and stared at me. Slowly he drawled, "Yeaaah, and I'll betcha you thought that pan had a bottom in it!"

CARMEN D'AMICO

WHEN WILL I BE THIN?

While standing in the locker room
    After training at the gym,
My girlfriend turned and said to me,
    "Oh, when will I be thin?"

I said to her, "You're gorgeous!
    There's more to life than looks—
A woman with a soul on fire
    Is one who really cooks!"

When you're feeling kinda funky
    And your chin's a little low,
Just use this little motto—
    Here's the way it goes:

Though our perky breasts may fall
    And our youthful skin may wrinkle,
What we have within our souls
    Is an everlasting twinkle!

So never doubt you're beautiful,
    Don't ever question that.
'Cause a soulful woman's gorgeous,
    Though her thighs are fat.

So don't give up the truffles
    If they're your heart's delight,
Just jog an extra mile
    While you twinkle in God's light.

MAUREEN GORSUCH

THE GREAT ZUCCHINI CAPER

He'd been on vacation only three days, and already the man was driving me crazy. My husband, Stan, usually oblivious to an overflowing trash can or squeaky doors, became an overzealous combination of Mr. Fix-It and Mr. Clean. He insisted on tidying every nook and cranny. He even took out the garbage with the rotten zucchini in it and placed a new paper bag in the trash can.

Used to having my mornings to myself, I especially needed some quiet time this particular day so I could review my program for a new client I hoped to impress. My employer was collaborating with a large franchise, and the chance for additional business looked promising. I'd spread the papers and documents entrusted to me across my coffee table, when my husband hit me with a barrage of suggestions.

"Let's get this place cleaned up, then take the boys for a ride in the country. We'll fish, have a picnic, pick some wild berries. . . . Come on, let's get cracking."

I finally conceded. Maybe togetherness and relaxation would do us all good. I felt keyed up and needed a little distraction.

As we headed out the door, I noticed that the coffee table was empty. "Stan," I began cautiously, "where are the papers that were on this table?"

"I don't know." His impatience sounded loud and clear. "I couldn't stand the clutter, so I cleared it off."

"But what did you do with my papers?" I persisted, my voice rising as my heart began to quicken.

"If they were on the table, then they probably got pitched in the trash along with the Sunday paper."

It was trash day, but the collectors weren't due for another couple of hours. I walked outside and stopped dead in my tracks. Two empty trash cans leered at me like a pair of hollow eyes. I stared into them, unable to comprehend the obvious. Then it hit me like a train engine crashing into my chest.

My valuable papers had been tossed away carelessly with the Sunday paper and the rotten zucchini and were now being carried off to God knows where. I tried to choke off my scream as I bolted into the house.

My husband's eyes grew wide as I stormed past. "What's the matter?"

"You threw away my outline, my notes, my objectives—everything! Don't you understand? You threw away my papers, and I don't know if they can be replaced. The administrator won't understand. He'll never believe I could be so incompetent." I ran to our bedroom and slammed the door and then, feeling the need for further isolation, locked myself in the bathroom. For several minutes, tears flooded down my cheeks, drenching the toilet paper I clutched tightly in my hand.

I kept asking myself whatever was I going to do. Then it struck me. It was obvious: there was only one thing I could do. Without an explanation to anyone, I raced out the door—no makeup, hair flying in all directions, dressed in my "farm" clothes. I jumped into my small station wagon and peeled out of the driveway.

As I barreled down the street, one thought crowded out all others: I have to find my papers. I got to the first intersection, when an overwhelming realization smacked me between the eyes. I had absolutely no idea where to start looking for the garbage man, what his route was, or even what his truck looked like. He could be anywhere by now.

I gazed toward the heavens, searching for some divine sign, and recognizing none, I took a fifty-fifty chance and headed up the street. I weaved in and out of the small side streets—down Meadowbrook, along Cherokee, out Pioneer Trail, up West Ely —investigating all the nearby subdivisions. I blinked to hold back any more tears. I couldn't believe this nightmare was really happening.

My choice of subdivisions and my hopes were both nearly exhausted. I had just about given up any chance of ever seeing my papers again, when at the top of the hill, barely disappearing over the crest, I spied a garbage truck. There was no way of knowing if it was *my* garbage truck, but it was the first good lead I'd had. I jammed my foot on the accelerator and tore up the street.

When I crested the hill, there was no garbage truck in sight. The cadence of a marching army pounded in my ears. My mouth was so dry I couldn't swallow. Then, out of the corner of my eye, I glimpsed the truck heading onto a dead-end street.

On two tires, I turned the corner, intent on running down that garbage truck, when a second one came rolling up the street. My thoughts became a blur as I tried to decide what to do. "I'll catch the other truck on his way out," I mumbled. I screeched to a halt in the middle of the street, blocking all traffic, and leapt from my car, flagging my arms wildly at the approaching garbage truck.

A Don Johnson look-alike started to roll down his window. His sparkling blue eyes were filled with alarm. "Something wrong, lady? Do you need help?"

"Have you picked up any trash from Heritage Road this morning?" I demanded as I raced up to his truck.

"You mean that road off Surrey Hill?"

"Yes, yes." I ran my tongue nervously over my dry lips.

"Yeah, I was there. I have an appointment this afternoon, so I had to start earlier than usual—" Interrupting him, I began scaling the back of his garbage truck. Without asking permission, I vaulted both legs over and sank past my thighs into warm, sticky plastic trash bags. Flies delighted in this smorgasbord, buzzing from one entrée to the next. The aroma of overripe fruit and oily, metallic machinery hung in the air.

"My husband threw away some very important papers," I called down to the young man, now standing at the side of his truck. With his mouth agape, he stared, then shook his head.

"There's a full load of garbage up there, ma'am. As a matter of fact, I was just heading to the dump to unload."

Reality began to sink in slowly as I settled deeper into the mire of trash bags. I tried to wade through the swell of garbage, then stopped when a thought struck. All our neighbors had been considerate enough to use tidy plastic garbage bags, most of them cinched neatly with twist ties. I struggled through the piles, casting bags aside as I went, until I spotted a stained brown paper bag, partially hidden.

"There." I pointed. "I think I see my zucchini." I dived toward the front of the sludge pile. Heaving a plastic bag aside, I screamed, "Yes, that's my zucchini!"

I grabbed the zucchini off the top of the paper bag and tossed it aside. Underneath, rolled in a bundle, was the Sunday paper. Gently I swept off a sprinkling of coffee grounds and unfolded the newspaper. There, nestled in the middle of the entertainment section, lay my papers, totally unscathed by the surrounding filth. Tilting my head back, I shrieked with delight.

Momentarily I regained my senses, and I realized what a spectacle I must have presented to the poor young man still standing beside his truck.

Weak-kneed and aromatic, I made my way to the edge of the oversize garbage bin, where the young man politely helped me down. I apologized and thanked him repeatedly as he lined my car seat with clean newspapers. I drove slowly home, marveling at the chain of events. To have turned down the right street into the right subdivision, found the right truck, and then finally the right trash, seemed inconceivable.

I pulled into the driveway and noticed my husband's truck was gone. Our nosy neighbor sauntered over. "Your husband took off right after you. Said something about finding a garbage truck."

"Let him look," I said, laughing, feeling giddy and smug. "I found my papers." I held up the evidence. I still couldn't believe it.

Just as I entered the front door, my husband pulled up to the house. "I found my papers," I boasted.

"I know," he said, stepping out of his truck.

Feeling somewhat cheated out of my glory, I approached him. "How'd you know?" I asked, unable to contain my curiosity.

"I started to flag down a garbage truck, when the driver stuck his head out the window and yelled, 'Mister, she's already been here!' "

KARYN BUXMAN

WARRANTY X

O ne of the many challenges I was confronted with after my first husband's death was people calling and asking to speak to him. Paul was an attorney, and calls from clients and others unaware of his death continued for months.

One evening a couple of months after Paul's death, the phone rang. "Hello. Kleine-Kracht residence," I stated.

"May I speak to Paul Kleine-Kracht?" the caller said. I caught my breath and said, "I'm sorry, Paul is deceased. I'm his wife, may I help you?"

Without any comment about what I'd just said, the caller jumped right in with, "I'm John Jones with your appliance warranty center. I'm calling to remind you that the warranty on your appliance is about to expire and you need to renew it."

"Thank you for calling, but that appliance is several years old and I've decided not to renew the warranty."

With a tone of impatience, he responded, "Well, I'm sure your dead husband would want you to renew."

"Funny you should mention it, but just hours before Paul died, he said, 'Honey, whatever you do, don't renew the appliance warranty!'"

There was silence, and then Mr. Jones said, "Oh, okay," and hung up.

ANN E. WEEKS

THE PURPLE PEOPLE

My son Austin has always had a unique approach to life. He has been described as "imaginative," "full of life," and "quite the little character." Some of the more negative adjectives used to describe Austin are "hyper," "wild," and even "out of control." Having been his mother for all his six years of life, I have learned to take these comments in stride. I try to accept Austin just the way he is.

Lately, his favorite game is to pretend that his father and I are his "evil stepparents" and his "true parents" are the purple people from another planet who will one day rescue him. On a daily basis, I am still amused and amazed by the way this child views his world.

When he was five, Austin bounded down our flight of stairs and announced, "It's time to move on with my life." His plan was to pack all his "important things" and head out to face the "real world." Austin then turned on his heel and headed up the stairs to begin his new venture. I was not blessed with an immediate response, so I calmly made lunch. I then called Austin downstairs for some nutrition and a chat.

My approach was quick and to the point. I explained to Austin that by law, he was required to live with his dad and me until he was at least eighteen years old. Until then, we would try to make his time with us as happy and adventurous as possible. He thought about this for a while.

"Will Dad teach me to sword fight so I can fight off the bad guys?" he asked with concern. I assured him that his dad would be honored to.

"And will you teach me how to make pancakes, sausage, and eggs so I won't get hungry?" he asked.

"Sure, honey, I'd love to," I replied, stroking his hair. Austin solemnly nodded.

I was confident that we had struck an agreement and that Austin would be staying on with us for a while longer. He was silent as he finished his sandwich, and I cleared his plate away. Left sitting before him was a place mat with a map of the United States on it.

"Mom, where do we live?" Austin asked quietly.

Thankful for the change of subject, I pointed to the upper left corner of the map. "We live here, honey, in the state of Washington," I replied with enthusiasm.

"Oh. Well . . . in that case, I want to live here when I'm eighteen." Austin was pointing to the bottom right corner of the map, the tip of Florida, and the place farthest from us that he could imagine.

It is at times like these that I, too, wonder when the purple people will arrive!

JENNIFER HOWARD

*"I base most of my fashion taste
on what doesn't itch."*
—Gilda Radner

A CHRISTMAS SURPRISE INDEED!

When you live abroad, one of the most important things in life is getting mail from the family back home. The Christmas box from my son contained a red-and-white jogging suit.

The cheerful outfit was a pleasant change from my standard attire, blue jeans. I received several compliments the first time I wore my sporty new clothing to the office, amid a couple of guffaws about my new "Santa suit." I remained proud of my son's fine gift selection.

Imagine my shock when I received his next letter, in which he asked how I liked my new pajamas!

Roberta B. Jacobson

CONTRIBUTORS

BURKY ACHILLES is a writer and recipient of a Walden Fellowship. She is working on her first novel, as well as a book of inspirational short stories. She and her husband are raising a daughter and a son on the brink of teenhood. (503) 638-4100.

ANN ALBERS is a traditional Reiki master, spiritual counselor, instructor, lecturer, and writer. She received her BS in Electrical Engineering from the University of Notre Dame and worked for eight years in the avionics industry before leaving to follow her spiritual calling. She is currently working on her first two books: *Whispers of the Spirit,* an inspiring and deeply human story of her spiritual awakening; and *No More Taboo!* to help women reclaim their bodies and their souls. (602) 485-1078.

BAILEY ALLARD is president of Allard Associates, Inc., an international seminar and consulting firm. She is a speaker, seminar leader, and business coach, who works with Fortune 500 companies on six continents. She speaks on influence and choicepoints in a downsized world. She is passionate about speaking to people—especially women—about understanding and acknowledging their value and increasing their influence. (919) 968-9900.

LORRI VAUGHTER ALLEN is a broadcast journalist and professional speaker. Her company, Good News!, helps people make more money and improve their image by mastering the media. (She's eaten a spudnut only once!) (972) 248-3610. <LorriA@wctv.com>

EMORY AUSTIN, Certified Speaking Professional, was featured in *Industry Week* magazine, along with fellow speakers Colin Powell, Margaret Thatcher, and Terry Anderson. She is a Phi Beta Kappa communications graduate of Wake Forest University and has keynoted in almost every industry, to rave reviews. For information regarding Emory's presentations and tapes, please call (704) 663-7575.

URSULA BACON fled Nazi Germany with her parents and spent the next nine years in China. She was interned, along with 18,000 European refugees, by Japanese occupation forces in Shanghai for four years. She emigrated to the United States at the end of WWII. Ursula is married to author Thorn Bacon, and they operate a small publishing house and write books. She is the coauthor of *Savage Shadows* (New York: New Horizon) and the author of *The Nervous Hostess Cookbook* (BookPartners, 1998). (503) 682-9821.

JENNIFER BROWN BANKS is a Chicago-based writer, poet, and speaker. She has been a contributing writer for *Being Single* magazine since 1995, providing insightful perspectives on love, relationships, self-esteem, and divine principles. She is founder of Poets United to Advance the Arts, and author of three collections of poetry: *Meet Me in the Middle, Amidst Quiet Hours,* and *Under the Influence of Love.* She credits her mother, Arabella, for motivation and her son, Jaremy, for inspiration. (773) 509-8018.

T. J. BANKS of Avon, Connecticut, has written fiction, poetry, book reviews, and essays for numerous publications, including *Poets and Writers, Cat Fancy, Just Cats!, Writing for Our Lives, Woman & Earth,* and *Our Mothers Our Selves: Writers and Poets Celebrate Motherhood.* She is an editorial associate with the Writer's Digest School and has won awards for her fiction and journalism from the Cat Writers' Association and *The Writing Self.* She has written a novel for young adults, *Houdini.* (860) 678-7978.

CAROLE BELLACERA is a writer living in Manassas, Virginia. Her fiction and articles have appeared in over 200 magazines in America and abroad. She recently optioned her first screenplay, *Border Crossings,* to Rialto Films for development as a cable-TV movie. In the years since she met Frank and became the mother of Leah, twenty-one, and Stephen, eighteen, she has worked as a medical technician, a sales clerk, a typist, a library aide, a secretary, and a receptionist for a congressman on Capitol Hill. But she is still proudest to be Frank's wife. <KaroBella@aol. com>

ANN BENSON is the author of the novel *The Plague Tales* and four best-sellers on beadwork. She is currently working on another novel.

DEBRA AYERS BROWN is the mother of an energetic second-grade student and is the senior vice president of Printgraphix. She has won numerous national design and writing awards. The author of several inspirational and children's stories, she is currently working on a mystery novel series. She is the mayor's wife and "First Lady of Hinesville, Georgia." (800) 257-9734.

ARLINE CRAWFORD BURTON is now a patient representative in a hospital in Georgia. She is a lover of mankind—God's greatest creation. Kindness, love, and understanding are her tools. The smiles her story "Angel of the Lord" brings are her reward.

KARYN BUXMAN, RN, MS, is from Hannibal, Missouri—home of the other great humorist, Mark Twain. She was editor for the American Association for Therapeutic Humor and is vice president of *Journal of Nursing Jocularity,* a national humor magazine for nurses. A leading national expert on therapeutic humor, Karyn Buxman wows audiences across the country with programs like "Is the Noise in My Head Bothering You?" and "JEST for Success." She has written countless articles and produced numerous audio and video tapes. To see how your group can benefit from some "mirth aid," contact Karyn at 1-800-8HUMORX. <www.humorx.com>

MARY CARROLL-HACKETT is a writer, a student, but first and foremost a mom, who lives with her family in eastern North

Carolina. When she's not chasing the three Irish-fairy children who inhabit her home, she is at work on her first novel.

MICHELLE COHEN is a former social worker with the developmentally disabled and a longtime public speaker and volunteer to the AIDS community. She has written a thriller and is currently working on a nonfiction collaborative work with her mother, Eileen Davis, titled *Dear Mush (Letters Between a Mother and Daughter)*. (973) 597-9212.

CONSTANCE CONACE worked full time and raised two sons as a single mother and has now returned to college to pursue a degree in English. Her goal is to write and enjoy life and her family to the fullest.

CARMEN D'AMICO resides in Fort Lauderdale, Florida, and is an international speaker, actress, author, and celebrity look-alike for Elizabeth Taylor. She has appeared on radio and television and has helped raise money for AIDS through numerous benefits and appearances. Her life experiences of triumphs over tragedies have made her a survivor. Her focus on restoring self-esteem has inspired her audiences. Her book, *Dust in the Wind*, is for anyone searching for hope, enlightenment, and strength. (954) 772-4111.

RITA DAVENPORT is president of Arbonne International, a personal care product company. She is a charter member of the National Speakers Association and has been awarded the Certified Speaking Professional (CSP) designation. She was honored by NSA with their highest lifetime award: the Council of Peers Award for Excellence (CPAE). She is a nationally known success-seminar leader, keynote speaker, humorist, and best-selling author of several books, including *Making Time, Making Money*. She produced and hosted her award-winning TV show for fifteen years in Phoenix. Her cable TV show, *Success Strategies*, was viewed in over 32 million homes. She has also appeared on

ABC's *Good Morning America* and other national shows. (602) 482-6919.

EILEEN DAVIS is a writer of poetry, short stories, and novels. She is working on a collaborative nonfiction work with her daughter, Michelle Cohen entitled *Dear Mush (Letters Between a Mother and Daughter)*. She has completed a collection of reflective short stories entitled *Of Me I Sing,* and a novel, *Yesterday I Woke Up Dead.*

LINDA DUNIVIN, MEd, has won several awards for lyrics in songwriting. She performed on the video of her collaborative children's musical, *Together,* which was published for Christian television. An inspirational and juvenile writer, she is currently writing a romantic historical novel. She is a former teacher of the visually impaired, has a Master of Education degree from Georgia State University, and lives on Colonel's Island, south of Savannah.

ANAMAE ELLEDGE is an elementary school teacher in the Hawaii public school system. In her spare time, she enjoys reading, quilting, and taking care of her six children.

LINDA G. ENGEL earned her master's degree in communication disorders and was a speech-language clinician and coordinator in public schools for twenty years prior to the adoption of a son and daughter. As a freelancer, she writes short stories for regional publications and is currently working on a book about grief. She resides with her husband and children in the heart of the Minnesota lakes, where she was born and raised. (218) 829-3433.

HOLLY ESPARZA, RN, MBA, has been a registered nurse, manager, and sometimes even a leader for many years. She is currently the director for Women's and Children's Services for two hospitals in Denver, Colorado. Her passion is health and wellness, and encouraging herself, her husband, and their two daughters to live a healthy, happy, balanced life. (303) 741-5203.

CANDIS FANCHER, MS, CCC in Speech Pathology, is the founder of Inner Sources. Audiences are inspired by her upbeat philosophy. Her Pleasure Pause seminars have energized participants to adopt more positive lifestyles. Her Staying Afloat in the Stresspools of Life seminars explore practical ideas for integrating humor into your personal and professional life. Her SNAC approach provides practical and humorous ways for Stopping, Noticing, Acting, and Creating heart-to-heart connections. She is also a speech/voice coach and is a member of the American Speech-Language Hearing Association and the National Speakers Association. (612) 890-3897.

JILL FANCHER, born in Seoul, Korea, attends school at Nicollet Junior High in Burnsville, Minnesota. She loves soccer, piano, oboe, and her dog, Ashley. Chad, her older brother, is her hero. She is enthusiastic, has a great sense of humor, and enjoys being with her friends. She is the daughter of Candis Fancher.

HOLLY FITZHARDINGE is a writer and film director in Vancouver, B.C., and has worked extensively in story development and production in both films and television. She is a member of the Directors Guild and Writers Guild and recently completed a film concerning Amnesty International prisoners of conscience, which is on the film festival circuit. She is currently working on another film. Fax: (604) 940-8814.

JOEANN FOSSLAND, President of Advantage Solutions Group, is a personal and business coach and professional speaker who lives in the beautiful Sonoran Desert of Tucson, Arizona. She delights in working with individuals, groups, and companies that are committed to discovering how to maximize their uniqueness. Through keynotes, workshops, and one-on-one coaching, Joeann's clients create abundance, love, and creativity

that ignite joy, self-expression, and aliveness! (520) 744-8731.
<Joeann@aol.com>

JUDITH MORTON FRASER, MA, is also a Marriage/Family/Child
Therapist and an actress. Her published works include the stories "Alone in the Woods Bearly" (*L.A. Times* and L.A. Times
Syndicate) and "Grammas Don't Die" (Everywomans Village);
a poem, "To Know You" (Hallmark); and articles dealing with
relationships and addictions (California Association of Marriage & Family Therapists newsletters). She is presently writing
a novel combining creativity, Native American ceremonies, and
life passages. Her musical director husband, Ian, is an eleven
Emmy Award winner; daughter Tiffany is an actress; son Neal
is a chef; grandchildren Grace, Chelsea, and Jenna are creative
works in progress. (213) 656-9800.

MARCI MADSEN FULLER is a writer, wife, and mother, currently
living in south Texas, with the wild parrots, and water snakes
and the geckos that bob their heads in greeting from the kitchen windowsill. She has just finished her first novel and is
now sorting inspirations for her second. (956) 399-3094.
<Wlflsprite@aol.com>

JILL GOODWIN considers herself to be a student of spirituality
on a guided journey by her Higher Power. She is a published
reporter and interviewer, and has hosted a television series. She
has a BS in communications and works as a public relations
practitioner in media relations. (703) 212-0486.

MAUREEN GORSUCH is a Licensed Massage Therapist who is
presently living and working in Kansas City, Missouri. She grew
up in New York, then moved to Kailua Kona, Hawaii, where
she continued her education and enjoyed great friends and sun-
sets. She loves skydiving, exercise, and meditation, and can
sometimes be found writing in her journal while sipping wine
in an ethnic restaurant. (816) 765-6297.

CINDY HANSON is an air personality at KINK-FM in Portland, Oregon. She is a seeker of cosmic truth, a believer in the healing powers of nature, the great outdoors, art, and music. She has an unbridled passion for the Oregon coast and other unspoiled wide-open spaces. She is an artist in the media of stained glass and watercolors, an aspiring poet and essayist, a singer of silly songs, avid cyclist and runner, and an occasional hospice volunteer. (503) 226-5100 x6224.

DONNA HARTLEY is an international speaker, a change specialist, and a member of the National Speakers Association. Owner and founder of Hartley International, she has been featured on NBC, ABC, PBS, The Learning Channel, and in the *New York Times*. Her popular book, video, and audio training series is called "Get What You Want." (800) 438-9428.

CHRISTINE HARVEY is a TV and radio personality and the author of five books in twenty languages, including *Secrets of the World's Top Sales Performers,* which has sold 150,000 copies. She is a keynote conference speaker, who addresses audiences small and large, including Sony, IBM, Toyota, Lloyds Bank, Mortgage Brokers Associations, Century 21, and writers conferences. She's an active director of the board of an investment bank and a venture capital company, and is a council member of the International Center of the National Speakers Association. She divides her time between her office in London, her home in Brussels, and her work in the U.S., including television programs in Los Angeles. (800) 813-7197.

MARIE HEGEMAN, CSW, holds a BS in psychology from the State University of New York at Oneonta and a master's degree in social work from SUNY-Albany. She is a clinical social worker (psychotherapist) who practices in Oneonta, New York. She is writing a book about her mother's extraordinary battle against cancer. (607) 432-7285.

LIZ CURTIS HIGGS is a Certified Speaking Professional and has earned the Council of Peers Award for Excellence with the National Speakers Association. She writes a bimonthly column for *Today's Christian Woman*, called "Life with Liz," and is a member of the American Association for Therapeutic Humor, the Fellowship of Merry Christians, and the National Association for Professionals in Women's Health. She is the author of four humorous books for women: *One Size Fits All and Other Fables; Only Angels Can Wing It, the Rest of Us Have to Practice; Mirror, Mirror on the Wall, Have I Got News for You!;* and *Forty Reasons Why Life Is More Fun After the Big 4-0.* Her four children's books include: *The Pumpkin Patch Parable; The Parable of the Lily; The Sunflower Parable;* and *The Pine Tree Parable.* (800) 762-6565.

ELLEN URBANI HILTEBRAND, MA, is an author and art therapist practicing in Portland, Oregon, where she specializes in developing art therapy programs to meet the psychosocial needs of physically ill patients and their families. Her company, Healing Arts, provides national contracting and consulting services to health care organizations interested in developing therapeutic arts programs, and she speaks regularly at medical conferences throughout the country. The therapeutic school art program she developed while serving as a Peace Corps Volunteer in Guatemala is now used worldwide by Peace Corps Volunteers and other development workers. A book about her experiences there should be completed within the next year. (503) 413-8404. <hiltebrand@juno.com>

JENNIFER HOWARD lives in White Salmon, Washington, with her husband and their four sons. She enjoys gardening, horseback riding, and spending time with her family and friends. Writing is a hobby that she uses to capture the milestones in her children's lives. (509) 493-4701.

SHEILA S. HUDSON, founder of Bright Ideas, is a freelance writer and speaker living in Athens, Georgia. An award-winning writer, she enjoys credits in magazines such as *Christian Stan-*

dard, *Lookout, Reminisce, Athens, Teddy Bear, Just Between Us,* and *The Pastor's Family.* She and Tim have been married twenty-nine years and have two grown daughters and a grandson; they begin their sixteenth year at the Christian Campus Fellowship at the University of Georgia. (706) 546-5085 voice/fax. <sheila@naccm.org>

ANTIONETTE VIGLIATURO ISHMAEL is the fifth–sixth grade language arts teacher at St. Bernadette Catholic School in Kansas City, Missouri. She was a 1997 recipient of the Excellence in Teaching Award in Missouri. She is also a writer, scout leader, the wife of Phil, and—most of all—the proud mother of Patrick (fourteen), Anthony (eleven), and Dominic (eight). (816) 231-4138.

ROBERTA B. JACOBSON, PhD, has lived in Europe for over twenty years. Her freelance writing reflects (mostly Western) European themes and has been published in *Transitions Abroad, True Experience, Cats, McCall's, Writer's Digest,* and *The American.* Her poems have appeared in *The Christian Science Monitor, Wry Bred!, Cicada, Krax,* and *Haiku.* <100601.3415@compuserve.com>

DEBB JANES is a radio news director and morning radio personality in Portland, Oregon. She successfully helped lobby for changes in Oregon's stalking laws when she encountered legal problems trying to prevent a stalker from harassing her. She is currently co-creating a talk show that features positive role models and programs for and about women. She's the mother of three terrific children. They are joined by an old soul cat and a wonder dog. (503) 226-9791.

SARAH JORDAN is a mother, wife, writer, and advocate for home education. As co-owner of Mindfull, she organizes ReThinking Education conferences and mothers' retreats and lectures on all types of family matters. She lives in the small town of Double Oak, Texas, just north of the Dallas–Fort Worth Metroplex, with her three home-schooled children and longtime friend, editor, and husband, Gary. (817) 430-4835.

LISA JUSCIK is the assistant director of athletic media services at Northwestern University in Evanston, Illinois (847) 733-8074.

KATHI J. KEMPER, MD, MPH, is an internationally known pediatrician, educator, author, and researcher. She is the author of the widely acclaimed book *The Holistic Pediatrician* and president-elect of the Ambulatory Pediatric Association. Her greatest life adventure and joy is being Daniel's mom.

NANCY KIERNAN, PhD, is an educator, a professional speaker, and a cancer survivor. She is committed to helping raise awareness for others with life-threatening problems by writing and speaking about the proved links between chronobiology and one's medical choices. Her current book in progress reveals many little-known truths about "perfect timing" and helps a woman plan strategically for a healthy life. (602) 391-9132. <AZ Kiernan@AOL.com>

SHARON KINDER is currently writing about her numerous spiritual experiences. Having successfully made the transformation from business owner and community leader to writer and hermit, she has recently moved to the Pacific Northwest from her home in the Sierra Nevada foothills of Central California. (503) 543-8262.

MARLENE L. KING, MA, is a professional writer, artist, and dreamologist. She currently publishes an interactive dream column in Dream Network and is writing a book exploring creation theories and symbology. She consults and does contract work for individuals, groups, and businesses. (541) 471-9337. <marlene@chatlink.com>

TAMMY KLING is a freelance writer, speaker, and the author of *Searching for a Piece of My Soul—How to Find a Missing Family*

Member or Loved One. She specializes in talks on adoption, family searches and reunions, and crisis management. She spent years serving on an emergency response team for a global airline and is currently working on her first novel, *Impact.* (972) 248-1429.

LON MY LAM is a teacher in Honolulu. She was born in Vietnam but raised in Oregon and California before settling in Hawaii. Her greatest ambition is to live each day fully with integrity, patience, and love. (808) 623-7897.

SUSAN LaMAIRE has spent the four years since college graduation trying various methods of rent payment (waitress, substitute teacher, bookseller). She relies on her quick wit, ingenuity, and God's power to get her from one trial to the next. She has a reputation for putting her foot in her mouth and rebelling against authority. She has a degree from Bucknell University and is a freelance writer currently working as a substitute teacher. (732) 477-6083.

CATHERINE LANIGAN has been writing for seventeen years and is the author of fifteen novels, including the novelizations of *Romancing the Stone* and *Jewel of the Nile.* She introduced a new breed of heroine into the literary fold, "The Evolving Woman," a woman who builds an arsenal of wisdom, dignity, and courage that will fortify her capacity to love and be loved despite her battles with very real tragedies and crises. Her self-empowerment stems from an abiding spiritual faith, which guides her and continually renews hope. (212) 929-1222.

STEPHANIE LAURIDSEN has been a news producer for Westcott Communications in Carrollton, Texas, since November 1992. She produces, reports, writes, shoots, and edits for the Automotive Satellite Television Network. As co-coordinator for the Westcott Communications Internship program, she frequently speaks at Texas universities to recruit new interns. As an automotive journalist, she also serves as the first female president of the Texas Automotive Writers Association. She is active in her

Christian life as a Senior High Youth Group Counselor and accompanies the group twice a year to continue the youth mission in Acuna, Mexico. (941) 540-9911.

MARY LOVERDE, MS, ANP, is a professional speaker and founder of Life Balance, Inc. Her passion is researching new ways to balance career success with a happy and healthy family. She is the author of *Stop Screaming at the Microwave: How to Connect Your Disconnected Life* (New York: Fireside/Simon & Schuster 1998) and has produced an audiotape series entitled *June Cleaver Never Fried Bacon in a Bill Blass Dress*. For information about her customized Memory Jar and Memory Cards, please call (303) 755-5806.

JILL LYNNE, a photographer and writer, is known internationally for her special portraits of VIPs, documentation of popular culture, environmental nature studies, use of cutting-edge technology and alternative photographic techniques. With twenty-one solo exhibitions, her photography is represented in prestigious collections, and her photography and writing have appeared in *Newsweek, Vogue Italia, Ms.,* and The *Miami Herald*. Based in New York City and Miami, she also produces special promotional and fund-raising events for such organizations as the United Nations, the Nature Conservancy, and the American Foundation for AIDS Research. (212) 741-2409 or (305) 532-8096.

CHRISTINE D. MAREK is a thirty-three-year-old mother and wife, who presently works as an industrial electrician. Christine began writing for therapeutic reasons while in counseling to end a violent marriage and to heal from her own childhood sexual abuse. Much to her surprise, as Christine began to heal, she began to connect with a gift that had heretofore remained under wraps. (815) 258-7788.

LYNNE MASSIE is a business consultant, speaker, and coach, who mobilizes people by training them in both personal and professional development. She is also a cancer survivor, who has written a book about her intense and inspiring journey through cancer, called *The Buttercup Has My Smile.* (503) 675-0058.

SUSAN MILES is a writer and photographer. Her current series, "The Heart of the Flower," depicts the inner beauty of nature through macrophotography. Her images are available as prints and on greeting cards. (503) 282-6266.

MARY MANIN MORRISSEY holds a master's degree in Psychology. Her growing global audience is a tribute to her inspirational speaking and teaching ministry. She counsels and leads seminars reaching thousands each year as the founder and spiritual leader of the Living Enrichment Center, often referred to as a model of the 21st Century Church. She is the author of *Building Your Field of Dreams.* (503) 682-5683.

YOLANDA NAVA is a television broadcaster, writer, and consultant. She is host of *Life and Times,* a nightly newscast that airs on KCET/TV in Los Angeles, and she writes a weekly column for Eastern Group Publications, the largest chain of bilingual newspapers in the nation. She is currently writing her first book, *It's All in the Frijoles: A Book of Hispanic Virtues,* to be published by Fireside/Simon & Schuster in 1999. (213) 256-7836.

O. C. O'CONNELL is a freelance writer who still struggles with her hair from time to time. She resides with her beloved and their twin angel babies in a perpetual state of chaos, passion, and negotiation, which are elemental in a house of four fiercely loving interdependent souls. She has led past lives as a teacher of English, algebra, and geometry, a market research analyst, and a vice president of corporate communications. She has never been a hairstylist. (303) 730-6745.

DEBORAH OLIVE, senior minister at Unity Center of Tacoma, in Tacoma, Washington, skillfully navigated the corporate world as a sales representative in the medical field prior to attending ministerial school. She holds a bachelor's degree in biochemistry and artfully bridges the arenas of spirituality, science, and business. Deborah's ministry, characterized by her integrity, humor, and commitment to spiritual transformation, supports people in clearing the obstacles to their heart's desires and achieving their dreams. (253) 460-9898. <Soulnheart@aol.com>

MARY OMWAKE has been the senior minister of Unity Church of Overland Park in Kansas since 1989. Under her leadership, the congregation has grown from under 200 to 2,450 members. She is a founding member of the Association for Global New Thought and is committed to supporting authentic spiritual growth and rendering genuine service to an awakening world. (913) 649-1750.

CHASSIDY A. F. PERSONS holds a BA in Latin American and Caribbean Studies. She is a preschool teacher working on her master's in Special Education. (518) 887-5898.

CINDY POTTER is the executive director of the Oregon State Mortuary and Cemetery Board, which is responsible for the professional licensing and regulation of the death care industry. She and her husband, Dan, reside in Beaverton, Oregon, and share their lives with three cats and three dogs. During their twenty-four-year marriage, they have rescued and either found the homes of or found new homes for over two hundred stray animals. Dazy Joy was their first. (503) 524-3614.

DIANE RIPSTEIN, MEd, is a speaker and trainer and the principal of Diane Ripstein Consulting in Newton, Massachusetts. She helps her clients give more powerful presentations, more succinct sales pitches, more compelling investment-raising road shows, and more credible interviews to the media. With both a highly successful sales career and several years of onstage performance experience behind her, Diane specializes in high energy. (617) 630-8630.

ROBIN RYAN is an international pilot for United Airlines, a wife and mother. She delights in giving inspirational speeches and motivating people of all ages to "go for the gold" and follow their dreams, no matter how seemingly difficult. She has begun an inspirational book using her life experiences as a basis for her message that if she can reach her goal, anyone can dig deep inside herself, dare to dream, and accomplish her dearest desires. (360) 576-5600.

JOANNA SLAN is a professional speaker and the author of *I'm Too Blessed to Be Depressed* and *Using Stories and Humor: Grab Your Audience*. Audiences around the world have enjoyed her uplifting and insightful stories on the topics of teamwork, change, communications, conflict, and workplace productivity. She still rocks Michael in their home in St. Louis, but now that's he's a big guy of eight, it's a lot harder to get all of him onto her lap. For more information about Joanna's speaking services or to order her books, call 1-888-BLESSED (253-7733). <JoannaSlan@aol.com>

JODY STEVENSON, director of Soul Purpose Ministries, teaches comprehensive technology that accelerates soulful awareness toward the discovery of your special contribution to humanity, your soul's purpose. Her delight is assisting you to awaken to your personal passions. Author of *Soul Purpose,* and *Solutions,* she is currently a counselor in private practice, speaking nationally and leading seminars on creative expression and Soul Purpose Principles. (503) 977-2235.

LINDA ROSS SWANSON is a freelance writer who frequently publishes essays and poetry. She is currently completing her first book, *Beheading the Hydrangea.* (503) 292-4755.

KATE McKERN VERIGIN is a licensed minister who focuses her energies on creating ritual and ceremony to celebrate all aspects of life. She is in her fourth year of leading moon ceremonies for women. On Friday nights, Kate serves as minister to a group called Heart & Soul, which sponsors eclectic ceremonies for women, men, and children designed to open the heart and celebrate the soul. By degree she is an educator and communicator. Through life experience she is an Emmy Award–winning television producer, publicist, spiritual counselor, and mentor, wife, stepmom, and cat lover. She lives in Portland, Oregon. (503) 256-9833.

ANN E. WEEKS, DNS, RN, is a nationally known speaker and nurse family therapist who gives her audiences and clients many everyday strategies to heal the stresses of life's passages. Her ever-present sense of humor and real-life stories always make her presentations a treat. She is the author of seven books and owns Passages Publishing, a small press dedicated to putting into print the stories that pass on our experience and heritage. She is a self-described "recovering academic" and is former dean and associate professor of the Lansing School of Nursing, Education and Health Sciences. She is a consultant on organizational communication and team building and innovative programs, and has twenty years' experience as a legal expert witness. (502) 458-2461. <healingpassages@ka.net>

ALICE STERN WEISER, a native Bostonian, is a graduate of Boston University. She received her certification from the International Society of Graphoanalysis. A leading expert in handwriting analysis, body language, and voice inflection, she was elected the 1995 International Handwriting Analyst. She is a popular motivational speaker, teacher, TV guest, workshop headliner, jury analyst, and personnel consultant. Her lectures not only entertain and inform but promote confidence through nonverbal communication skills. (713) 355-4546.

JEAN WENZEL has lived in Sierra Leone, Iceland, Germany, the Faeroe Islands, and Pakistan before settling in what she believes to be the most beautiful place of all, Oregon. She writes for magazines, newspapers, and web sites, teaches writing, and hosts and anchors on community radio. She is an all-weather hiker, a voracious reader, and a master knitter.

ACKNOWLEDGMENTS

My deepest gratitude goes to the contributors of this book. Their unique and contagious enthusiasm and their willingness to share their favorite "heart" stories created the magic and universal appeal of Chocolate for a Woman's Heart.

Many thanks and the warmest regards to my agent, Peter Miller, who opens doors and makes things happen, and my editor, Becky Cabaza, for her expertise, friendship, and belief in me.

A special thanks to: Ellen Hiltebrand, a gifted writer and friend, for reworking several stories; motivational speakers Mary LoVerde, Candis Fancher, Donna Hartley, Emory Austin, Irene Levitt. April Kemp, Maggie Bedrosian, and Joanna Slan for their special love of the Chocolate series and their understanding of its value to readers. My love and appreciation go to my publicist extraordinaire Joanne McCall, and to Kathie Millett, Linda Kemp, Jody Stevenson, Susan Miles, Linda Swanson, Michelle Hayhurst, Ursula Bacon, Mary Jo Evans, and Jacqui Elliott for their support, feedback, and friendship.

As always, my heartfelt love and appreciation to my one-in-a-million husband, Eric, whose integrity and commitment in his professional and personal life is beyond reproach. He makes our journey together a playful adventure.

Thanks to my family for their understanding and patience during the "creative process"—and to my daddy, to whom this book is dedicated.

The sweet, delicious bonus from compiling these stories has been the new friendships of seventy-four women from around the country. I am grateful for their generosity, and I'm honored to have their stories in Chocolate for a Woman's Heart.

PART TWO

Chocolate

for a Woman's

Soul

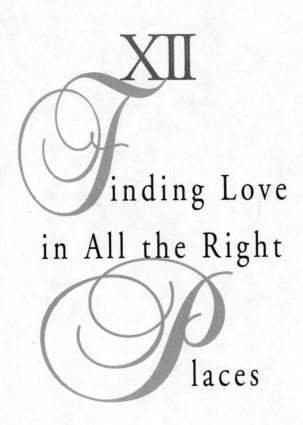

XII

Finding Love in All the Right Places

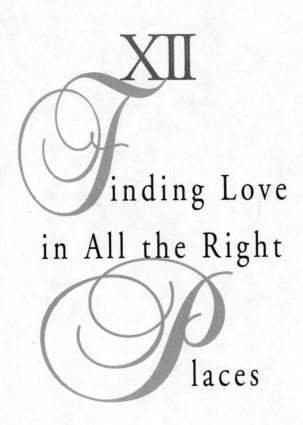

"For your ship to come in, you must first build a dock."

—Author unknown

How to Find Your Perfect Mate

Dear Abby always said that husbands don't leave their wives for the other woman—mine did, and he married her. Suddenly single at thirty-eight, I looked for refuge in my work. Work helped me forget my painful divorce. I suppose I could have been interested in a partner, but for three years I was not attracted to anyone I met.

A friend of mine had just been to a workshop called "How to Find Your Perfect Mate." She cautioned that if I did not feel worthy enough to have my perfect partner, or did not believe wholeheartedly that he was on his way, this was not the time to go forward with the process.

She described the steps this way: 1. Make a long list of attributes you'd like in your partner. 2. Study that list carefully, and pare the number down to about fifteen qualities that are essential to you in a mate. 3. Review that list again to see if you have all those qualities you are seeking in someone else. (This is the time for your own personal growth.) 4. Create an open space in your life for this person to come in by freeing yourself from dead-end relationships and casual dates. 5. Be in gratitude to your Higher Power, for your perfect mate is on the way. You won't need to seek your partner out or force the process along. You can watch as events unfold and not be concerned about the outcome. You can relax now.

I was ready to make my list. It included such things as: A spiritual man, a man with a good sense of humor, a man who makes a difference in the world by what he does, a man who is loyal, a man I respect, a man who wants to live on the water, and a man who knows how to take good care of his lady.

As I drove to work each day, I felt grace wash over me as I expressed my gratitude in how Spirit was working in my life. It was an inside-out process of looking at who I was and what I wanted to create in my life. I was able to see my future and rejoice. And instead of just looking for my perfect mate, I began working on myself to become the kind of partner that I wanted in return.

During this time, I was attending a management development class at the hospital where I worked. Eric, our consultant, was teaching us about mission, vision, values, and partnership. I really admired his work. I also admired his cute buns. However, my thoughts did not go any further because at nearly five feet eight inches tall, I envisioned a taller man, perhaps six feet. Eric was coming in at 5 feet 7 inches.

I continued identifying my personal and professional values as I attended Eric's class. Personally, I decided I would never again be in a marriage that had no spiritual foundation or shared values.

I also met with a psychic for the fun of it , and he asked me, "How do you feel about short men?" My response was "Do I have to?" He went on to say that my life partner really knew how to take care of his lady, was highly intelligent, and there was something about a country club. He said our courtship would be easy.

Months later, I hired Eric to do a weekend team-building at the beach for my staff. He offered to drive me there so we could plan the session. During casual conversation, I asked him the location of his office, in a city two hours from me. He told me his office was on Country Club Road.

During that weekend, we noticed each other in a new way. There was attraction there, but neither of us knew what to do with it. He asked if he could drive me home—it was only four hours out of his way!

On the way home, I worked up the courage to tell him I was attracted to him. Fortunately, he felt the same toward me. When Eric walked me to the door, he looked very confused. Later, he told me he hadn't known whether to kiss me or shake my hand. We compromised on a hug. He had a rule that you don't date your clients. But he didn't know that Divine Providence was moving in. He found himself calling my boss the next week to ask permission to date me. After a year's courtship, during which Eric caught up with what I already knew, one hundred friends and our four sons joined us in celebrating our wedding and in blessing our house on the water.

If I had not gone through the process of identifying and living my own values, I could not have asked for them in another person. OK, so I forgot to put "a tall man" on my list. But if I had, I may have missed Eric, my "Find Your Perfect Mate" guy. He may be short in stature, but he's a giant in the way he lives his life and in the way he takes care of his lady.

KAY ALLENBAUGH

"I'm not shooting for a successful relationship at this point.
I'm just looking for something that will prevent me from throwing myself in
front of a bus. I'm keeping my expectations very, very low. Basically, I'm just
looking for a mammal. That's my bottom line, and I'm really very flexible
on that, too."

—Lucille, in the movie *Bye Bye Love*

Sleepless in San Francisco

BY AGE THIRTY-FOUR, I WAS LIVING MOST OF MY
girlhood dreams. I had a quaint apartment in San Francisco, an interesting job, and great friends. But there was one thing I'd dreamed of
that still eluded me—finding someone to love and marry.

I didn't have boyfriends in high school. And in college, it often fell
on my roommates to fix me up with blind dates for important weekends. Even in my twenties, long after the asthma, pimples, and fat were
gone—when I was actually quite pretty and accomplished—I still
didn't see myself as someone another person would want to share a life
with. Chalk it up to childhood traumas, big and small. A multitude of
things had chipped away at my self-esteem.

Of course, I wasn't aware of the inner beliefs that were keeping true
love out of my reach. Now and then someone came along with enough
glib charm to put me at ease, and I'd fall head over heels. But these

were usually brief romances, brightening my hopes, then dimming them.

Once I launched my career and began working side by side with a lot of fascinating males, I began to really enjoy men as friends. But my love life still consisted mostly of short-term, loose connections with lonely spells in between.

I rarely let myself dream about the big "M" word anymore. This was the commitment-phobic early eighties, when a monogamous relationship that would last through Christmas seemed like too much to ask. Then *Newsweek* came out with the man-shortage article that said a career woman in her thirties had about as much chance of getting married as getting killed by terrorists.

The news was perversely comforting. With simple demographics to blame, I stopped wondering what was wrong with me and started grappling with the idea that I might remain single.

I settled for another tenuous relationship, this time with a man I'd met on vacation in Mexico. Jon was a political aide in San Francisco, a weekend pilot, introspective, good-looking, and fun.

He made it clear that he didn't want me to get serious. Thoughts of a house, kids, and a lawn mower made his skin crawl. Actually, he hoped to be working overseas within a year. It saddens me now to recall how easily I assured him that I had no expectations of a long-term commitment. We continued to see each other off and on, like two planets in orbit, sometimes close but never completely in each other's worlds.

On my birthday, however, Jon was there with lovely gifts of clothes and jewelry, taking me out for dinner and dancing. It seemed to me that we were closer than we'd ever been, and I started to wonder if things might work out after all. Then the next day, he bluntly announced that he was bringing another woman to a party we both planned to attend the following weekend.

I usually cry when I'm angry, but that day my fury was like dry ice as I asked him to leave my apartment. My anger stayed hard and frozen inside me for weeks, even when he called to make amends. He told me that a job had come through—a yearlong assignment in Africa. He wanted things to be right between us before he left, so wouldn't I please have dinner with him?

"No way," I said, surprised that my resolve wasn't melting. "If I let myself feel close to you again, I'll spend another year waiting with hope and doubt and I can't afford to do that. Besides, I expect to be married by the time you get back!" *Married!* Where had *that* come from? Jon couldn't have been more stunned than I was by my proclamation. But he left the country, and while he was gone, miracles happened to me.

Everywhere I went, it seemed I met another attractive man who wanted my phone number. Some of them I met at parties, others came up to me politely on the train, even on the street. These were men who seemed almost old-fashioned in their manners, attentiveness, and regard for me. For the first time in my life, my calendar was crammed with "real dates." One of the men was David, a neighbor in my apartment complex.

An hour into our first date, I felt I'd known David for years. We discovered we shared many hobbies and interests. Before the day was through, we'd already planned our next outing. Soon I was finding flowers at my door and romantic cards in the mail while he was away on business trips. I'd never known a man who was so sweetly persistent, so blatantly smitten, so dependable and generous. Of course I fell in love with him.

Jon returned to San Francisco, bewildered to find me engrossed in wedding plans. I don't know what's happened to him since, but David and I have been married for six happy years.

People used to tell me when I was single that I'd find love when I was "ready." I'd thought I was ready all along, but now I know I wasn't —not until that day on the phone when I loved myself enough to claim what I truly wanted and deserved.

PENELOPE PIETRAS

The Second Time Around

*S*USAN IS A HOPELESS ROMANTIC," I TOLD MY CONGRE-
gation. I centered my Sunday talk around Susan and Warren's story.
My message was on how love works in mysterious ways. It was a good
time to tell this story, because I was renewing my parents' thirty-third-
year marriage vows at the end of the service.

At the time Susan entered ministerial school, there was one hard-
and-fast rule: If you're married, stay married; if you're divorced, stay
divorced. Students were warned this was not the time to be making
long-term relationship decisions.

Susan was never one to play by the rules. Partway through her first
term of school, she returned home to marry her sweetheart. She
brought Warren back with her to school. They seemed the perfect
couple.

Susan's friends were shocked when she announced, a short time after
her graduation, that she had made a rush decision to get married and
it wasn't working out for them. All she could think of was starting her
own church and the people she would serve. Susan didn't feel ready to
walk that path with Warren. They divorced, and she immersed herself
in her new ministerial duties.

Years later, the church was flourishing, yet Susan was searching for a
long-term, loving relationship. She bemoaned the reality that most
single ministers face—it's awkward to date someone in your congregation, yet difficult to meet anyone "out there." Warren had married
someone else after he and Susan parted. She had not seen him for seven
years. Susan admitted that in her heart she knew if she had it to do

again, she would have stayed with Warren. She realized he had been perfect for her. Now she was looking for someone just like him to marry. Susan felt that if she set her intention on what she really wanted, voiced it, and believed in it, miracles would happen. And so she did.

"I have good news to report," I told my congregation. "Susan and Warren are getting married today." I continued my story, filling in the missing pieces for the congregation. After Warren's second marriage failed, he went through his own spiritual awakening and longed to reconnect with Susan, the love of his life. Warren found Susan's church and tried to work up the nerve to walk in several times. On the third try, he opened the door cautiously and sat in the back row. Susan's heart jumped to her throat when she saw him. She knew intuitively that her prayer had been answered in a most special way. They secretly got reacquainted, and Warren quietly became more active in the church as a volunteer usher.

"I'm a hopeless romantic too," I concluded to my congregation, circling slowly so they could admire my beautiful beaded dress. I could have passed for a bride. I was dressed to the nines to honor my parents and the power of long-term love in their lives. We were all wearing flowers for the upcoming ceremony.

I brought the congregation back to the present and told them that, like Susan, it's been hard for me to date anyone from the church. I even joked that I had heard them all talking behind my back about how John, a new usher, and I would make a great couple. I told them, "Now you know how difficult it is to think of being involved with anyone in the congregation with this kind of gossip!" The congregation roared, and John blushed as bright as the red carnation pinned to his lapel. The service ended, and the ushers moved to the back of the church. I reminded everyone to remain seated so that I could perform the renewal vows for my parents.

I walked to the back of the church and disappeared momentarily around a corner into the lobby. The organist filled the church with the familiar strains of the "Wedding March." The congregation gasped in amazement as I reappeared, walking down the aisle arm in arm with

John. My father walked up to the podium and explained, "There are two ceremonies today. Mine plus Susan and Warren's. Susan and Warren are here today for you to meet. Susan is your minister, Wendy Susan Craig, and Warren is that handsome usher, John Warren Purcell." We walked the length of the center aisle amid laughter, tears of joy, and celebration. Seven years later, I still don't play by the rules.

A visiting minister I had secretly invited to perform the ceremony stood up and met us at the altar. He asked us to repeat after him, and we exchanged our marriage vows to one another—for the second time. "Do you, John, take thee, Wendy . . ." We lit two candles and joined them into one. We kissed tenderly, then placed a banner on the wall behind the altar. As we walked back down the aisle as husband and wife, the congregation read what the banner said: "Love is lovelier the second time around."

REV. WENDY CRAIG-PURCELL

No Signature Required

JP

I'M A PROFESSIONAL HANDWRITING ANALYST. WHILE A great source of financial security, this unique talent wreaked havoc on my love life! Every time I was attracted to a new guy, I immediately analyzed his handwriting in terms of potential for a long and lasting relationship. I didn't want any surprises.

Handwriting analysis proved to be an easy way to eliminate men before I became remotely interested in them. Why bother if we have nothing important in common? Having heard so many stories from my women friends about meeting men who turned out to be "jerks," I felt confident that by using my professional handwriting expertise, I was covering my bases.

On the downside, I kept running out of men to run through my system. After years of hopeful dating and analyzing, I finally admitted to myself that "Mr. Right" probably didn't exist for me.

At a tennis match for singles, I was surprised to meet a man who seemed to have everything I was looking for—sensitivity, intelligence, and financial independence. My intuition told me that this guy looked promising, but I needed to be sure. Aha, I thought. I'll find out what he is really like right away. I'll give him the acid test. I'll have him write something for me and find out the truth.

He adamantly refused! He even laughed. "Why," he asked, "would I do that? You can read things into my handwriting and cut me off before we've really gotten to know each other. No, I want this to be as equal as possible. We can talk, but I'm not going to write for you. At least, not now."

Thus this guy took away my control. By removing the crutch I used to tell me how I felt about a man, he was forcing me to depend on observation, intuition, and feelings. Without my knowledge of graphology, I didn't trust myself, so how was I supposed to trust him?

Handwriting analysis had always enabled me to probe into a man's inner secrets. I could tell whether he forgave easily or held on to grudges. I knew if he was naturally generous or a penny-pincher. I could tell if he was sensitive to the feelings of others or was self-protective and self-absorbed. Many years of study had shown me that first impressions are not always the right ones. I reasoned that if he refused to write for me, it was probably best to forget him. Perhaps he had something to hide! A tug-of-war continued between my heart and my head. "He seems perfect for you," my heart said. "Why not give him a chance?" My ego chimed in at that point: "Be careful. You're on foreign ground."

Handwriting self-analysis had made me painfully aware of my own personality: I was likely never to love again, because of past hurts. A small, quiet voice inside me asked, "Is that the way you want to live the rest of your life?" I knew I had to break with the past, or there would be no future. While my heart and my head battled on, I decided to tough it out. It was time to let go—and trust. I followed my intuition for the first time and continued to see "Mr. Possibly Right."

I now know there are some things in life that I can't control or analyze. When I allowed my heart to open, I learned to be in a relationship fully without knowing the outcome.

I watched this man relate to his children. I respected his sharing and caring ways with his son and daughter. I adored the way his hair curled in the back of his head, the look of love and tenderness in his eyes when he looked at me, the way he never stopped rubbing my thumb with his fingers when we held hands in the movies. At last I knew, with no handwriting to back me up: "Mr. Possibly Right" was "Mr. Right."

And his handwriting, when finally I saw it, merely confirmed what I had already discovered about him by trusting myself.

By design, nothing was in writing as we exchanged our marriage vows. At our wedding ceremony, we simply spoke from our hearts.

IRENE B. LEVITT

"You have forgotten yourself,
and that is your only fault."

—Author unknown

Five-Dollar Psychic

I VOLUNTEERED TO DRIVE OUR CONFERENCE SPEAKER, A professor who spoke on death and dying, to the airport, three hours away. The professor held degrees in sociology and psychology, and he fascinated me with his insights on what made people tick and what was really important in life. I didn't share a lot as we drove, yet he read between the lines. Though I held back, he told me about his personal life and his family. I was surprisingly comfortable with him. It felt as though we had a lot in common. He encouraged me to fulfill my dream of completing my degree in sociology and was making me think about my life in a new way. Out of the blue, he turned to me and said, "You don't have any idea how attractive and charming you are, do you?" He wasn't flirting; he was just observing me. Why didn't I feel attractive? And why had I settled for working for my husband in a job I did not enjoy?

My mind flashed on Allen. My family had warned me against him. "He's not your type," they had all said. At twenty-eight, in a marriage that wasn't exactly sizzling, I was trying hard to convince myself all was well.

A few days later, Jeanne and Darlene commented on how distracted I was at our cooking class. I told my friends I had an unusual feeling of expectancy. They looked at each other and began to speak in unison.

I needed to see Reverend Marty, they told me. She is really good at what she does, and she's credible. She's even helped in some investigations with the police and the FBI. Reverend Marty was a psychic.

"Hold on now," I told them. Given my traditional religious beliefs, I could feel myself resisting their advice: "Something is trying to happen for you. You are ripe for a reading!"

I followed them as they drove to Reverend Marty's house. We had decided that I would go first. Resolved to make it tough for Reverend Marty, I wasn't going to say anything—she would have to "know" things on her own.

We pulled up to a small house with a lace curtain on the window. I couldn't believe they had talked me into this. Reluctantly, I followed Jeanne and Darlene to Reverend Marty's front door. A small sign read: REVEREND MARTY, PSYCHIC. READINGS $5.

My cooking pals waited in another room as I stared incredulously at Reverend Marty in her quaint, linoleum-floored kitchen. Reverend Marty was not looking into a crystal ball. Her demeanor surprised me. She was like a grandma—tiny, soft-spoken, and empathic. Reverend Marty came straight to the point by telling me that I had recently met a man from the East Coast who was as comfortable as an old shoe. I was shell-shocked. She described his family perfectly. Again right on target, Reverend Marty said my husband would be taking a trip in a few days. Gently disclosing the heartbreaking news that Allen was being unfaithful, she described several of my friends he had been trying to seduce; and I knew who she meant. I was frozen in my chair. She told me I would have a double loss—my marriage and my job. And I would have a double victory—a new career and a new marriage.

Reverend Marty said I would be happily married to a man who was perfectly suited to me; and we would have a boy and a girl. I was having trouble absorbing all this information. The next voice I heard seemed to be that of my deceased mother-in-law! Although our bond had never been strong, her words sounded tender and wise as she told me to move on with my life without her son. "Honey"—my mother-in-law had always called me that—"he will never change his ways."

Speechless, I felt as if I were in a helicopter, looking down on my life. I saw for the first time that my marriage was a disaster, in which I had felt alone for a long time. I faced what I'd never wanted to see—Allen's repeated pattern of chasing after women and putting me down. My heart ached with the conscious realization.

I was holding back tears when I stepped off Reverend Marty's porch into the night. I spoke briefly to my friends, then rushed to my car. I found the nearest phone booth and called my best friend, Kris. "You'll never believe what I just did," I told her. Kris confirmed my worst fears. "I was approached by Allen," she said gently. "I've struggled a long time whether to tell you this; but I wasn't sure you were ready to hear it. Jan, I'm not the only friend of yours that Allen has approached." She began naming names. It was obvious how much Kris cared for me and how hard it was for her to tell me.

I now knew I wasn't intended to live out my life with Allen. Just hours before, I had been willing to remain stuck in this short-term fraudulent marriage forever because that's what I'd been taught. I was placing a higher value on never divorcing than on the quality of my life. It had taken two encounters—with the professor and with a psychic—to dissolve Allen's hold on me.

When I got home, Allen wasn't there. I scooped up my two dogs, packed a suitcase, and left the house. I never turned back.

One and a half years later, I met and married Jim, the love of my life. I've long since finished school, and Jim finds me irresistible. After twenty years, we're still best friends and lovers. We are blessed with two well-rounded kids, a boy and a girl.

I'm grateful to the professor who unknowingly made a chink in my protective armor. And thank you, Reverend Marty. The five dollars I spent so many years ago was the bargain of a lifetime.

JAN HIBBARD

The Completion

❧

$\mathcal{B}$RUCE AND I HAD A CONVERSATION ONE AFTERNOON about past intimate partners who had been important to each of us. Our intention in being open and honest, sharing our past, was to deepen the intimacy in our own relationship. This level of honesty was refreshing and scary.

I told Bruce about my special relationship with Tom, in my own personal version of *The Bridges of Madison County*. Tom and I had met in the late seventies, when I was assigned to a project thousands of miles from home. We had one of those cosmic attractions. Born on the same day of the same year, we thoroughly enjoyed each other's company. And what passion! Six months later, my project was completed, and I returned home with a heavy heart. Tom and I continued our long-distance romance for the next five years. We spent time together whenever he came to the West Coast in his work as a theatrical producer.

Some time later, Tom relocated to New York, and I went to visit him. Although I loved Tom and enjoyed Manhattan, I couldn't see raising my son in the asphalt jungle, so far away from the quiet forests of Oregon. The relationship seemed to drift. Neither of us was willing to state the obvious. One day we just stopped writing and calling.

From time to time over the next twelve years, I would feel the longing in my heart as I wondered about him. I tried to contact him. New York showed no listing, nor did Washington, D.C., or Los Angeles. I had no idea where Tom could have gone. What had happened to my cosmic love?

At this point in my story, Bruce looked at me with a completely bewildered expression and said, "You mean to tell me that if you were to see this Tom guy today, you might consider being with him again?" Hmm. I really didn't know the answer to that question. But I did know the relationship was unfinished and still occupying a space in my heart. I began to pray and ask for closure—but I had no idea where to find Tom.

Five months later, someone said something that reminded me of Tom, who remained on my mind for the next several days. I renewed my conviction to seek to resolve our relationship. In the middle of that same week, Bruce and I were flying to visit his parents in Montana. We went to the airport, checked in at the counter, and turned to head for the gate. There he was! Tom was standing no more than ten feet away from me. Simultaneously our eyes locked on each other. My heart was beating like crazy. "Tom?" "Alex?" And Bruce gasped, "Tom?"

Our exchange was brief. He had just landed and was changing planes. He was married, had a family, and lived in a large city. His career had followed his passion: the theater. It was midafternoon, and he had the smell of alcohol on his breath. I am in recovery.

As Bruce and I continued on down the corridor to board our flight, I felt a great sense of spaciousness. Bruce looked perplexed. His eyes asked a million questions. I quietly looked at him and said, "Wait, you must understand. God just helped me free an enormous new space for me to be fully in our relationship." I had not truly realized how much space Tom had occupied in my heart.

Seeing Tom and letting him go had renewed my faith in the power of prayer. I had determined *what* to pray for, and like a scene from a superbly crafted play written only for me, God determined *how*.

ALEX MERRIN

Black Belt in Dating

 ᔕᔑ

 MILE, TAKE A DEEP BREATH, WALK SLOWLY AND
surely . . .

How many times have I had to give myself this pep talk? Ten times?
A hundred? Oh, I don't even want to think about it. It's too terrifying
for words. The first date. There, I've said it.

You'd think that after twenty years of widowhood I'd get used to the
jitters, dry mouth, and mild GI disturbance. You know what I'm
talking about—that silly hope and silent prayer that this man will be
"the one."

Well, I have learned a few things about dating. I've got bad news
and I've got good news. The bad news is it's a numbers game. The good
news is . . . it's a numbers game. The secret is persistence, patience, and
planning. You've got to suit up and show up. And keep showing up.

I got it down to a science after a while. I always had a "first date"
outfit that was appropriate for most situations (usually a brief meeting
for coffee or lunch), and I felt I looked fairly decent. I always suggested
meeting in the same restaurant. I liked having my own wheels if I
suddenly needed to exit. If the waiters ever thought it was odd that I
appeared frequently with different men, they never let on. They smiled
sympathetically the few times my date decided we would share a main
course. Or when, in the case of blind dates, I had to walk across the
restaurant to a man who had gained fifty pounds and lost most of his
hair since he described himself to me the night before. Smile, take a
deep breath, walk slowly and surely . . .

Talk about a numbers game. Some were truly forgettable . . . and yet

I remember them: The tall, gorgeous man who told me the people who killed his wife were out to get him too—as we dined on an outdoor patio facing the street. The usher I had met at church who proceeded to drink seven (yes, seven!) glasses of champagne at brunch and then wanted to drive me to my car. And the pump company president who arrived early for our date. I thought he was the plumber, coming to fix my broken sewer pump. Smile, take a deep breath, walk slowly and surely . . .

Of course, not all first dates were nightmares. There was the world-renowned plastic surgeon who picked me up in a Rolls-Royce and let me drive it around my small town for a week. An oilman who sent his plane to pick me up for a gourmet dinner he cooked for me himself. A policeman who brought ten pounds of carrots and made fresh juice before the date; then checked out my house with gun drawn when we returned after a power failure. The successful restaurant owner who took me to Park City to ski. Smile, take a deep breath, walk slowly and surely . . .

From time to time, I'd get dating burnout and need a "dating fast." During one of my fasts, a no-nonsense counselor helped me surrender many issues that were holding me back from the right relationship. Then my dating became more focused. With that focus came the pain of knowing I'd been picking the wrong men. I needed to look at what kind of man would "wear well" for the rest of my life. Well, for me it wasn't some high-flying businessman. (Oh, darn, you mean he'll have a regular job, not always be working on some big deal?) It wasn't someone who'd been married a couple of times. And I wasn't going to meet him any place I was frequenting. I let everyone know I was open to dating again. Smile, take a deep breath, walk slowly and surely . . .

I don't want to count the nights I wrote in my journal that God must be playing a cruel joke on me. Otherwise why would I have such a longing in my heart for a mate? Year after year, I prayed that either the longing would go away or my soul mate would come into my life. And I kept on dating. Smile, take a deep breath, walk slowly and surely . . .

Now I'm at a crucial moment. I look across the room and see the man who suggested our golden retrievers meet for a walk on our first date. The man who wrote down the names of my friends and relatives, so he'd remember the people who were important to me. The same man who talked about money and sex and fears and hopes and dreams before he even tried to kiss me. The man who contradicted all the preconceived notions I'd ever had about a forty-seven-year-old never-married man.

In this room, I also see our close friends and dear family members. I see our moms crying. I hear Pachelbel's Canon in D playing. I hear my heart beating wildly in my ears. As I begin to cross the room to join him and the pastor, I feel the presence of God, telling me, "Smile, take a deep breath, walk slowly and surely."

CONNIE MERRITT

Soul Mates

CRASH! A GLASS SPILLED OFF MY TRAY ONTO THE FLOOR, breaking and spilling milk all over. My face red, I stooped to pick up some of the glass fragments. "Don't worry, I'll get it," said a male voice. When I looked up, I saw bright blue eyes and a glorious smile looking down upon me. That's how Don and I met—at the University of Colorado campus, summer of 1952. I was there for summer school. Don was in summer school too. He worked busing tables at my sorority dining room.

Don was soon calling me for dates, and I was so smitten that I couldn't eat when in his presence. He was serious and very intelligent, as well as handsome as a prince. I hung on his every word as he showed me Boulder and drove me to the peaks, showing off Colorado's mountainous splendor. I was surprised that he was attracted to me. I felt so young and inadequate. Don treated me like a princess. He treated me as a thinking adult. He was very open, and we could talk feelings—something foreign to me.

That summer was a combination of classes that lasted too long and time with Don that seemed too short. We danced to "I Only Have Eyes for You." And when it came time to return home to Houston, I felt overwhelmed with sadness.

We wrote to each other daily. In September, Don and his brother drove down to Texas to visit me. I was excited and nervous. Scared, actually. The long-distance romance had been like a dream. Now it was reality.

After they left, my dad called me in for a talk. "Trish," he began,

"I want you to know that I like your boyfriend. He seems to be a well-mannered, intelligent young man, and I think he will go far in the legal profession. However . . ." And that *however* said it all. "Too many obstacles," my dad said. "Number one, he is Catholic. Number two, he is Italian. And number three, he lives too far away." I was stunned. My heart was in my throat. As if I were far away, I heard Dad talking about Catholics and their lack of birth control, the difference in our backgrounds, and the necessity of my finishing college in Texas. And as though it were all now settled, he finished by saying, "Now I think you had better write that young man and tell him."

In all my eighteen years, I had never crossed my father on anything. It was 1952, and you did what you were told.

My brother had been "the rebel" all our lives, and I had assumed the opposite role. I cried as I wrote that letter, telling Don it was too difficult to continue our relationship. Part of me was scared, anyway. I was in awe that this bright, handsome, outgoing boy could be in love with me. I could not imagine moving away from my family and friends.

I received a nine-page letter back. He told me it was something he had already guessed and how sad he was about it. The letter was tender and understanding, and made gentle efforts to console me. He told me he wanted to leave me with the sweetest and most fragrant memories of the short time we had together. He wanted me to always be able to think back on my summer in Colorado as one of the happiest times of my life.

The letter was so beautiful that I couldn't throw it away. I never did. I kept Don's picture and that letter with my private diaries.

My father died of a heart attack five months later. I wrote to Don to tell him, but I did not hear back.

I began to date and eventually married another man. Someone close to home. Someone who had known Dad and had his approval. Someone who helped carry me through my dad's death. We had four wonderful, beautiful children and many good early years. But we were on different philosophical and spiritual paths, which eventually could no longer be ignored, and after twenty-seven years, our marriage ended.

We sold our house, and I bought a town house. I was putting books on the shelf when I ran across my diary, the picture of Don, and that letter. I unfolded the thin, yellowed pages again and saw tearstains on the letter. I felt compelled to write him—to say hello across the thirty years.

I sat up half the night writing and revising that letter. I told him what had gone on with me. I felt a surge of energy. The words just tumbled onto the page. I told Don that he didn't need to answer that letter, but I needed to write it.

Years earlier, he had told me he would like to practice law in Denver. I looked in a Denver phone book, and there was his name. I sent the letter with excitement and anticipation, assured that somehow I would receive an answer back.

When I saw the familiar handwriting on an envelope a week later, I postponed the moment. I just looked at the letter for some time before opening it. He told me that he had lost his wife three months before, and they had no children. Don had moved to another address after his visit to Houston thirty years before. He had not received my letter telling him about my father's death.

Several months and numerous phone calls later, we decided to meet. We chose a neutral place, Santa Fe. Neither of us had ever been there. When I got off the plane, I looked for Don. I then saw the same smiling face and bright blue eyes, the hair now gray. My heart was in my throat, and my hands shook as we walked toward each other. When we hugged, we bridged thirty years. We immediately fell into a familiar patter of communication, finishing each other's sentences, knowing each other's hearts.

We had a long-distance romance for a year, while I made arrangements to move and he dealt with his loss. We were like soul mates. We married the following April. To my many amazed friends and family who asked, "How can you just pick up and leave family and friends?" my answer was a smile. Inside, to myself, I said, "Watch me."

By this time in my life, I had learned how to know my heart. I had learned how to listen to that small, still voice within, to heed the strong intuitive part of me. I had learned to trust myself.

PATRICIA FORBES GIACOMINI

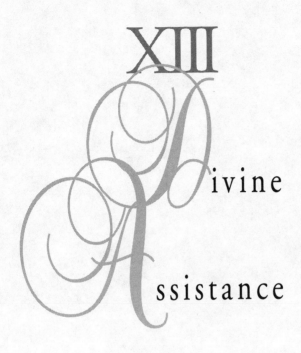

XIII

Divine Assistance

✧

"You can let the same force
that makes flowers grow and planets move
run your life, or you can do it yourself."

—Marianne Williamson

> "I'm convinced that sometimes we have to die a little
> before we really live a lot."
>
> —Rosita Perez

Flight #603

JP

I HEARD ALARMING SOUNDS AS THE CONTINENTAL DC-10 took off down the runway. Accelerating to 167 mph, it started its ascent. Suddenly there was an explosion. In terror, I put my head between my knees, and hugged my legs in the crash position. The plane crashed to the ground in flames. In a split second, fire engulfed the entire left side of the aircraft. The flames shot hundreds of feet into the air, and black soot covered everything.

For the previous seven years, I had led the life of a struggling actress in Los Angeles. Emotionally, financially, spiritually, and mentally, I had hit rock bottom. I didn't want to live. As a former Miss Hawaii, I was on my way back to Honolulu to emcee the Miss Hawaii pageant. When I boarded the plane, I said to myself over and over again, "Let my life change; let it never be the same, or let me die." At the moment of the explosion, the focus of my reality shifted dramatically.

From nowhere, an all-encompassing calm descended on me. I felt protected. It was as if a shield surrounded me. I was the center of a white light. Instead of cringing in fear at what was going to happen to the plane and to me, I was suddenly filled with joy and peace. I felt unconditional love.

A white light surrounded me and I heard a message: "You were given this life. What have you done with it?" And then four questions shot through my mind. "Do you love yourself? Do you love your family and friends? Are you living your goals and dreams? And, if you die today, have you left this planet a better place for having been here?" I screamed, "No! I want to live!"

As the flames raged closer, I scrambled to the exit, and I was the last one to make it down my evacuation slide. As I limped away from the burning aircraft, I realized that I had a second chance at life. Anything from now on was a bonus. It was as if all the wrong decisions I'd made in my life were printed on a blackboard, and with an eraser I had wiped them away. With this clean slate, I would be responsible for anything I did from this day forward.

An explosion shattered the aircraft. Survivors ran past me, screaming and crying. Slowly, I limped after them, toward a wire fence. I had walked away from death.

A disaster cuts right to the heart of life. It separates the chaff of pretense from the wheat of truth. It brings out a common denominator of love and compassion for fellow sufferers. A young woman, shaken and crying uncontrollably, clung to the arm of a man who comforted her. An elderly woman sobbed in the arms of a lady friend, who rocked her dearly, as if she were a child. Husbands held their wives as they never had before. Straight from their souls came love, each person giving and receiving in unashamed need.

I now know it's not what you are given in life but what you make of it. Life is a precious gift; and I create my own results.

What am I doing differently? I *never* put off saying "I'm sorry" or "I love you." I look to myself rather than to others for what is happening in my life. I don't know if I'll have a tomorrow, so I live each day as if it were my last.

DONNA HARTLEY

Let Me Know

ॐ

JESSIE SAT AT THE KITCHEN TABLE, WRITING NOTES. As I walked through the door, I spotted Reed lying on a pallet beside Jessie's chair. Reed was Jessie's schnauzer and constant companion for the past eleven years. They had spent those years joined at the hip. Now Reed was dying.

Tears springing to my eyes, I slumped in the nearest kitchen chair and listened as Jessie recalled the memories of bathing Reed while singing "Sweet Violets." She leaned over and patted his still body and talked to him in the loving tone of a mother knowing that this would be the last time he would hear her words. His ears barely twitched in recognition of the soothing voice he had grown to love over the years.

I couldn't control my grief as I watched my friend go through this heart-wrenching experience. Finding no words of solace, I bent down, patted Reed, told him I loved him, and slowly retreated out the door. I mumbled that I would call later. I drove home, emotionally wrung out by that sad scene and by the flood of my own painful memories when my beloved Pepper died.

Hours later, the vet humanely performed the deed we all dread; and Jessie took Reed home and buried him in the backyard, close to her flower bed. Such a fitting place for a dog who had been so loyal and loving. After a brief prayer, Jessie walked into the house and began her life without Reed.

Later, near bedtime, Jessie went into the kitchen to drink her warm milk—an evening ritual that had always included small gray paws fanning the air, begging for an evening treat. Only tonight, and from now on, there would be no popcorn treat and no Reed. Now there would be only the creaking sounds of an old house that for one person was too big, too lonely, and now too empty.

Drying tears that fell all too easily and too fast, Jessie turned on the evening news for distraction and went to take a shower. As she came out of the bathroom at the end of the hall, she stopped dead in her tracks. There at the top of the stairs was Reed!

"Reed! What are you doing here? You're not supposed to be here!" Jessie cried.

In his usual stiff-legged gait, Reed ran to Jessie, and as she bent down, he eagerly sniffed her face as if nothing had ever happened.

Not knowing what to think, Jessie repeated in an anxious whisper, "Reed, you're not supposed to be here!" Before she could take a breath, Reed was gone.

When Jessie told me what had happened, I automatically asked, "Are you sure it was Reed, Jessie?"

"Yes, I know it was Reed. Just before I carried him out to the car to take him to the vet, I held him to my heart and said, 'I don't know what they do with little fellers like you, so you let me know if you are all right.' Reed was the most obedient dog I've ever had. I told him to let me know—and he did."

SHIRLEY ELKIN

The Sweat Lodge

I COULDN'T BELIEVE I WAS ENTERING A SWEAT LODGE, A place of Native American ritual. I'm blond, blue-eyed, and mostly German. I was forty-three, the mother of four grown boys, and working at a hospital when my husband, Eric, and I took a vacation to the beach with a group of alternative healers.

When we were offered the opportunity of participating in the Indian ceremony, Eric didn't hesitate. He's like that—an "I'll try anything once" kind of guy when it comes to new adventures. Me, I need to be prodded along.

I was still resisting as the twelve of us sat cross-legged in a circle inside the tiny, five-foot-high tentlike structure made up of poles and branches. The Indian medicine woman began chanting and giving praise to the spirits. My heart raced. I watched fearfully as fiery rocks were piled in the center of our circle. Can rocks explode? Will we run out of air? Will I pass out? Everything felt too tight. I tried desperately to control my wild breathing. It was so hot that, in sheer panic, I leaned forward, placing my face in the dirt to cool off.

An hour later, I stumbled out of the lodge. I was totally drained and exhausted. I collapsed outstretched on the sand. Yes. That was it. I was safe and in fresh air. I expected no more. Then suddenly, as I gazed up at the stars, my mother's image appeared before me. I was stunned. (My mother had died young, at forty, when I was just fifteen years old.) Her smiling face took up the space of the full moon.

She began speaking to me in words only I heard. "Look at you!" she said. "You've done so much and come so far. You've had opportunities

I never had." She was very pleased with me, and I could feel her love envelop me.

There flashed through my mind all the important events I had not shared with her: my anguish at the time of her death; finding my stoic twin brother outstretched across his bed, sobbing and grieving, six months later; my senior prom, my high school graduation, my college graduation; Mother's Day each year, my wedding day, Mom's grandchildren; a painful divorce, a wonderful second marriage, career changes. I had also wanted to share my spiritual hunger, my tears and laughter, my love of movies, seeing mothers and daughters together. I thought she had missed them all. Now I knew she had been there with me all my life.

She faded away after a few minutes, and I lay there feeling sheer joy and wonder, bathing in the warm afterglow. I can't explain it, yet I know it was real.

If I had chickened out of that sweat lodge, I would have missed one of the most memorable experiences of my life. I was given this sweet opportunity to heal, and to hear Mom say, "I love you, dear daughter."

KAY ALLENBAUGH

What Do You Need?

IP

I GOT OFF TO AN EARLY START. BEFORE MY FIRST AP-
pointment, I took a friend to Kansas City International Airport and
drove back by my usual route. Approaching the fork where I would
turn left, I was in the left of four lanes. Then my car began to move
right, almost involuntarily, as if someone had taken the wheel from my
hand and was steering for me.

I spoke to myself out loud, saying, "Why did you do that?" as I
continued to drive along.

My white suit was perfect for this beautiful summer day. Knowing
my tendency to speed in good weather, I put on my cruise control and
enjoyed the scenery. I continued down the highway, singing, when a
voice in my head said, "Slow down." I looked at my speedometer and
saw I was only going sixty mph, so I thought, I'm fine, and waved my
hand dismissively.

A moment later, a voice that sounded as if it came from the back
seat yelled, *"Slow down!"*

Startled, I slammed on my brakes, which brought me to a near stop.
I had just enough time to utter, "What was that all about?" when the
little white car in front of me started losing control.

I immediately moved to the side of the highway, sensing a bad
accident was about to happen. By the time the white car crossed all
three lanes and slammed into the guardrail, going about seventy, I was
at a stop.

The minute I jumped out of my car, another car stopped beside me.
A man rushed over and asked, "Why did you slam on your brakes?

Nothing had happened yet." I answered, "I don't know." Then he said, "Thank you. You saved my life!" I asked how, and he went on to say, "I was speeding, going about eighty-five—I'm late and was trying to make up time. I've had so many speeding tickets that when I saw you slam on your brakes, I assumed you saw a cop. So I hit my brakes too. I would have been directly beside that car when it started to lose control."

Still stunned, he got into his car and drove away.

As I approached the wrecked car in the middle of the highway, I whispered to God, "Why me? What do I know about first aid?"

The driver, a pregnant young woman, and her husband were sitting in the white car, both looking badly injured. Blood was everywhere. His teeth were broken, and they were crying and scared. I knew we needed help and an ambulance.

A car stopped, and a woman asked, "What do you need?" I answered, "We need to call the police and an ambulance. These two people are badly injured!" She drove away to find a roadside phone.

As I walked back to the couple to tell them help was on the way, someone yelled from a passing car: "You've got to get them out. There's fluid leaking under the car!"

I went to open the driver's crushed door, when the woman told me it wouldn't budge. There was jagged glass in her window, so I knew she had to exit by the door. Using all my strength, I pulled on it. Unbelievably, the door gave way.

I helped the frightened woman out of her car and set her down, then I ran back for her husband. The passenger door was jammed against the guardrail, and an obstruction blocked the front seat. He could not slide across to get out the driver's side. I shouldered his weight while he hoisted himself up and out the window. I helped him lie down on the road next to his wife.

He was bleeding so badly that I thought to myself: We desperately need two towels. At that moment, a woman stopped her car and yelled, "What do you need?" I told her, and she reached in the back seat for a Kmart bag, which contained two towels she had just purchased. Returning to the couple, I applied a towel tourniquet on the man's arm and placed the other towel under his head.

They were going into shock, and I knew they needed blankets to stay warm. Another woman pulled up and asked, "What do you need?" I said I needed two blankets. She walked to the back of her van, pulled out two blankets from a laundry basket filled with clean bedding, and said she had to leave.

As I covered the man and woman, I realized I had done all I could do on my own. I thought: I need a medic—I need someone right now! I looked up and saw a man in a white uniform on the side of the highway, running toward us. I didn't see any vehicle; he seemed to have appeared out of thin air. He told me he was an off-duty medic. I stepped back as he began to administer first aid to the couple.

I'm sure I looked confused when the police came and told me I could leave. My mind flooded with the grace of the miracle. I had received everything I needed the moment I asked for it. For the first time in my life, I comprehended how safe we really are. Our angels are only a whisper away, to do God's work in our lives.

I realized I had just enough time to get to my appointment. When I arrived, I suddenly remembered, starting through the office door, that I was dressed completely in white. I looked down in disbelief. After all I'd been through, my clothing was spotless.

DIANN ROCHE

"What we are is God's gift to us.
What we become is our gift to God."

—Author unknown

Not Guilty

SP

STRESSED AND TIRED, I WAS DRIVING TO THE MOUNtains in southern California. I was a novice, working the twelve-step program. Even though I had seen miracles in my life, I still struggled to understand a Higher Power that could and would respond to me personally.

As I pondered the words of the eleventh step, "We sought through prayer and meditation to improve our conscious contact with God," the word *conscious* kept jumping out. It was at a time when I was asking, "How does God directly communicate with me by this thing called 'conscious contact'?" To know, without a doubt, the presence and power of God was just too much for my intellect to grasp.

At this point in time, there was one thing I knew for certain: The wreckage of every aspect of my life demonstrated how deeply, profoundly, and irreversibly *guilty* I felt! Shame had permeated my whole life, from beatings and rape to alcoholism and financial ruin.

So there on the California freeway, cruising toward the refuge of the mountains, I yelled out to the Creator of the Universe: "OK, I need a sign. Let's have conscious contact! Something concrete! Something now! Let me know that you are real! Reach me. Get a message to me and help me, so there will be no doubt in my mind that you exist." (When you're ignorant, you get away with this approach!)

As I stopped yelling, a silver compact car pulled ahead of me. The personalized California license plate read NT GILTY. I was frozen with the certainty that this was the message my Higher Power wanted me to get. God was sending a message of love and reconciliation, a message that we are not our mistakes, we are not our wounds. We are not our circumstances. We are beloved.

I began to believe I was destined for a life with purpose. I knew I was meant for more than I had experienced in the past.

I attended church the next weekend, and we were invited to stand and state our highest intention for ourselves. I stood and heard myself saying, "I am going to be a minister!" What? Was this true? But truly, I knew. And since I had already received one sign from God, I knew this unexpected intention was simply a more subtle sign, another reminder of how loved I was. I was ready to move beyond myself.

But that's not all. . . .

Years later, a young woman, who had also been sexually abused and battered, was visiting my congregation in Kansas when I shared this story. The next week, as she was eating lunch, she noticed a small silver compact car parking in front of the window where she was sitting. The personalized Kansas license plate read: NT GILTY. The friend who had brought her to my church called me excitedly and said, "Your Sunday message of forgiveness and love has deeply touched my friend's life." I said, Thanks for telling me, and thought to myself, for just a moment: Sure, uh-huh. After years of miracles and thousands of coincidences that had guided me into a fulfilling, purposeful, and joyous life, there was a part of me that still doubted the "invisible helping hands." The hands of the Divine that work constantly to wake us up and guide us. .

Driving home from work that night, my doubt was permanently erased. As I joined in the rush-hour traffic inching onto the freeway, a certain silver compact car I've never seen since slipped right in front of me. And like the car in California—you guessed it—the personalized Kansas license plate once again carried God's eternal message to us all: NT GILTY!

REV. MARY OMWAKE

Co-Creating the Future

ⵗ

$\mathcal{I}$N 1965, I WAS THIRTY-FIVE YEARS OLD AND HAD FIVE
young children. My lot in life seemed set—I was a full-time mom. I
loved my children very much, but something was definitely missing.
As a child and then as a young woman, I had been exposed to a rich
and varied education, one that had trained me to question and explore
and exercise my intellect. The years trickled by, and I grew increasingly
depressed—then I turned to books as a cure. I read voraciously, until I
hit upon Abraham H. Maslow's seminal book, *Toward a Psychology of
Being*, his study of what makes people joyful, well, and productive—
"self-actualizing," he called it. He found that without exception, these
people had one thing in common: they valued their work.

I realized I was not neurotic; I was underdeveloped, intellectually
and spiritually. Motherhood was not my vocation! I valued and enjoyed
family life, but having children was not my "calling." In the mid 1960s,
this thought bordered on the radical.

Not long after this epiphany, I was taking a walk in the Connecticut
countryside one fateful day in February, still pondering my true purpose in life. The temperature was below zero. I lifted my eyes upward
to the heavens, suddenly inspired by the cold but starkly beautiful day,
and asked the universe some questions: What's our story? How did we
get here? What event in our age is comparable to the birth of Christ?
What is happening to our planet? Born of a Jewish agnostic family, I
had no religious or metaphysical background whatsoever, but I felt
increasingly compelled to explore these broader life issues.

As I reflected on these questions that seemed to have no answers, I felt a message coming back to me, as if I was about to be gifted with a brilliant glimpse of how the world really works. First I saw visions of war, of pollution, of pain. I felt the earth gasping for breath, struggling to carry its load. And then I saw a light in my mind's eye—a planetary light, such as mystics throughout history have seen. I felt that light bathe the earth with love and, in one second, capture everyone's attention. We were one people, we were healed, and we were one with the earth—radiant, alive with joy.

I heard the words *Our story is a birth. What Christ and all the great avatars have come to earth to reveal is happening now. We are one body. We are being born to universal life. Go tell the story, Barbara.*

I was overwhelmed with joy. I had received my vocation!

To me, the meaning of my vision was simple and clear: We are one with God and with nature, and we will not survive as a planet unless we love one another.

My vision has motivated me for more than thirty years. Through lecturing, writing books, and organizing groups, I have talked to people, telling them the story of our birth, teaching them the importance of love and peace. Before I embarked on my journey, I remember telling my still-young children that their mother was a pioneer, that I would never abandon them but I had to go forth and tell the story. My nine-year-old son, Wade, put his arms around me and said, "That's what mothers are for—they are to create the future."

I've never been content to merely observe. Instead, I decided to be an active participant with others in co-creating a loving consciousness for this and future generations.

BARBARA MARX HUBBARD

A Forever Friend

ᘒ

ENDED UP SITTING NEXT TO JULIE BY CHANCE AT A
motivational seminar. We had ample opportunity to tell stories about
ourselves and found that we shared a common interest: passion for
the spiritual and "unseen" parts of life. I told her I was studying
dreamwork. This interest was to become the glue that bound our paths
together. At the end of the day, we exchanged business cards and
promised to meet again soon.

When we got together for lunch, Julie casually mentioned that she'd
been having random and disturbing pains in her lower legs. The next
few months proved to be an emotional and pivotal time in Julie's life.
She was becoming increasingly immobilized from the pain and from
muscle spasms. A litany of physicians, then neurologists, attempted to
diagnose her growing lack of control of her extremities. After endless
and agonizing tests, Julie had no conclusive answers. She began doing
research of her own.

I had never really understood what Lou Gehrig's disease (or ALS)
was until it became the focus of Julie's growing suspicions that she was
afflicted with this insidious illness. She educated me about the symptoms, treatments, side effects, and, worst of all, prognosis. Unfortunately, her suspicions were confirmed.

Five years after I met Julie, she knew her time was short. We had
many conversations concerning her beliefs about death and dying,
and how she did not want to be a burden, and how she wanted to
pass from this existence with dignity. Julie also had conversations with

God with increasing frequency. Near the end, she heard a voice tell her it was time for her to move from her home into a hospice care facility.

Julie talked often about wanting to leave this earth, and that she was ready to go. This was a difficult, yet special time for me, as I learned to honor the present moment when visiting with her. Time was running out for us. My dear friend was in the active stages of dying. During our last visit together, we made a pact. She said she would contact me, if at all possible, after her death. Due to an out-of-town commitment that could not be postponed, I was not present at Julie's memorial service. A month later, my husband and I went to our beach cabin for the weekend. There, I was able to heal and reflect on this amazingly strong and courageous woman who had taught me so much about the miracle of the human spirit.

On our second night there, I had a very real and intense dream of Julie actually standing in our bedroom. She was radiant, whole, vibrant, and smiling. She held her arms out to me and hugged me hard, and then held me at arms' length so that I could see her eyes and her joy. Julie said clearly, "We do not die!" This was more than a dream—I knew I had experienced something very real. It made sense for Julie to contact me this way. She knew my lifework was based around art and dreams. I shook my husband awake and told him that Julie had visited me, what she said, and how wonderful she looked.

On the way home, I could not stop thinking about the feeling and image of Julie. I began to cry and thought to myself: Julie, your strength and spirit and amazing courage touched many lives and hearts. I, for one, will never be the same for having known you.

Before reaching home, we stopped by our offices to pick up the weekend mail. I found that I had been sent a program from Julie's memorial service. When I opened the envelope, there was Julie's radiant, smiling face on the cover of the leaflet. It was the exact image of her I had seen in my dream! A Native American poem that Julie had selected before her death was printed on the inside page. It began with the words: "Do not stand at my grave and weep, for I am not there," and the last line read: "Do not stand at my grave and weep, for *we do not die.*"

MARLENE L. KING

XIV

A Woman's Intuition

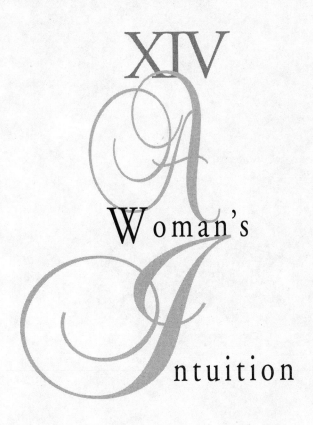

*"Peace is seeing a sunset
and knowing whom to thank."*

—Author unknown

Letter of Love

❦

THE OCTOBER DAY WAS CRISP AND SUNNY, PERFECT FOR a late-afternoon ride. My daughter, Janice, rode her favorite horse, Lady, and I brought along the dog. We followed the pasture fences, leaves crackling under hooves and feet, and talked about life and love and changes. We talked about how lucky we were to live in such a beautiful place. She told me about the new license plate she had just ordered. SA LA VIE, it would declare. "This is life." It would arrive in January. She had wanted to replace her current plate, PARTY N, with something new, like BLONDIE or SUN FUN. When I expressed surprise at her final choice, she explained that it had come to her at the last minute. I was proud of Janice's poise and grace, the gentle and loving adult she had become. At twenty-two, she was beautiful both inside and out.

Returning home, I felt closer than ever to her. I realized how much a part of each other we are and always have been. When I shared this with my husband and a friend, they suggested that I write Janice a letter, telling her how connected I felt to her. What a wonderful idea, I thought—I'll do it soon. As the holidays came and went, my good intentions faded.

On December 28, at 11:30 P.M., I woke from a fitful sleep. My husband and I were vacationing in Phoenix. I quietly slipped out of the hotel bed and hoped the light from the lamp would not awaken him. I had been thinking of Janice and decided to write that letter of love. My thoughts poured out on the paper, telling her how special our horseback ride had been, how connected I felt to her, and how much I would always love her. Folding the note into an envelope, I relaxed and fell into a peaceful sleep.

At 2:00 A.M., the phone call came that tore our world apart. Janice's heart had failed, the aftermath of a childhood heart murmur. We needed to get home. Our daughter had not survived.

On my way home, I clutched the letter tightly, as if it would somehow keep us connected. As we approached the driveway, a rainbow curved gracefully over the gate: a gift from Janice. I heard her voice in my head, saying, "It's beautiful where I am, Mom." Later that day, the friend who was with her last told me what had happened. They had been driving in his car, and she was laughing when she collapsed and died. He noticed that the dashboard clock had flashed 11:38. It was then that I realized I had been writing the letter during that time. The comfort I felt knowing that at the moment of her transition we were connected through pure love was immeasurable. I knew then that the words I wrote to her were also meant for me. We exist in a new and different relationship now, feeling closer and more a part of each other than ever. And we always will be—connected through pure love.

Her new license plate arrived shortly after her death. SA LA VIE, it read. This is life.

SUSAN MILES

Gifts of the Heart

❦

GIFTS OF THE HEART ARE ESPECIALLY NEEDED DURING the holidays. In this hustle-bustle world, it's so much easier to charge something on a credit card than to give a gift of the heart.

A few years ago, I began to prepare my four children with the notion that that Christmas was going to be a small one. If you have kids like mine, you know the response was "Yeah, sure, Mom, we've heard that before!" I had lost my credibility because I'd told them the same thing the previous year, when I was going through my divorce, but then had gone out and charged every credit card to the max and even invented some creative financing techniques. This year was definitely going to be different, but they weren't buying it.

A week before Christmas, I asked myself, "What do I have that will make this Christmas special?" In all the houses we had lived in before the divorce, I'd made time to be the interior decorator. I learned how to wallpaper, lay ceramic tile, sew curtains out of sheets with matching bedspreads, and more. In this house, there was little time and a lot less money. Plus, I was angry about this ugly rental house, with its red-and-orange carpeting and its turquoise-and-green walls. I refused to put money into it because I had this inner voice that shouted, "We're not going to be here that long!"

Nobody seemed to mind except my daughter Lisa. Though she was only eight years old, I'd always sensed that Lisa was perhaps more family-oriented than any of my other children. The move had been particularly hard on her. She'd lost the security of her old home, and to top it off, had left behind a wonderfully decorated bedroom—papered with daisies—that had been her special haven.

It was time to put my talents to use. I called my ex-husband to discuss gifts for the kids. For Lisa, I asked that he buy a specific bedspread, and I bought the sheets to match.

On Christmas Eve, I spent fifteen dollars on a gallon of paint and also bought the prettiest stationery I'd ever seen. My goal was simple: I'd paint and sew and stay busy till Christmas morning, so I wouldn't have time to feel sorry for myself on such a special family holiday.

That night, I gave each of the children three pieces of stationery with envelopes. At the top of each page were the words: "What I love about my sister Mia," or "What I love about my brother Kris," or "What I love about my sister Lisa," or "What I love about my brother Erik." The kids were fifteen, thirteen, eight, and six, and it took some convincing on my part that they could find even one thing they liked about each other. As they wrote in privacy, I went to my bedroom and wrapped the few store-bought gifts.

When I returned to the kitchen, they had finished their notes and sealed the envelopes, and we exchanged hugs and good-night kisses. The children hurried off to bed, and Lisa was given special permission to sleep in my bed, with the promise not to peek in her room until Christmas morning.

I got started. I finished the curtains, painted the walls, and, in the wee hours of Christmas morn, stepped back to admire my masterpiece. Wait—why not put rainbows and clouds on the walls to match the sheets? So out came my makeup brushes and sponges, and at 5 A.M. I was finished. Too exhausted to think about our poor broken home, I went to my room, where I found Lisa sprawled in my bed. I decided I couldn't sleep with arms and legs all over me, so I gently lifted her up and carried her into her room. As I laid her head on the pillow, she said, "Mommy, is it morning yet?"

"No, sweetie. Keep your eyes closed until Santa comes."

I awoke to Lisa's thank-you. "Wow, Mom, it's beautiful!" We all got up and sat around the tree and opened the few wrapped presents. Then each child was given three envelopes. We read the words with teary eyes and red noses. Then we got to the "baby" of the family, Erik, who, as the youngest, wasn't expecting to be told anything nice. Kris had written: "What I love about my brother Erik is that he's not afraid of anything." Mia wrote: "What I love about my brother Erik is he can talk to anybody." Lisa wrote: "What I love about my brother Erik is he can climb trees higher than anyone!"

Gifts of the heart are what memories are made of. I'm back on my feet financially, and we've since had "big" Christmases, with lots of presents under the tree . . . but when reminiscing about favorite Christmases, we all talk of that one.

I especially remember feeling a gentle tug at my sleeve, a small hand cupped around my ear, and Erik whispering, "Gee, Mom, I didn't even know they liked me!"

SHERYL NICHOLSON

No Simple Solution

ᏭᏭ

LAST WEEK JESSIE WANTED A NEW BARBIE MATTRESS TO replace the one her brother hacked up for his Z-Bots and Mighty Morphin Power Rangers.

This week Jessie wants Ryan, a boy she's just met. "Mom, it was so cool," Jessie says as she chews around her fingernail. I hand her a carrot, which she gnaws with equal resolve. "I'm glad I went to church camp. And this guy Ryan is just so cool. He was in my family group, and we walked around camp, arm in arm, all weekend. He said I was his little sister."

"How old is Ryan?"

"Seventeen. He has this kinky blond hair you can do anything with. He puts in like five hair scrunchies at a time. His ponytail sticks straight up on top of his head, and his hair never gets caught in his earring."

"Hmm. Where does Ryan live?"

"Across the river. He just called and said if I wanted a ride to youth group on Wednesday nights, he'd drive me."

"You don't think this Ryan thing's serious, do you? You just said goodbye to him at camp—what?—a couple of hours ago?"

"Yeah, but you know, he's just being nice, and he wanted to let me know he'll be at youth group this Wednesday, and . . . I was wondering if I could go."

I feel my daughter's childhood slipping away. It's possible. Five years' difference between Jessie and Ryan is nothing. Nothing like the seventeen-year difference between her father and me. It could happen.

"Wednesday service?" I ask. "What about that after-school job you just took on for the Tensfeldts? If you have to leave for youth group at six, when would you do your homework? And track's starting up. A mile or two every day in those brand-new fifty-nine-dollar-on-sale Reeboks is going to eat up a lot of time."

"But Mom, I have to go Wednesday. He still has my blue hair scrunchie."

From Barbie to Ryan, all in one weekend. This isn't supposed to happen until at least eighth grade.

"Wednesday sounds OK." OK for doing homework and jumping on the trampoline and being twelve, *not* fifteen. "Why don't you call and tell him you'll meet him there."

"Really? That is so cool." Jessie dances off with the portable phone.

After showering, I find Jessie sitting against the wall on her bed, surrounded by her collection of stuffed animals. Duke, our greyhound, is sprawled among the colorful heap, with his head in Jessie's lap. "What's up?" I ask as I drop into the swivel rocker next to her bed.

"Mom, a girl answered, and it wasn't Ryan's mother."

"Maybe he has a sister," I offer into the silence.

Jessie rolls her eyes. "Mom, he doesn't have a sister, only little brothers. It was Andrea."

"Who's Andrea?" I feel like I'm trying to read a novel with every other page glued together.

"She was at camp. She's seventeen too, and sometimes I'd see her and Ryan down by the stream, holding hands." I watch the tears form in Jessie's eyes as she chews her pinkie nail down past the quick. I reach for the injured hand, and Jessie lets me hold it as she climbs into my lap. Instead of following my impulse to ask her more questions or put a damper on this whole Ryan thing, I relax and rock her, because there is nothing else to do.

I remember what it was like not to be sure of myself. How important it was to know that someone besides my parents loved me. And how it mattered what everyone but my parents thought. At her age I didn't know what I wanted, but I went after it with a vengeance just the same.

"I just want Ryan and everybody to like me." Jessie strings together the words between ragged breaths and wipes the side of her face against the shoulder of my robe. She lets me rock her and finger the ends of her coarse black hair. I hum a bedtime song we used to sing together, but now I sing alone. I know there is no simple solution.

Love is an inside job.

BURKY ACHILLES

Flower Power

⟡

*I*T IS NOT OUR ENEMIES WHO DO US THE GREATEST harm. Sometimes we permit our uniqueness, individuality, and self-esteem to be eroded little by little, day by day, by those who love us most. I realized that the day I decided why I did not want flowers at my funeral.

I was to speak at a Conference on Human Rights. I went in to kiss our youngest daughter, who was still sleeping, goodbye.

She opened one eye and groaned, "Gross."

I was puzzled. "What's gross?"

"The flowers in your hair, Mom. It's too early for that."

I smiled and headed for the garage. On my way past the kitchen, daughter number two looked up from the morning paper and also communicated with one word: "Tacky."

I stopped smiling. One "gross" and one "tacky" is about all I can take first thing in the morning. As I consulted with the mirror, daughter number three's words haunted me: "How many of the three hundred people there today will have flowers in their hair, Mom? Doesn't that *tell* you something?"

I kept the flowers in my hair. I knew it was not too early. If truth be told, it was almost too late.

Many years later, after having done a session on Creative Living for a board of realtors, I received a card in the mail. It said: "I want you to know that ever since I heard you speak last week, I've been wearing flowers in my hair."

It was signed: "Wayne Cochran, Realtor."

ROSITA PEREZ

⟡

Angel on Patrol

ЯP

POLICE OFFICER BERNIECE JOHNSON WAS WORKING the graveyard shift in downtown Portland, Oregon, one wet, cold night. While cruising, she heard a call go out over the radio about an accident on one of Portland's eight bridges.

Officer Johnson was twenty minutes away from the site of the accident, but she had a strong gut feeling to assist the responding officer. There was no logic to the tug she was feeling. Backup had not been requested, and there were officers closer to the scene than she was. But she proceeded anyway across the Marquam, one of the bridges crossing the Willamette River, separating Portland east from west.

The call was handled quickly, and she started driving back toward the other side of town. Again, she had a strong gut feeling, which held her back from taking the next two bridge entrances. As she was nearing the Fremont Bridge, she heard a voice inside her say, "Turn here."

As Officer Johnson started across the Fremont, she noticed a small car parked illegally off the side of the roadway. The car had its flashing lights on.

Seeing a man and a woman in the parked car, she began her routine check. She peered in the car and asked, "Is there a problem here?"

"Yes," the woman responded, tears streaming down her face. "My husband wants to kill himself by jumping off the bridge."

Procedure calls for the officer to take a suicidal person into custody for an evaluation. Officer Johnson's intuition told her to talk to the despondent man who was sitting behind the steering wheel, staring straight ahead.

She began by giving him reasons why he shouldn't take his life. She told him that nothing was so bad that he needed to take his life over it. Fifteen minutes later, she didn't know what else to say. He looked like he was about to cry. She reassured him by saying, "It takes a strong and sensitive man to be willing to cry. That's how we get our grief out." The man placed his head in his hands, slumped over, and began to weep. Officer Johnson silently prayed, "What do I do now?"

In the back seat, Officer Johnson noticed a baby boy. She told the young father about her own hurt as she grew up with a dad who was emotionally unavailable. The officer reminded him that no matter what he was going through, he could still love and care for his little boy. He could be there to nurture his child, to encourage this small boy as he grows, and to make his son feel safe in the world.

The man cried even harder, and this time Officer Johnson heard God's voice say, "Be quiet!" She prayed silently again: "What do I do now?" It came to her to consciously send this anguished man healing white light. Whether she was moving traffic along, or just standing near the car, shivering, she continued to see him surrounded by white light.

An hour later, like a flower responding to a good watering, the suicidal man rose up from the shower of loving white light being beamed on him by Officer Johnson.

The officer asked the young man to come sit in her patrol car. She had a feeling he wanted to talk with her alone before she let him go. He told her about all the mistakes he'd made in his life. He talked of his problems with his mom and dad. He shared his feelings of despair. His demeanor became soft and peaceful—as if he'd gone through an emotional cleansing.

This once suicidal man turned to the officer and thanked her for being there for him. She touched his arm and whispered gently, "Before you go, I want to tell you something. No matter where you would have gone tonight . . . I would have found you."

KAY ALLENBAUGH

"What you focus on increases."

—Author unknown

The Power of Visualization

WHEN I BEGAN TO WRITE MY BOOK, I DECIDED TO visualize myself signing autographs. Four weeks later, I was invited to attend a Dodger Christmas party given for Los Angeles inner-city children. My date, a former Dodger pitcher, the owner, the manager, and other players would be there to sign autographs for the children.

The children received small baseball helmets when they arrived. The baseball celebrities would sign each of the children's helmets. Lines of small, excited children began to form in front of each player. It was a special Christmas gift for all these young Dodger fans.

A little girl walked over to me and handed me her helmet to sign. I explained to her that I was not a celebrity, but she would not take no for an answer. I decided it would be easier just to sign my name.

Everyone seemed to be looking my way. All kinds of things went through my head. I imagined the players wondering: Who is this woman? I assumed they were thinking: What right does she have to sign her name on a Dodger helmet? What would the parents say when they looked at the helmet and saw all the well-known Dodgers on it, and there would be my name!

Then it hit me. I was actually signing an autograph! This was what I had asked for. I looked up, unprepared for what I saw. In the few seconds it took for me to sign one autograph, a long line of small, beautiful children formed in front of me. Their numbers had multiplied. They were each holding a helmet in their outstretched arms, waiting for my autograph. As I stood there talking with the children, signing autograph after autograph, I was filled with excitement and gratitude. The Christmas party was for the children; but they were giving me a wonderful gift. I now knew the thrill of signing autographs.

Now when I practice the power of visualization, I always see an image of innocent, happy children in the background of my mind. For it is the children who know: anything you dream of can come true.

DANIELLE MARIE

Grandma Knows Best

MY MOM BELIEVED IN THE MOST OLD-FASHIONED OF all principles of etiquette, the written thank-you note.

When my niece, Maura, had her first child, my mother sent a card and a check as a gift to her new great-granddaughter.

The check cleared the bank, so Mom knew someone had received it. But she heard nothing from Maura.

Several months later, I told my mom about Maura's impatient response when I asked her if she'd sent a thank-you card to her grandma: "Aunt Maggie, I sent Grandma a 'cosmic' thank-you."

Mom paused.

"Tell Maura that next time, I'll send her a cosmic check."

MAGGIE BEDROSIAN

Master Plan

I formed a master plan for life
   In the green years' dawning glow,
Not comprehending, naively,
   The truth I could not know.

I only planned for happy hours,
   I sketched in sunny days;
On my horizon not a cloud
   Presaged the storm god's ways.

I left no place, no room at all,
   For grief; could not foresee
That pain and loss were down the way,
   Just waiting there for me.

I could not know my firstborn son
   Would have a stay so brief
And leave behind an emptiness
   Akin to a fallen leaf.

I hadn't left a space for loss,
   I only planned for gain,
But I expected rainbows
   Though unprepared for rain.

My plan was aimed for large success,
   No page contained defeat;
No slow, discouraged footsteps
   Trudged down my private street.

Then when life didn't follow through
   The blueprint I had made,
I couldn't understand at all
   And found myself dismayed.

But life wrote other plans for me,
   Which, wisely, it withheld
Until I learned I needed more
   Than what I'd blithely spelled.

And now in life's gray twilight,
   By pain and sorrow blessed,
I know how wisely life has planned:
   I know its plan was best.

GLADYS LAWLER (AGE 93)

XV

Soaring Through Barriers

❦

"When you get into a tight place and everything goes against you, till it seems as though you could not hang on a minute longer, never give up then, for that is just the place and time that the tide will turn."

—Harriet Beecher Stowe

Joe's Picture

ᴎᴘ

MOST OF US ARE AWARE THAT THE FIRST FEW YEARS of school can matter for a lifetime. We know that they are often essential to our success in life and to our self-esteem. Joe's parents were no exception. They saw to it that Joe had a loving and nurturing home life; that his experiences were stimulating and enriching; and that he knew the alphabet and could count to ten. He was indeed ready for first grade.

Joe entered school with great enthusiasm. He liked his classmates and they liked him. He liked his teacher and received encouragement from her and from his parents. All signs pointed to success, and yet success eluded Joe.

He had a hard time grasping the rapid pace of his surroundings. Just as he was on the edge of understanding, the teacher moved to another subject or to another hard lesson. By the end of first grade, he was behind many of his classmates and discouraged. His parents hoped summer would bring growth and maturity and second grade would be better.

But it was not, and by the end of the school year the teacher suggested retention, but Joe's parents said no. At the end of third grade, with Joe falling further behind, the principal suggested that Joe should repeat. Again, his parents said no.

Fourth grade started, and Joe was a nervous wreck. He didn't want to go to school. He had suffered through three years at the bottom of the class, and he certainly did not want to be there again. He had heard that fourth was supposed to be a very hard grade. And it was. He struggled every day and studied every night, but he remained at the bottom—until one black, dreary, rainy afternoon.

Teachers have a sixth sense about the weather. Difficult concepts like fractions call for the sunniest of days. The day began that way, but as the teacher started the lesson, a blackness covered the sky, and the downpour set in. Try as she might to keep them working on their math, thunder and lightning won the battle for their attention. Distracted by the storm, the children were not grasping the math. Except for Joe. He understood. He had all the answers correct. She patted him on the back and told him to go around to the others and explain what he had done. Smiling and happy with his newfound success, Joe moved quickly throughout the room.

As math time ended, the teacher handed each child a sheet of white paper. It was time for art. And all the children did the expected—dark, dreary days always called for dark crayons and dark pictures. And today was no exception. Except for Joe. Joe used bright yellow, orange, and red. A big, bright, glowing sun filled his paper.

Joe started improving and earned his promotion that year. His fourth-grade teacher was curious about the changes in him, and she followed his progress through his high-school years. Why had that one dark and dreary day changed Joe? Who knows what moment a teacher will touch a student?

Joe was not at the top of his class. He did not have to be. He had succeeded and he knew it, and after graduation Joe joined the service and was sent to Vietnam. He did not make it home.

Hearing of Joe's death, the fourth-grade teacher went to his home to pay her respects. Joe's mother welcomed her and told her there was something in Joe's room she wanted to show her. As they entered his room, the mother pointed to Joe's most cherished possession. Hanging on the wall over his bed, neatly matted and framed, was his picture of the big, bright yellow, orange, and red glowing sun. It celebrated the rainy day when he woke up to his own brightness. At the bottom of his picture, in big capital letters, Joe had printed: THIS IS THE DAY I GOT SMART.

PHYLLIS MABRY

Into the Cave

WHAT GETS IN THE WAY OF YOUR DOING ALL THE things you dream of? Could it be fear? It is for me. That's why I signed up for a "Push Through Your Fears and Limiting Beliefs" workshop in California. I was ready to make the effort to push through another layer of fear in my life.

I don't really know what I expected. I pictured sitting around and having meaningful conversations about our fears, praying about them, and that would be it!

So here I am, having just arrived at the lodge, and the first thing they do is load us all on this bus and take us out in the middle of "nowhere" California. Then they tell us that we are going to rappel through a thirty-inch crevass one hundred eighty feet down into a dark cave on our own power! Well now, no one told me *this* was part of the program. Here I am in my nice clothes and gold tennis shoes, jewelry to match, and every hair in place.

Heights are not my thing. All my life I've told myself I get dizzy when I stand on a step stool. I've never broken a bone in my body, nor do I ever intend to. I'd never done anything the least bit physically threatening. I've got to tell you, my "stuff" was really up! It's much easier to *talk* about our fears than to push through them.

This cannot be happening, I remember thinking. "Pure terror" puts it mildly. I was scared to death. Every facade, every pretense, just flew out the window. I was like a babbling, sniveling idiot. I was thinking: How can I get out of this without making a total ass of myself?

They were saying things like, "If you don't do this, you'll have to go home, and you won't get a refund." Well, right away they had my attention!

I knew it was way beyond the money stuff. This jump was really touching a core fear issue for me. Although I knew I had to do this, *I did not want to do it!* They gave us five minutes of instruction. That's it? I felt so inadequate. Like, where's the "real" information that tells me how to do this?

They gave me gloves and harnessed me up in this sling thing. I literally started babbling incoherently to myself. Too afraid to cry, I was feeling crazy . . . victimized . . . angry . . . dumb . . . scared . . . alone. *I had to do this myself!*

I remembered hearing them say, "The next step you take will be the point of no return."

I responded, "Oh my God!"

"Once you step off this ledge, you are absolutely on your own," they cautioned. "If you do not move this rope, you will hang there in space for the rest of your life!"

I'm an Alabama girl. Being in the middle of California with all these strangers, and at least two hundred miles from the nearest Neiman Marcus, I was totally out of my element.

One guy in our group was a career navy officer in air-sea rescue. This man is whistling! I just wanted to slap the snot out of him.

So it was finally my turn, and I *knew* I had to go for it. If you can just imagine the terror I was experiencing and what it took for me to step off that ledge! I had never felt more fear in my *life*—but I stepped off and started going down that rope.

About halfway down, the people who had already descended started yelling up to me, "Look around, it's b-e-a-u-t-i-f-u-l"—and I'm deep in concentration, repeating, "Jesus Christ, Jesus Christ, Jesus Christ." It felt like hours, although it was probably less than thirty minutes as I inched my way down to the cavern floor.

When I finally got to the bottom and they unhooked me, I fell on the ground and kissed the bottom of the cave and said, "Thank you, God," while experiencing an old-fashioned Southern hissy fit—shaking, crying, screaming. The man who worked there, who was un-hooking me, said, "Lady, are you all right?" I said, "Just leave me alone. I'm fine."

I knew then that if someone else had been trapped at the bottom of that cave, I would have done whatever it took to rescue that person. I'd always been there for others. However, standing in that cave, I discovered I could be there for myself. I had faced my fear and rescued the frightened little girl in me.

A wise one once said that true courage is not the absence of fear but learning to act in the presence of fear.

An even wiser one has instructed, "Fear not, little flock. Lo, I am with you always."

REV. EDWENE GAINES

The Perfect Wedding

❧

J'D WAITED A LONG TIME FOR MY WONDERFUL DAVID, and I wanted our wedding to be perfect. To offset my prenuptial jitters, I set out to be the most organized bride in history. Every imaginable detail about the ceremony and reception went into my computer. But there was one thing I couldn't control, and it bothered me a lot.

Mindy, David's teenage daughter back in Chicago, was coming to California for our wedding. In recent months, communication with my soon-to-be stepdaughter had been fraught with both outbursts and silences, as she struggled to come to grips with her dad's new life.

I could empathize with her confusion, but David and I were trying our best to help her feel included in our lives. In those moments when she didn't seem ready to meet us halfway, we wondered if it was even wise to encourage her to attend our wedding. Nevertheless, we sent her a plane ticket and hoped for the best.

On our wedding day, while I was getting dressed, I could hear Mindy and her aunt Jan in the next room, arguing over what Mindy should wear. I knew I should stay out of the fray, but my curiosity got the best of me. Peeking in on their dispute, my heart sank. Mindy was wearing a baggy 1950s vintage housedress, with dark-blue ankle socks and shoes that closely resembled combat boots. "Don't take it personally," I told myself. "Don't let this spoil your day." Still, I was relieved when Jan finally coaxed Mindy into a navy dress with pearls and pumps.

At the church, Mindy stood stoically through the photographs. She said her shoes were hurting her feet, but I knew her discomfort went deeper. I didn't know how else to reach out to her, and a lot of the time

I was too caught up in the flurry of events to mind her moods. But at the hotel, as the band began to play for the first dance, I realized she had disappeared.

"Have you seen her?" I asked David.

"Uh-huh. She asked for the key to our room."

I moaned. I had visions of a toilet-papered room or a short-sheeted bed.

"She wanted to change her clothes." David shrugged.

Just as the band announced that it was time for our families to join us on the dance floor, Mindy reappeared, wearing the baggy dress and combat boots. David took her by the hand and led her around the room in a careful box step. In her self-conscious moves, I saw all of my own awkward adolescence, and in my husband's face, the pride and delight every father feels dancing with his daughter. David obviously didn't care what Mindy was wearing, and at that moment, neither did I. I was happy she was there.

When the reception was over and we went to the bridal suite, the only thing out of place was a piece of hotel stationery, folded on the bed. David opened it and handed it to me with tears in his eyes. "Dear Dad and Penny: Congratulations. I love you both very much. Love, Mindy."

Our wedding was perfect after all.

PENELOPE PIETRAS

"Life is either a daring adventure—or nothing."

—Helen Keller

Close Encounters

Y KAYAKING PARTNER GOT A CALL FROM A RAFTING friend in the Midwest. They'd just gotten a permit to run the highly sought after Selway River in Idaho—a river that could just as easily put you in a body bag as lift your spirits. Forty permits were given out each year to run this river, and we were always among the fourteen thousand people who applied. We'd hit the jackpot. The "put in" date for our six-day wilderness kayak trip was the following Sunday.

My anxiety rose as I remembered the deaths on the Selway three summers before at the same time of year. My kayaking friends had been the unfortunate boaters to be the first on the scene. Graphic details were never spared in kayak war stories, and before I ever met the Selway River, I knew exactly where the boating accident had happened and where the bodies were found.

We met our friends thirty miles from the put in point and discussed the details of the trip. The river was three to four times faster than I had expected a high mountain river to be. My stomach was in knots. I walked to the river's edge and focused on the task at hand. I prayed to God for a safe journey. I had to know in my heart that I was ready and capable to meet the Selway at high water.

I was nervous for good reason. There was five miles of unrelenting Class IV and Class V water—water that foamed, frothed, and curled up into house-size waves and created bus-size keeper holes to eat the unsuspecting. It had rained two days straight, and the river had been rising steadily, along with my anxiety.

My kayaking friends, all men, had tried to quell my jitters by telling me that if I didn't want to run the "juice," I could walk the trail along the river. However, the last time one of them had walked the trail carrying his boat, a rattlesnake had struck the kayak. Choose your death, I thought to myself.

I was edgy, jerky, hyperventilating, and everything that you can't be when you need to muster your focus on reading the water. At one hundred twenty pounds, I float higher on the water than my male counterparts; one of their paddle strokes is equal to two and a half of my strokes.

I pried myself out of the safe little eddy just above the biggest fear of the day—the drop named Ladle. I heard my buddies shout that familiar call, "You gotta want it!"

I'd pulled out too close behind the boater in front of me. This was dangerous for both of us. I wasn't reading the water, I was following another boater, and that's where it started to unravel.

My boat was swept across the foaming water. I was twenty feet to the right of where the safe passage was. Before I knew it, the ledge with the forty-foot-long hole that looked like a keeper from the bank was right underneath me. Time stood still as my boat pitched forward into dead airspace. I began my somersault over the five-foot ledge into the frothing water below. I landed upside down in what felt like a Maytag washing machine. I was being sucked at, pushed up, and pulled down by unexplainable powerful, random forces. My paddle was ripped out of my hand. Miraculously it was stuffed back into my hand by the next torrent. *Yes, you gotta want it.* I righted the kayak with one strong, swift motion.

With that motion, I found myself in the middle of this huge piece of white water, surrounded by total calm. I composed myself, thanked

God, laughed nervously, took two strokes backward, and launched myself into the rest of the drop. Sitting forward, I paddled aggressively, and seconds later, I was united with the other boaters in the eddy below Ladle. The whoops and the cheers made me cry. The pleasure of being alive was overwhelming; I'd survived because of my own skills and the grace of God.

That first night at camp, I again walked to the river's edge, saying my thanks, praying for safety on the river miles ahead.

The rest of the trip was not easy by any stretch, as any of the next drops of white water could have easily kicked my rear. But I paddled into each drop with more certainty than the one before.

Was that my last risky trip? No way. I continue to seek out adventure, over and over. Some may say it was a disaster when I somersaulted into dead airspace and "luckily" paddled myself out of the hole. However, I prefer to think of it as my finest moment.

KIMBERLY JACOBSEN

A Jewel from Mrs. Goldberg

ℳORE THAN EIGHTEEN THOUSAND MIDDLE EUROPEAN Jews fled the Hitler regime and found refuge in the city of Shanghai, China—my parents and I among them.

For years, Shanghai had been the receptacle of human flotsam and jetsam discarded by the rest of the world for one reason or another. The arrival of European Jews between 1938 and 1939 was the latest contribution to the already overcrowded, teeming metropolis on the China coast.

By the time my parents realized they had to leave Germany or perish, most countries had closed their doors to emigrants. Passage on the few available ocean liners traveling to the Orient was at a premium, if at all obtainable.

Miraculous circumstances, strange happenings, and unexplainable events led my parents to secure passage at the last minute on a German luxury liner scheduled to sail to China within twelve hours. We had to be ready. We made it.

Upon arriving in Shanghai, we were greeted by a huge black swastika riding boldly in the center of the red-and-white flag of the Thousand-Year Reich as it whipped in the wind high above the harbor from the roof of the German consulate. Perhaps Adolf Hitler's promise had come true and his "arm reached wide and far."

The moment we set foot on Chinese soil we were declared stateless citizens—an awkward position for strangers in a strange land. Like the rest of the refugees, our little family struggled to survive, and whatever life my father was able to provide for us came to an abrupt end when America went to war with Japan.

On Pearl Harbor Day, Japanese troops occupied Shanghai. The axis between Germany, Italy, and Japan was formed and once again, Jewish lives were threatened. The Japanese ordered the entire Jewish refugee population to move into a designated area (the worst part of town, already occupied by thousands of locals), allowing little time to find nooks and crannies to call home.

The first thing I learned about being "incarcerated" was that men raged against their confinement and women made curtains. My mother cut up a useless evening gown to make flounces and panels for the one window in the nine-by-twelve cubicle that would house us for the next six years.

We lived on top of each other under the most difficult conditions and learned quickly to make the best of them. Some did better than others, and among those who made a difference in my eleven-year-old life was the round-faced, roly-poly, middle-aged Mrs. Rosa Goldberg.

To find some relief from the steamy-hot, and breathless air of Shanghai's endless summer days, Rosa Goldberg would place her three-legged stool in a shady spot in our garbage-cluttered, stinking lane, seemingly oblivious to its rivers of urine and rows of "honeypots," filled to overflowing with human refuse. Friendly and outgoing, she knew most of the inhabitants of our little "lane" by name. She greeted us each morning with a cheerful smile, a warm twinkle in her deep-brown eyes, and in her "Jewish delicatessen" English accent dispatched us on our way with one bit of wisdom or another. Her message to me never varied.

Each morning as I was on my way to our makeshift warehouse classroom, she would stop me, reach out her hand to grasp mine, pull me to a stop at her side, look up into my face, and ask, "So! What does Mrs. Goldberg tell you every day, little girl?"

Knowing her game well, I shook my head, voiced a quiet I-don't-know, and waited.

"Well, darlink, Mrs. Goldberg will have to tell you again. Now listen and remember what I'm telling you," she instructed. *"Go out and make a miracle today. God's busy, he can't do it all."*

Her face beamed up at me, her hand let go of mine. With a friendly parting pat on my backside, she sent me on my way, giving me a purpose for the day and meaning to my life that will be mine as long as I shall live. She handed me wings to fly, opened my eyes to a world that needed miracles, and gave me the assurance that I could do God's work.

To this moment, every day of my life, each time I leave my house, I hear the raspy, heavy voice of Rosa Goldberg calling to me, and I remember to *go out and make a miracle today. God's busy, he can't do it all.*

URSULA BACON

Mom's Special Day

N THE EARLY EIGHTIES, WHEN MY TWO SONS WERE toddlers, I put them in day care when I went to work. Like thousands of other working moms, I too was plagued by the articles and news stories about the negative impact of children growing up in day care. Despite the growing ranks of women in the workplace, society's message still seemed to be: "Mothers belong at home with their children." Period! End of discussion.

Although I was doing my best to balance wholesome family life with an aggressive career track, I was filled with guilt and self-doubt. "Am I ruining my kids for life by sending them to day care? Will they resent me? Should I be a stay-at-home mom?"

On Mother's Day 1993, at the traditional eighth-grade Mother's Day tea, the answers to my questions came in a very unexpected way. To celebrate this day, the children had written poems about their mothers. I sat there, listening to poems describing cookie-baking, Halloween-costume-making, birthday-party-giving, and car-pool-driving Moms. There was laughter and plenty of tears as we all heard how our teenage children saw us.

Then it was Justin's turn. As he walked to the front of the room, I held my breath, and my stomach did a flip-flop. How would his poem describe me?

My Mom

How will you be remembered?
Only by the memories you leave behind.
Your memories will be as soft and colorful as a young rose petal.

A woman who owned her own business and became very successful,
You will be remembered by the way you fulfilled all your dreams,
How you spent time looking after kids while you reached the top—

Two young boys, rowdy as monkeys.
You were a great mom, a great wife, a great person—
Mom, how on earth did you do it?

Legends will be told about you, Mom.
When I needed help, you were there.
Your shoulder was a place where I could rest my head.

What would I do without you?
How would I survive?
What I'm trying to tell you is, I love you, Mom.

—Justin

In those few glorious moments, as I heard his words, all my doubts and fears about being a working mom were put to rest. Then and there, I knew, after years of baby-sitters, camps, and day care, that my son did not resent me. To the contrary, he let me know that through it all, I was always there when he needed me. He let me know that he was proud of me.

When he finished reading his poem, he looked over at me, sitting in the front row of the audience. He smiled that wide glimmering, silvery smile that only kids with braces are capable of. My first impulse was to race up and wrap my arms around him—like you would a small child —yet I resisted. Justin was a thirteen-year-old young man, and the process of "letting go" had begun. A thumbs-up from one proud mom said it all.

CONNIE HILL

Reaching Beyond

Do you reach beyond to touch the sky,
   or lag behind, afraid to try?
Do you reach beyond to learn anew,
   or hesitate—the same old you?
Do you reach beyond to test your limit,
   or do you tell yourself, I'm timid?
Do you reach beyond to lead the pack,
   or do you waste time looking back?
Do you reach beyond and strive to find
   better ways to stretch your mind?
Do you reach beyond to care and share
   and help some others do and dare?
Do you reach beyond, expect the best,
   or have you given up the quest?
Do you reach beyond and claim your space,
   here and now, this time, this place?
Do you reach beyond and try to soar,
   or, sadly, play it safe once more?

SUZY SUTTON

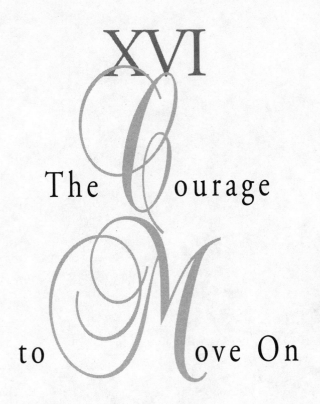

XVI

The Courage to Move On

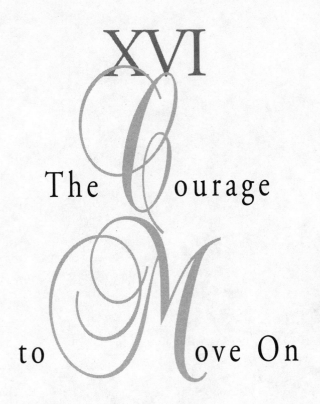

"Life shrinks or expands in proportion to one's courage."

—Anaïs Nin

Beyond Twin Peaks

*I*ALWAYS THOUGHT THAT NIGHTMARES HAD ONE THING going for them.

You woke up. Safe.

With the reassuring reality of day, you snuggle deeper into the blankets while your heartbeat slows to normal. This is the way nightmares are *supposed* to progress: first the nightmare, then the relief, and finally the comfortable feeling that the really b-a-d things happen to you only in dreams.

At least that's the way nightmares happened with me until the day I woke up in the recovery room at Duke University Medical Center, to see my husband, George, bending over me. I had asked him to tell me the truth as soon as I opened my eyes. I couldn't bear having to look to see if all of me was still there, if my "twin peaks" were still familiarly in place. To see if I was still "whole." George said, "I love you," and then said, "It was malignant." I remember lying on that bed, flinging my head back and forth on the pillow and screaming, *"No!"* as loudly as the waning anesthesia allowed. And I remember thinking: *This is a nightmare—and I am awake!*

What I had was breast cancer, and it changed my life. Suddenly and completely and forever. I was not safe. Not anymore.

As I lay in my hospital room that day, only dimly aware of the numbing flurry of activity around me, I watched with despair as my lifelong sense of security just floated out the window. Here, in addition to the cancer and the mastectomy, was the nightmare that would never fade: no more security—ever. At first fear colored every aspect of my life, including my language. Even my sentences became jerky and choppy as I grew increasingly anxious.

But then, one day, I thought of my unusual parents. My college professor father and my teacher mother never chose the well-worn paths. Every time I had a problem, faced a crisis, or ran into the various and sundry brick walls that are always a part of growing up, one or the other of them would exclaim: "Isn't that *fascinating!* I wonder how many ways you can deal with this?" And off we would go, exploring possibilities and turning problems into adventures.

Thus, with the terror of a life-threatening, life-altering disease, began the fascination of how to deal with it. Of how to face new challenges. I started hesitantly to confront my new self and the new view that others had of me.

My doctor during this time at Duke was, without question, the most unapproachable man I had ever met. He looked like a Russian czar, massive and dramatic, with a lion's mane of flowing white hair. Everywhere he went, a worshipful, white-coated entourage trotted behind, notebooks in hand, writing down every word he uttered. I would have sworn that even the plants in my room stood straighter when he strode in. He was brusque, all business, always in a hurry. My stomach-turning panic was that this man, in charge of my health—*my life*—scared me to tears. In an abnormal situation, with a desperate need for reassurance and a warm hand on my shaking shoulder, I was totally intimidated by this imposing, off-putting doctor. I began thinking about what I could do to make him think of me as an individual and not a disease, somehow sensing that such a bond would enhance my chances of recovery. (*How fascinating—what are my options?*) I got permission to leave the hospital, went to the mall, and had a T-shirt made for him. A big black T-shirt with big white letters that said: ONE OF AMERICA'S 10 BEST BREAST MEN.

You can only begin to imagine the lump-in-the-throat nervousness with which I presented this silly shirt to Duke's most powerful surgeon. He took one look at it, laughed, and said with quiet astonishment, "You . . . did this . . . for *me?*"

And one more time it hit me: We are all alike. Whatever our role, whatever our profession, whatever our lot in life, all of us are looking for someone to make us feel important. That T-shirt made my brilliant, world-renowned doctor feel important. Imagine that!

The honest facing of reality and the effort to deal with it creatively started affecting other areas of my life. My family relationships became closer and more open. Two weeks after the mastectomy, my ten-year-old son and several of his friends joined me in the kitchen. They looked at me searchingly, and Joe finally blurted out, "Are you wearing your artificial breast today?" "No"—I laughed—"I left it in the bedroom." And off they went outside. My visiting mom asked, "Are you sure you want your sons and friends discussing your breast?" "He's having to face the fact he might lose his mother," I responded. "If he needs to take me to school for show-and-tell to deal with this, I'll be there. Now, there," I said to her, remembering all the times she had said it to me, "is a *fascinating* idea!"

Marvelous things began to happen. I entered upon a speaking career, which has plunged me into the business community and into the fields of medicine, education, charitable institutions, and government. My presentations are not *about* cancer, just *because* of cancer. *(Fascinating! I wonder how many ways there are to deal with each day's celebration of new possibilities, of each day's wonder at what lies ahead.)* Rejoice in your willingness to step out and watch the unfolding.

Having cancer has freed me forever from what I call the Scarlett O'Hara syndrome: "I can make a new friend . . . tomorrow. I can make an impact . . . tomorrow. I can start a new business . . . tomorrow. I can take more risks . . . tomorrow." I've had a smack-in-the-face realization that there may not be three score and ten cards in my deck. Because I am not guaranteed a tomorrow, my life has taken a unique and enriching direction. Today.

Isn't that . . . *fascinating?* I'd always thought that life was about building security. And then a great teacher—cancer—taught me that this is not what life is all about. It taught me that nightmares can become springboards.

How much difference does it make to step outside the bounds of the expected and the ordinary? Five years after finishing the prescribed radiation therapy, I read in the paper that the "doctor from Duke" was coming to Charlotte to do a symposium on breast cancer. As I stepped into the back of the auditorium to hear him speak, he saw me and called out my name: "Emory! Emory Austin!" Five years later, five thousand patients later, he remembered *me*. "My goodness," I thought, "this truly is *fascinating*."

EMORY AUSTIN

"And the day came when the risk to remain tight in a bud was more painful than the risk it took to blossom."

—Author unknown

Riding the River of Abundance

ᴅᴜʀɪɴɢ ᴛʜᴇ "Bᴀᴛᴛʟᴇ ғᴏʀ Cʜɪʟᴅ Sᴜᴘᴘᴏʀᴛ," I ʜᴀᴅ completed my bachelor's, master's, and PhD degrees, while working as a therapist. Although I was very successful in the rest of my life, and happily remarried, I seemed completely inept in the area of getting child support.

My son was twelve, and I had been divorced from his father for eleven years. At one point I triumphed in a court appearance and had the monthly amount raised from $100 to $125. In spite of my efforts, he came through with payments on the average of three months out of twelve.

One day my husband suggested that I fire Chris's father from his apparently reluctant role as provider. When I considered not asking for child support anymore, I uncovered an entrenched set of beliefs:

Women aren't supposed to provide; men are. . . . He means well, give him another chance. . . . He's the only father Chris has. . . . Life is hard work, and you should be grateful for any money that he provides. . . .

As I honestly began to look at my beliefs and feelings, I realized that

I had been angry for years. I was angry at the unfairness of having to grovel for my meager monthly check. I was angry at the beliefs and blinders that had shaped my dependence.

It was very difficult to look at the payoffs for continuing to expect that monthly check. I did not want to let go of the anger. And most difficult, I didn't want to see that my anger had limited Chris's ability to have a relationship with his father. Chris could not form a bond with his step-father, Gay, without resolving his relationship with his father.

I decided to take a leap of faith. Taking a deep breath, I sat down and wrote Chris's father, firing him from any further financial responsibility. Without blame, I added that I was stepping out of the role of mediator in their relationship. Any contact and relationship was up to them.

When I mailed the letter, I felt both exhilarated and blank. Could I really take full responsibility for my financial well-being? The familiarity of feeling like a victim was comfortable; the possibility of creating abundance was not.

I spent many days seeing new possibilities for myself. I needed to jettison the anchor of the past. I realized that I had spent years dragging my bucket to a dry well and complaining about the lack of abundance. When I let go of my small vision of possibility, I began to open to the magical resources of the universe and the rivers and oceans of flow that could carry me toward my deepest dreams.

The next year, my income doubled—along with my self-respect; the year after, it tripled.

With no response from his father, Chris finally closed that door and was adopted by Gay. I watched in gratitude as Chris began to reach out to Gay in both touching and amusing ways—by having rowdy philosophical conversations, or by making fart jokes while playing croquet.

People meeting Gay and Chris for the first time now say, "Chris, you look so much like your father."

KATHLYN HENDRICKS

"Hurdles are in your life for jumping."

—Rev. Sharon Poindexter

Ann's Story

𝒥𝒫

FATE PAID ME A VISIT ON SEPTEMBER 10, 1984, AND MY life—as I had been living it—came to a crashing halt. On that Monday morning, while I was getting ready to go to work, I certainly thought of myself as self-sufficient and independent. I had a job, I drove a car, I had reared a family successfully, I had many interests and friends. My life was full and busy.

Then I fell . . . and couldn't move. . . .

Ever since an automobile accident the year before, I had experienced discomfort in my neck and increasing numbness of my left arm and hand. I found I could relieve the pain and pressure in my neck by dangling my head over the edge of the bed. This is what I was doing on that fateful morning when I slid off the bed and landed on the back of my neck. As my body hit the floor, I felt an excruciating pain—as if my spinal cord had been cut by a knife—followed by a lightning-like sensation surging down my spine and exiting through every nerve ending. Then nothing—no sensation, no movement! I lay crumpled on the floor the way I had fallen and could not move. A horrible realization dawned on me: *I am paralyzed!*

The shock of this discovery was instantaneous. The anguish I felt during those moments was nothing short of despair. "Oh, God, not this!" In less than ten seconds, my life had changed from self-sufficiency to total helplessness. The telephone rang only two feet away from me; and I couldn't move a hand, an arm, or any body part to answer it or to dislodge the receiver. I couldn't summon help. I lay there terrified. Suddenly everything was out of reach and beyond my control. I was fully conscious and painfully aware of my predicament. It was 7:30 A.M. Everyone had left for the day. I was alone. No one was expected to be back before evening. Would I still be alive?

I began to imagine the course this process was likely to take. Given the loss of motor function and sensation I was experiencing, it was probable that my entire body would soon begin to shut down. Breathing would become more and more labored . . . until I lost consciousness. My mind raced on: What if I was comatose when found and couldn't object to being kept alive through mechanical means? The thought of impending death wasn't nearly as frightening as the possibility of having to live totally dependent on the mercy and goodwill of others. Terror engulfed me. An intense rush of self-pity overwhelmed me.

Then something from deep within me stepped forth and took charge, as if to say, "Stop your sniveling! You can't wipe your nose or dry your tears; you will choke. This is not the time to feel sorry for yourself. Use what little time you have left to put your inner house in order." Emotions did not have to run the show. A higher wisdom could prevail. I began to take a good look at my life, now that the end seemed near.

How does one prepare to die—consciously? Not some day when I'm old, but *now*, perhaps in a matter of hours. The thought occurred to me to do a "general confession with an act of contrition," as I had been taught in my Catholic childhood: to ask forgiveness wherever I knew I had wronged someone and to extend mine where I harbored resentment.

After I finished my life review, I felt great relief. I saw my life as having been rich in meaningful experiences; some were very happy, many painful, but it had been an eventful life, with a number of challenges and opportunities for soul growth. I could forgive myself for my shortcomings, which had loomed so large before.

I began to say my goodbyes in my mind. This was truly wrenching. I was so attached to the people I loved. With deep love and caring, I took my leave from those closest to me. I was amazed to see how many people had influenced my life. I began to understand how interconnected we all are. At that moment, it was easy to love the whole world and everybody in it.

Floating on that wave of acceptance and love, my sense was: "It was a good life!" Tranquillity and stillness washed over me. I was at peace. All fear of death had vanished. The sun was high on the horizon now. My breathing was shallow and labored. Death would be a welcome visitor. My last conscious thought was: Into your hands I commend my spirit, O Lord.

The next few weeks were largely shrouded in amnesia. I was told that my coworkers had sent out a "Where is Ann?" alarm when I hadn't come to work that Monday morning. They reached my sister, who also "sensed" that something was wrong. She found me around noon. The first few days I spent in intensive care, my condition critical. Later, I was transferred to a neurological rehabilitation unit.

A major transformation occurred during my six months of immobilization. Often I drifted at will in another dimension of consciousness. I emerged with a new appreciation of life and a renewed sense of purpose. There was something for me to do yet, very different from anything I had done before. Something I could do from a wheelchair if need be.

The next two years were spent convalescing. My medical records state, in part: "Fracture/dislocation of the C5–6 vertebrae with resultant quadriparesis, flaccid paralysis, incomplete spinal cord lesion." What this means is that I couldn't turn a page in a book, brush my teeth, push a button on a telephone, or feed myself. My legs wouldn't carry me. I lived with a catheter.

After months in traction, a spinal fusion, further immobilization in a Halo body jacket, physical rehabilitation, alternative healers, and loving support from kindred spirits, my recovery exceeded the most optimistic medical prognosis. This was verified by a call from an emergency room physician, who said, "I've been going through our records, and I find you've made remarkable progress in your recovery since your accident two years ago. To satisfy my curiosity, would you answer some questions for me? When you were brought to the ER with a traumatic spinal cord injury, all we could do was immobilize you and keep your spine in alignment. The *healing* was up to you. How did you do it?"

I told her of the inner experience, the attitude shift that had occurred in me. Having so little energy, I learned not to waste any. I learned to look for what is central and meaningful. I learned the grace of appreciation. I learned to be still and listen—to live inner-directed. This brush with death was a wake-up call to life.

What does that have to do with getting better physically? Everything! I became more open to new possibilities and receptive to an inflow of goodwill and mercy offered by others. Along with conventional medicine, I also used complementary healing methods, from acupuncture to lovingly made chicken soup. Professionally I retrained so I could counsel those who need a lift in spirit.

Through my work, I now encourage ordinary people to live extraordinary lives. My wheelchair is a thing of the past. I largely forget about my remaining physical challenges, for my life is richer and deeper than I once would have believed possible. What may appear as a setback to many was merely a transformative hurdle God knew I could jump.

ANN V. GRABER

The World Upside Down

*I*HAD JUST TURNED SIXTEEN WHEN MY MOTHER, SISTER, and I were taken into the infamous Auschwitz concentration camp. I watched with despair as my mother was escorted to the gas chambers. At that point, I felt my world turn upside down.

What sustained me during this time warp of horrors were my mother's words. As she was led away, she appealed to my sister and me to live a full life. Her last words to us were, "Remember, they can take *everything* from you *except* what you put in your mind."

I went from feeling victimized by our keepers to the realization that I quite possibly had the inner resources to outlast them. Somehow, with my determination to live, I would overcome their collective decision to eliminate us.

So even as I put on a striped uniform and submitted my hair to the razor, I mentally committed to a return to normalcy, home, and my training classes in gymnastics and dance.

A Nazi officer came to "welcome" the newcomers, and he asked what "talents" we had brought to the camp. My inmates pushed me forward because of my training in ballet. I was forced to dance. With my eyes closed, I envisioned this grotesque prison of horrors as the Budapest Opera House, and I gave the performance of my life. That evening I discovered the power of "doing within when you are without."

Our barracks received some extra rations the next day from the Nazi officer I had danced for—who was none other than Dr. Mengele, Hitler's "Angel of Death," who was known to send people to the "showers" to die if their shoelace was untied.

Is it any wonder that when life and death become as casual as flipping a coin, a personality would undergo radical changes? The tenets of "good behavior" learned in my sheltered childhood were replaced by a kind of animal instinct, which instantly smelled out danger and acted to deflect it. During a work detail, my sister was assigned to a brigade that was to leave for another camp. I could not allow us to be separated, and quickly cartwheeled over to her side. I thought I noticed a hint of amusement on the guard's face as he turned the other way, ignoring our clutched hands.

Confronting fear and taking action helped me fight off the numbness that a persistent contact with arbitrary authority can create. Learning to "face the fear and do it anyway" became my way to recapture my self-esteem.

The inhumanity continued, and months later, unconscious from starvation, I was thrown on a heap of corpses and presumed dead. Later that day, the American troops entered the death camp. I was too weak to realize what was happening. A GI looked my way as my hand moved. At the infirmary, he watched over me until I was declared out of danger.

After several months in the hospital, I returned to my hometown of Kassa, on the Hungarian-Czech border. Out of fifteen thousand deportees, seventy of us returned. A neighbor greeted me on the street, saying, "Surprised to see you made it. You were already such a skinny kid when you left."

Several years ago, I traveled back to Auschwitz on those same railroad tracks that took countless thousands to their death. I came to mourn the dead and celebrate the living. I needed to touch the walls, see the bunk beds where we lay those endless nights while the stench of the latrines wafted over us. I needed to relive the dreadful events in as much detail as memory allowed, while feeling the emotional and physical response.

The next step in recovery for me was to go public with my story. Recently, when I asked an audience of three hundred University of

Texas students how many knew what happened at Auschwitz, four hands went up!

I hope that someday my grandchildren will ask me questions about the time when the world was upside down. So that if it starts tilting again, they and millions of others can pour out their collective love and spin the world right side up.

EDITH EVA EGER

Thanks for the Miracle, Sis

MY DEAR SISTER SALLY,

This is a thank-you letter, shared in public because—as you say—it may hold out hope to others.

When I left you in the rehab center in mid-November, a week and a half after your second stroke, at age forty-six, you were paralyzed on your left side, confined to bed, confused about what was happening. Doctors said you could die, or at best subsist with extensive brain damage.

Thank you for proving them wrong.

Oh, the joy of having you and our younger sister, Jill, meet me at the airport in mid-January, just two months later! Precious, upright you—leaning on your cane, your hair freshly cut and styled; tears running down your face. Were your cheeks wetter than mine?

We came to make sure that you would be safe at home alone until your son got home from school and your husband from work. Those few days showed us you would, and taught me far more than I can tell you.

Yes, you still have weakness in your left arm and a slight hearing loss. You mispronounce some words and get confused if we talk too fast, but *you* are intact: your keen intelligence, your delicious sense of humor, your thoughtfulness and generosity, your sweet soul. More folks should be as whole as you are.

And now we see a new side to the shy and sometimes fearful middle sister who preferred to stick close to home, while Jill and I ventured forth and got in trouble. Thank you for your example in courage, fortitude, and the ability to keep putting one foot in front of the other in the face of great odds.

I watched you exercising several times daily to strengthen your left arm: stacking dice and paper cups, moving a dish towel around the table in figure eights, laboriously picking up paper clips and small screws to drop into a cup.

I saw you punch numbers into the automatic teller machine to get your bank balance, then do it all again when you forgot the sum. And I was suddenly ashamed that some days simply getting out of bed seems like too much work for me.

Thank you for the laughter. When you went to have your blood checked weekly to make sure your blood thinner was working, you said you had an appointment at "the vampire's." When you looked at the bleak hospital photos I'd snapped of you attached to snakelike tubes, you said, "I was *really* having a bad hair day!" Boy, are you a lesson in lightening up.

Stopping by your office gave us the opportunity to see how much others care about you (something some folks never discover until a funeral). Your coworkers told me how helpful you'd been when their relatives suffered strokes. They talked about your enthusiasm and generosity when they had babies, or adopted a family at Christmas. Such an outpouring of love!

Several times you apologized for "being trouble." Don't you know how grateful we are, dear Sally, to finally be able to give back to you? Who else but you would present Christmas gifts in January—gifts you'd purchased long before the stroke, now wrapped in paper bags with bows because you couldn't manage gift-wrapping?

Thank you for pointing out what's truly important—and for saying that you've dropped from your list nagging your teenager about his room. "I used to worry about things I thought were problems—like being fat," you said. "Fat isn't a problem. Being healthy is the most important thing in the world." Let me remember that the next time I climb on the scale.

And thanks, too, for the lesson in gentleness with yourself. When you pulled your shirt on inside-out and we called it to your attention, you didn't beat yourself up for making a mistake, as the rest of us do so often when we don't do something perfectly. You simply said, *"Oops, I flunked shirt!"* and fixed it.

I'm the wordsmith, but you say things better. Like when you read through all the nice letters that readers sent when I wrote about your stroke. "People are really nice, aren't they?" you said through tears. And over cocoa, you remarked, "I'm so glad I didn't die. I woulda missed you guys."

We would have missed you, too, Sal. But I want you to know: as painful and as frustrating as this whole experience has been for you and everyone who cares about you, it has been rich in love and lessons. I'm thankful for that.

Because of you, I'll be more patient with the person walking slowly in front of me, or trying to figure out change. Who knows what odds that stranger contends with, that stranger who is some one's father or mother or sister.

And I'm so glad you're mine, my miracle sister. I love you, Sal.

Janny

JANN MITCHELL

to college. He was telling me to go on with my life and fulfill a dream. On my graduation day four years later, I walked across the stage to accept my diploma. I could feel him giving me a standing ovation.

MILDRED COHN

Will You Be Healed?

*ℛ*EBECCA HAD A KIDNEY TRANSPLANT A FEW YEARS ago. Her body went into acute rejection several times, damaging the new kidney so much that this last year it has only been functioning at eight percent.

She'd been losing weight and energy all year. With reservations, Rebecca put her name on the transplant list at a university hospital, but she knew she wasn't totally committed to yet another transplant.

All that she had been through—years of illness and pain, dialysis, surgeries, a rejected transplant—left her depressed and questioning whether or not she wanted to live. A kidney didn't come the first month . . . the second month. It didn't come the third month.

One afternoon, lying in bed alone with her pain and weakness, she realized that she could *choose* to live or die. It was a powerful moment. She was dancing with death. She knew God was near as she relaxed into a deep sense of peace.

Suddenly a jolt of fear and sadness brought her back to the present. She felt regret at the prospect of not fulfilling her dreams. She thought to herself: It's not time yet. I can't let go of my dreams! Dreams of love, a full life, joy, and adventure. At that point, she made a decision. She was choosing life. With a deep resolve, and total commitment, she decided to do whatever it took to be healed.

Miracles began happening. She knew she couldn't go through the emotional and physical healing process alone. She reached out to her best friend, who immediately organized a prayer vigil. Family, friends, and church members prayed for her.

The next day she prayed, "What do I need for healing to happen?" The message she got was that she needed to be with others, to release, surrender, and share her story aloud. But how?

Friends heard her prayer, reached out to her, and bundled her into their car. They drove her to the coast, to an ongoing weekend retreat; its theme was Healing. She silently promised herself she would share her pain on the first night of the retreat, no matter how uncomfortable it felt to her.

Rebecca confided to the group that in the past, she had suffered in silence. On this magical night, however, she opened her heart, and her struggle poured out. Rebecca asked for support. The group listened and shouldered her burden. She found herself going from "Please, God, heal me" to "Yes! Yes! I will be healed."

On Sunday morning, one of the women Rebecca had met during the weekend needed to leave early to drive the two hours back home. Packed, she decided to stay until after the morning meditation. During the meditation, the call came for Rebecca. A new kidney awaited her! She now had a ride ready to go.

Before they left, Rebecca stood in the middle of a healing circle with a group of forty people who sang "Alleluia" as they blessed her, loved her, and sent her healing light for a successful transplant.

Rebecca had the kidney transplant that evening. The next morning, a kidney function test was done. The test results came back high, indicating a need for dialysis. After a dialysis treatment, they tested her again, and the results seemed too good to be true. So they tested a third time, and the even lower rating amazed the medical staff. She was doing better than anyone had imagined was possible. They had not factored in the power of prayer.

Rebecca has a scar on her left side, pointing slightly downward, from the first transplant. Now there is a connecting scar on her right side. They make what she fondly calls "my wonderful smile right in the middle of my belly."

REV. MARY MANIN MORRISSEY

XVII

Crossroads

𝓙𝓟

*"Having your way is a lot easier
when you have more than one way."*

—Jennifer James

Better Than a Stocking Stuffer

ᴊᴘ

KIDS DO NOT REALLY BELIEVE THAT THEIR PARENTS will ever die. They don't even like you to get sick. Kids expect Mom to be there always, no matter what.

How well this struck home when I was told I had cancer. I burst out crying when I told my husband, Hank. I worried about how to break the news to our four grown sons. I decided to approach it in the same "blurt it out" fashion we always used in our family . . . so when the first one called on the phone:

"Hi, Mom."

"Hi, babe."

"How are you?"

"Not too good. I just got bad news. The doctor says I have cancer."

Long pause . . . and then the kid says, "Does that mean you're going to die?"

The second one calls:

"Hi, Mom."

"Hi, babe."

"What's up?"

"Nothing good, I'm afraid. I've just been told I have breast cancer."

Long pause . . . and then the kid says, "But, Mom . . . you don't even eat fat."

The third one calls:

"Hi, Mom."

"Hi, babe."

"How's life treating you?"

"Not well. I just found out I have breast cancer."

Long pause . . . and then the kid says, "This isn't going to bother Dad, is it?"

The fourth one calls:

"Hi, Mom."

"Hi, babe."

"What's new?"

"Nothing good. The doctor says I have cancer."

Long pause . . . and then the kid says, "Why couldn't it have been Mrs. Walcott?" (Mrs. Walcott was a neighbor who loved chasing the kids off her sidewalk, screaming and waving a broom.)

Well, that all took place on December 4, 1987. On Saturday, December 5, two days before the removal of my breast, I went in for a chest X ray and a bone scan. I had announced to my family that if the cancer had spread through my body, I was not having the surgery. Hank wanted to go with me for the tests. I said, "No, I can only handle my own emotions this time. I don't need a husband pacing back and forth in the waiting room. It would be just our luck to be billed for a hole in the carpet."

I spent the whole day taking my clothes off and putting them on again. Each test was conducted inside a cold cubicle. With each test, the nurses would glide in on squeakless shoes to take blood from my arm or X-ray my chest. Then, as quickly and as quietly, they would leave me with my terror, without even a trace of perfume to mark their exit.

Men in white coats marched in, with their cold hands and vacant smiles. They poked and prodded, while I sat in quiet terror, waiting for the doctor to deliver the final crushing blow, telling me that the cancer had spread. I was terrified as I waited.

Suddenly the doctor appeared. He said, "I see no other cancer in the rest of your body." Oh, how I prayed this man had twenty-twenty vision.

I drove home as if by magic. I skidded into our driveway, jumped out of the car, and ran toward our front door. And then I heard music bellowing out from our living room. It was Mahalia Jackson, singing "Silent Night." I threw open the door and stepped inside. In the corner of the living room stood the largest Christmas tree we had ever had, decorated with all the ornaments the kids had ever made . . . even the ugly ones. Standing there was my family, each one dressed in a suit and tie. They looked as if they were ready to carry me down the aisle in a box.

"Merry Christmas, Mom," they shouted.

"Merry Christmas," I whispered, "and a Happy New Year . . . I know we have lots more to come." We hugged each other as we sobbed. And then I saw the dining room table set with the good china, the good silver, and all the chipped crystal.

That night together was one of the best we've ever had. My family never looked so precious . . . and Domino's Pizza never tasted so good.

LOLA D. GILLEBAARD

"For something new to begin, something must end."

—Kris King

The Interview

ॐ

S A YOUNG WOMAN IN THE EARLY SEVENTIES, I
worked at a job in a small southern Louisiana town, doing door-to-door
interviews. I was collecting political-sociological research data for a
PhD candidate. I had a letter of introduction from the mayor and the
chief of police, to put residents at ease.

I will never forget one man whom I interviewed. He was the owner
of a major business in town and highly respected by the community.
He invited me into his home for the twenty-minute interview. It was a
hot, humid summer day.

One part of the interview involved rating groups of people on a scale
of one to ten. There were twenty categories, including business people
and farmers, men and women, Republicans and Democrats. He was
answering right along, until I asked him about Catholics and Protes-
tants.

He stopped. He asked me what religion I practiced. I explained that
it was best not to tell him, so as not to bias his responses. Apparently
not wishing to offend me, he rated both religious groups equally high.

The next category was Jews. Not knowing that I was Jewish, he began to tell me that he knew all about "those people," because he had served with them in the army. "You know," he told me, "there's probably a prince or two among them, but other than that, every last one of them are dirty and evil-spirited."

I began to feel frightened. I was a young Jewish woman alone in a house with a man who was not only anti-Semitic but self-righteous about his bigotry. All I wanted to do was finish the interview and get out of the house and as far away from him as I could.

He continued ranting about Jews and, at the same time, asking me if I was Catholic or Protestant. I continued to smile and explain why it was best I not answer. He went on, "You know them Jews. They're dirty and they stink. They'll go days and days without even changing their socks or underwear. And talk about greed. Why, they'll rob you of your last drop of blood if it'll get them a dime."

My fear rising, I finished the interview and said goodbye. When I got outside, he asked me one more time about my religion. I wanted to run away from his house, from his hatred. But I couldn't bring myself to leave him with his arrogant, "knowing" prejudice. So, feeling some safety with the screen door between us, I told him the truth. "Sir," I said, "I am Jewish."

He looked at me for a second and then said, "Well, I told you there was a prince or two among them. I must have just met one."

"No, sir," I replied, "you have met a human being who happens to be Jewish. No prince, not even a princess. A human being just like you."

His smile disappeared, and my fear came back. But after what seemed like eternity, with the two of us staring at one another, his voice got soft and his head bowed. "Ma'am," he said, "I'm sorry."

SHELLY MARKS

And I Almost Didn't Go

WHAT ARE YOU GOING TO WEAR?" MY HUSBAND HAD that innocent look on his face that typically masked his emotions. But after fifteen years of marriage, I knew what he was really wondering: Is it appropriate?

Not that I dress inappropriately. In fact, I "gussy up" real fine, thank you. But David was nervous. After all, it isn't often that you invite legendary pianist Van Cliburn to dinner.

"Look . . ." I was spoiling for a fight. "If you'd rather I stay home, I'd be glad to. You waited so long to get a sitter that I sorta think you don't want me, anyway."

The second salvo was launched. The tension in our home had been growing ever since David called Cliburn's personal manager. He invited Van first to dinner with VIPs from the Saint Louis music community, and then to appear the next day to sign Steinways at our piano store. Needless to say, David was tightly strung. Cliburn is a national treasure, an immortal in the music world; and we had moved to Saint Louis to start this business only two years before. If the dinner and appearance went well, it would be the climax of the great start our piano gallery had enjoyed here. If it went poorly, the repair work could be extensive.

I also had reason to feel panic. As David once said, "People seem to either love you or hate you." There seemed to be no middle road, no lukewarm feelings, when it came to *moi*.

Then, too, my knowledge of music was rather limited. True, my mother had been a professional ballerina. I had grown up hearing the classics. But when it came to naming what I heard, or recalling who conducted the Chicago Symphony, or even telling the difference between Bach and Beethoven, I was lost. As I dressed for the dinner, I gnashed my teeth and muttered, "I will be charming. I will be charming. I will be charming."

I had visions of a very short, very embarrassing, stab at conversation: *So, Mr. Cliburn, your piano has eighty-eight keys . . . ?*

At the restaurant, our dinner party was so large that we had to be split into two tables. David told me I would sit next to Mr. Cliburn.

"Call me Van," said the long, tall Texan who had taken Russia by storm.

He chatted gracefully with everyone at the table. Mainly they discussed conductors and symphony halls around the world. I excused myself to check on Franz, one of my friends at the other table. He was eating a large, succulent Portobello mushroom. I helped myself to a bite.

When I returned to my seat, I explained my absence.

"Sorry. I just can't seem to resist food on other people's plates."

Van looked at me curiously. "Neither can I. I'm afraid I'm positively shameless."

And so began a friendship born, if not in heaven, at least at Tony's, a five-star restaurant, an earthly version of paradise for those of us who love food. Van sipped my tomato soup. I ate one of his scallops. Back and forth we went all evening, eating and discussing . . . performing. You see, I'm a speaker, and his thoughts on audiences, practice, and nerves were music to my ears.

We munched and sipped our way through the courses and sealed our friendship with—what else?—dessert. He insisted I taste a frothy Italian delicacy, and I enticed him into spoonfuls of an ice cream pie smothered in caramel sauce. Finally, I pushed the plate away.

Van looked at it lustfully. "You aren't going to finish that?"

I giggled. "No, but you are!" and I slid my plate over in front of him.

Well, I suppose that strictly speaking, one dinner does not a friendship make. But I don't know, maybe it does when you meet a kindred spirit over chow. Someone who likes the same food and worries the same worries you do is hard to find.

And to think I almost didn't go.

JOANNA SLAN

Stranded at the Truck Stop

I WAS DRIVING HOME TO TAHOE CITY FROM SAN Francisco after a speaking engagement. Weather reports predicted a major snowstorm on the pass, and I was hoping to be ahead of it. As I pulled into Auburn, California, I was surprised to see that the highway patrol had blocked the roads due to "whiteout" blizzard conditions. No one was getting through the barricades. Well, this was a new one for me. I went to the first, second, and third motels in Auburn, and there was no room at the inn! Finally, I found space at the fourth motel—a truck stop.

I checked in, turned to leave the lobby, and bumped into a fabulous-looking gentleman. He introduced himself as Dennis.

"Since we're stranded," he said, "how about we have dinner together?" I quickly gave him the once-over and felt safe.

"Sure," I said. "Let me just go up to my room and unpack, and I'll meet you in the restaurant across the street."

I was so relieved to have a room, I didn't even mind the paper-thin walls of this low-budget motel. I was happy just to have a roof over my head!

I heard a man's voice next door. He's talking on the phone. In this deep, husky voice, I hear, "Yeah, I'm on overtime. I'm stranded in Auburn and had to park my rig. Don't get me wrong, though, all's not lost. I just met this redhead in the lobby. I'm going to take her out to dinner, give her some liquor, and look out later!"

I couldn't believe I was hearing this. It was Dennis! Then I realized I was in one of those suites with connecting doors.

I knocked on his adjoining door.

"Dennis, can you do me a favor?" I asked.

"Where are you?" he questioned.

"Right here," I responded. "We have connecting rooms."

He opened his door and said, "Sure, you need something? Just name it."

"Well, listen," I told him. "When you bring that redhead back from dinner, will you promise to keep it down. I can hear everything through these walls."

I missed dinner that night; and by morning I was starving. Knowing there was safety in numbers, I went to breakfast in the coffee shop— with twenty-five truckers.

I peered out the window, and there was Dennis. He was getting into his truck. No wonder I suspected something was up after hearing that phone call the night before. The sign on the side read: FRITO LAY.

DONNA HARTLEY

High-Tech Wisdom

"MOM, GO OUT OF YOUR ROOM AND DON'T PEEK. I'VE got a surprise for you. You're going to love it."

I waited joyfully in another part of my tiny house. My adult kids always know what kind of toys I like, and I imagined a new meditation candle, a Native American ceremonial object, a plant—probably something spiritual. Several minutes passed, and my curiosity grew.

"It isn't totally ready, but you can come in now." Carol's eyes were dancing in anticipation of my reaction. I immediately spotted the monstrosity sitting on top of my formerly uncluttered desk, taking up most of the space.

"Isn't it great, Mom! My school is involved in a special project, and all the teachers get the latest-model computers. I want you to have my old model. It's perfect for you. I'll even give you personal instructions."

I longed to give my daughter the enthusiastic reaction she expected, but she would see through my lies. The aversion was all over my face, and the truth spilled out of my mouth. "Honey, thank you, but I don't do computers. I'm from the dinosaur age of manual typewriters and carbon paper. My first television was black and white, and my first 'plane ride' was on a train."

"Mom, I know you can learn this, and you'll love it. I even brought you a mouse." I was hoping she meant a rodent, but I knew she was referring to that ugly object with a tangled gray cord for a tail.

The computer sat there, a silent reminder of my incompetence and unwillingness to enter the electronic age. I was always considered to be "with-it" by my kids and their friends, but now my reputation was tarnished.

Months passed. My typewriter met my needs just fine, even though I was on a constant drug high from white-out fumes. That obsolete friend must have known its days were numbered when it broke down and died. I couldn't find a typewriter repair store that was still in business. I knew that the time had come to enter the world of Macs, modems, and mice.

"Carol, I'm ready to learn to be a computer whiz. Help!" She came immediately, triumph oozing from every pore. She was ready to take on her most challenging pupil. I sort of understood what she was explaining, and by the end of the day, I could work the on and off switch. The truth is I took to the computer like peanut butter takes to jelly and within weeks was an addict, spending hours writing to every-one. Actually, that is an exaggeration; the hours were spent playing computer solitaire. I spent more time with my mouse than my spouse.

It is such a thrill to open my mind to the new computer age—using the delete key on my "I can't do it" killer self-talk. My next milestone will be to go on-line and float around in cyberspace.

I'm glad the computer takes up so much room. There are moments in my life when I need a big reminder that opportunities for growth are always there.

LYNNE GOLDKLANG

Little Glass Angel

ઝૈરૂ

*L*ISA HOPPED INTO THE BACK SEAT OF THE CAR, BUB-
bling over with excitement. She'd found the *perfect* Christmas gift for
every member of our family.

As we pulled away from the curb, Lisa whispered to me, "Oh,
Mama, I got Daddy a shirt for fifteen dollars, I bought Joey a race car
for ten dollars, and I bought Rags a bag of bones to chew on for six
ninety-five. And Mama, I think you're gonna *love* what I bought you."

I knew how much money Lisa had taken to the mall. Now I knew
what she'd spent for Christmas gifts. Quickly adding up what she'd
spent on her dad, her brother, and the dog, I became clearly aware that
what she'd spent on the dog was more than she'd spent on me.

I felt a slow, growing sickness in the pit of my stomach. *Lisa, how
could you spend more money on the dog than you did on me? I've loved
you, cared for you, would gladly give my life for you! How could you think
so little of me?* The unspoken turned from hurt to anger. She and her
brother chattered away. I said nothing, resentment growing inside.

We arrived home and got out of the car in silence. The kids followed
me inside. Lisa was still giddy with excitement over Christmas, and she
was proud of her gifts. She asked if I'd like to see the presents she'd
bought the others.

"No," I snapped. "I don't want to see anything."

"Mama, what's wrong?"

"Nothing." My lie was obvious.

"Mama, I know something's wrong. What is it?"

I could hardly stand myself. I was nearly forty years old and churning inside because my daughter had spent more money on the dog than on me. I couldn't believe my own immaturity, but I couldn't seem to do anything about my feelings.

"Lisa, I'm acting like a child right now because you spent more for the dog's Christmas present than you did on me. I wish I didn't feel like this, but I do. I'm going upstairs, and when I feel like acting like an adult, I'll be back down. In the meantime, that's how I feel."

"Mama," she shrieked incredulously, "I didn't even think about how much it cost. I found your gift *first,* and I bought it because I knew you would love it." She then burst into tears. "Now I don't feel like giving anybody anything. I wish I hadn't even gone shopping."

I felt horrible . . . but the feelings kept coming. I bolted to my bedroom, fell on the bed, and sobbed. After the tears were gone, I lay in the darkness thinking: *How* could *I have behaved so badly with Lisa, whom I dearly love?* Perhaps It was because I didn't feel loved. But I knew she loved me. I washed my face, slipped downstairs, apologized to my daughter, and asked her forgiveness. Although I could never take back the hurt I had caused her, it was the best I could do.

I shared this story years later with a friend, who said, "Don't you see, Mary Jane? She didn't need to buy your love; she already had it."

I did not love myself enough at that time to see the beauty of her inexpensive gift. Lisa's glass angel was a gift of love. Love has no price tag.

That happened years ago. Yet every Christmas when I gingerly unfold the tissue that holds my little glass angel with the Wedgwood-blue candle, I am reminded of the greatest gift of all . . . and of the priceless child who gave it.

MARY JANE MAPES

Cool Blades on the Boardwalk

IT WAS A VAGUE FAMILIAR FEELING—A FEELING OF freedom experienced a lifetime ago. Motion. Speed. Wind. Excitement. Small but present danger. Oh, yes! That same exhilaration that comes with competence. I was doing it!

I was rollerblading on the boardwalk at Seaside, Oregon, on a glorious late-summer afternoon. Two miles of flat, smooth pavement, sunshine, ocean air. I couldn't help but smile; it was as ridiculously relentless as a yellow happy face. My body moved with relative ease and a modicum of grace. Push, glide, push, glide . . . don't lift the feet so high. Swing the hips. *Oops!* Too much push means too much glide. Let's get more control here. Up and down! Up and down! Miles and miles . . . every once in a while picking up the scent of a cigar, as I once again whizzed past my husband, reading Tom Clancy on a bench.

Getting tired, I informed my husband that on the next pass I wanted to stop. "OK," he said. "I'll be ready." Stopping is not yet a skill I have mastered. As I approached him, I slowed to a more manageable speed. He stood up, swung his arms wide, and enfolded me in a great hug. "I am your stopping place," he whispered. And I thought: Yes. What a wonderful metaphor. You are my safe, comfortable stopping post.

I sat for a while on the bench, enjoying that moment in my life. Some teenagers sauntered past, talking quietly among themselves. The last, a young man about thirteen, looked admiringly at my skates, bent down, and murmured just so we could hear, "Cool blades." Then he picked up his pace to catch his friends. My husband and I said in unison, "Cool blades!?" And we laughed.

The sunset watchers began converging like 49er fans on Super Bowl Sunday. I hoisted myself off the bench to make the most of the fading sunlight with another run. Up and down, push and glide. Lost in the exquisite rhythm and the elegant air, I almost missed the group of women. But out of the corner of my eye, I glimpsed a bicycle surrey pulled up close to the boardwalk. Four women nested there comfortably, in that distinctly women's way of companionable silence. I thought they were completely absorbed in the inch-by-inch disappearance of the day. But as I moved past, almost out of earshot, I heard the soft call of support, "Go, girl!" To acknowledge, I signaled with a "thumbs up" and continued on.

Now, whenever I put on my skates, I hear the voice saying, "Cool blades," and I smile. When I think of my husband as a safe stopping place, I smile. When I replay the sisterly words of support, I smile. I'm sure glad I didn't take seriously those people who predicted, "Rollerblade? You're nearly sixty! You'll kill yourself!"

Kill myself? I'd say I was very much alive and well on the boardwalk!

PAM GROSS

XVIII

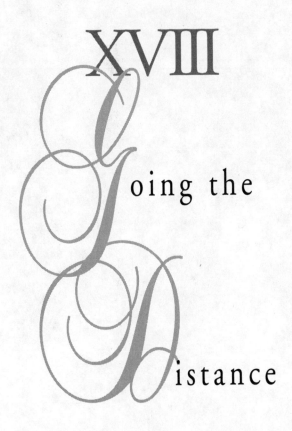

Going the Distance

*"I'm not afraid of storms,
for I am learning how to sail my ship."*

—Louisa May Alcott

Raggedy Ann and Me

ᔐᕈ

ONE DAY, WHEN I WAS SIX AND MY SISTER WAS EIGHT, my mother brought home a beautiful handmade Raggedy Ann and Raggedy Andy. Mother had us whisper in her ear which one we wanted. Of course, I wanted the little girl with the red heart that said "I love you." Yet, when it was my turn, knowing my sister wanted Raggedy Ann, I murmured, "Raggedy Andy." For years, I pretended to myself and others that I loved my Raggedy Andy.

I had plenty of reasons for choosing Raggedy Andy. Aware it would be too hard on Mother if my sister and I chose the same doll, I took care of Mother. Also, I feared my sister's anger and envy if I won. I didn't feel brave enough to have something for myself at her expense! For all these reasons, it just wasn't safe. The way I resolved my dilemma was to accommodate and not want at all.

It's significant that I couldn't let myself choose the doll I wanted, but even more crucial was my inability to let *myself* know for more than a moment that I wanted her. I not only fooled them, I fooled myself!

Later, in the course of therapy as a young woman, I told my husband the story of how I didn't choose Raggedy Ann. I was astonished to find myself weeping, releasing tears that had been locked up for twenty years. I wept for the loss of Raggedy Ann, and even more for the loss of the little girl who had to give up herself to keep peace in her family. Not being able to be who I was and want what I wanted was a source of great suffering for me.

On my next birthday, my husband watched as I opened his gift. The box was sealed with children's wrapping paper. I tore the paper off the box and lifted the lid. There she was peeking out of the tissue—my very own Raggedy Ann.

I now have a small collection of Raggedy Ann dolls. She has become a symbol to me of my reclaimed self. My newest Raggedy Ann is three feet tall and graces a small rocker in my bedroom. She happily reminds me that it's OK to know what I want, and it's OK to give to myself. It's now safe to be me.

CHRISTINE B. EVANS

"Love is an endless act of forgiveness."

—Author unknown

A Legacy of Love

ᏬᏢ

FROM TIME TO TIME, AN EXPERIENCE OF ASTONISHING grace can instantaneously transform our relationship to self, others, and the universe in a way that leaves us renewed. The story of my mother's death and our mutual rebirth was that kind of luminous event.

My mother's answer to the perennial question of why bad things happen to good people was deeply affected by her losing most of her family in the Holocaust. Her faith was shattered by Hitler. To her, the world was a Godless place where nice guys finished last. After my father fell ill with leukemia and committed suicide when medical treatments had rendered his life unbearable, my mother became a hermit. She saw only family for the last thirteen years of her life.

When my mother's health failed and she became bedridden, I wondered how she felt about death. After all, my entire professional life consisted of working with people in passages like my mother's. But with her, I felt stymied. It was a case of the shoemaker's children having no shoes.

I wanted my mother to taste the healing, the peace of mind and forgiveness that I had witnessed in hundreds of other people. In retrospect, this was my need, not hers. Perhaps it was really a need of forgiveness before her death. But our track record for intimate conversation was poor, and discussion of our mutual feelings about life and death were no exception. We had no shared vocabulary for feelings. So for the most part, our conversations centered on politics, family, and sports.

Sitting in my mother's bedroom, watching television and making small talk, I continued to search for some way to make a deeper spiritual connection. One evening my former husband crawled into bed next to her, held her in his arms, and lovingly recounted inspiring near-death experiences we had heard. She pushed these away with good humor, commenting that we could believe in such things if it made us feel better, but they didn't speak to her in the least.

A few weeks before she died, Spirit provided an experience that spoke to her. Mom, an avid baseball fan, was a Bostonian, and the Red Sox were naturally her team. Like most of Boston, she had followed the saga of Wade Boggs, a third baseman, with great interest. Boggs's mistress had spilled to the newspaper some nasty gossip he had told her about his teammates, and he was publicly humiliated.

The media had a field day with his indiscretions. Even though I'm not a baseball fan, my attention was caught one day by a newspaper article that queried why Boggs was doing so well in the stressful situation. The answer was nothing short of astonishing. Boggs's mother had recently died, and he reported that she had come back to him as a full three-dimensional apparition! She assured him that we learn from our mistakes and that he should take responsibility for what he'd done and go on. At the same time, she had appeared to Boggs's sister, who was confined to a wheelchair with multiple sclerosis so advanced that even her vocal cords were paralyzed. She asked her daughter to give the eulogy at her funeral, and her daughter recovered sufficiently to do so!

Filled with the most delicious excitement, I phoned my mother and read her the article. For once she was speechless. Just a few weeks later, I was with her when she went into respiratory distress. I called an ambulance, and we rode through the snow to the hospital for the last time.

In the ER, a very kind nurse, whom she knew well from previous stays, told Mom that she was close to death and asked if she was at peace with that. Barely conscious up to this point, Mother was fairly resurrected with her own version of the good news. "Am I at peace with death?" she crowed. "Have you heard about Wade Boggs's mother?"

As she lay dying, Mom pondered the perennial questions in a new way. Never once did she question that her soul would live on—apparently the apparition of Mrs. Boggs convinced her of that. Instead, she pondered about whether my father, her brother, and her parents would be there on the other side to greet her. The hope of reunion gave her tremendous peace.

The morning of her death, she was taken down to the hospital basement, where the radiology department was located. She was bleeding internally, and they wanted to diagnose the source of the bleeding. When she had not reappeared after several hours, the family dispatched me to look for her. I found her alone, on a stretcher, in the hospital corridor. She was waiting her turn for X ray.

Although I'm not usually an assertive person, I lambasted the young doctor in charge and demanded that they let my mother go back to her room, where the family was waiting to say goodbye. He commented dryly that first they needed a diagnosis for her bleeding. Mom retorted, "You mean I've been waiting here all day for a diagnosis? Why didn't you just ask me. I'm dying—that's your diagnosis." He couldn't argue with her logic, and surprisingly he let her go.

I rode up in the elevator next to her stretcher. Holding hands on that brief ascent, we accomplished the work of a lifetime—the exchange of forgiveness and the realization of a deep mutual love.

JOAN BORYSENKO

Guts and Glory

To celebrate my fiftieth birthday, I decided to buy a Harley-Davidson motorcycle, pack my sleeping bag and tent, and ride through all fifty states—one for each year of my life.

The blue-eyed, red-haired image in the mirror looked remarkably calm for a woman who had just made this life-changing decision. I knew I wanted to do something outrageous to celebrate my milestone, but there were still obstacles, fears, and doubts.

Preparing for a three-month adventure was no small undertaking. I had never been alone. After a marriage that lasted seventeen years, my two sons lived with me for the next ten. My oldest son was in college, and my nineteen-year-old would need to find a place to stay. I worried about his lack of experience and if he would be OK.

What about my law practice? After my divorce, at age forty, I earned a law degree and developed a successful practice. To walk away from this seemed almost irresponsible.

And then there was this important relationship. I loved the guy, but it was hard. I was tense much of the time. Our talks of commitment were always accompanied with that uncomfortable gut feeling. I began wondering if I was with him to compensate for my loneliness. That relentless inner voice knew our relationship would not survive the three-month separation.

Finally, I knew the woman who returned would not be the same woman who left. That bothered me. I rather liked the woman I was. A 14,200-mile journey alone through all fifty states would clearly be a life-changing event. In what ways would the trip change me? Would I even return?

Yet I had a lot going for me. Physically, I was in good shape. Mechanically, my bike was sound. I had confidence in the goodwill of the people I was sure to meet along the way. I also had an underlying confidence in myself.

To push through my veil of fear, I had to risk everything that was known and secure to me. I kept hearing in my mind the phrase: "Do the thing you fear, and death of fear is certain." So I took off on my long journey, including special side trips to Alaska and Hawaii.

My trip was magical! I felt as if I were living out a fantasy. I swam with the manatees in Florida, encountered a tarantula on my bathroom floor in Oklahoma, saw the high plains of Kansas, rode through howling winds in Montana, felt the magnificence of Bryce Canyon, and touched the glaciers of Alaska.

But the most important part was what happened within me. This trip put my life in perspective. My soul and spirit was fed. Inner peace and contentment replaced my fear of loneliness. I learned to treasure my time alone. My pace is slower now. No longer practicing law, I'm writing instead. My sons are beginning the adventure of their own lives.

I decided to move back to my rural home in Oregon to spend time with my parents. Before my trip, I would never have considered moving home. I now know that where we live is not as important as spending time with those we love.

While on the trip, I ended the relationship I'd been in, and we went our separate ways.

No longer driven by fear of loneliness, I met "Mr. Wonderful" in, of all places, that small hometown I once resisted. When I first saw him, he was leaning against his Harley-Davidson, surveying the crowd at a local bike rally. As I pulled off my helmet, our eyes met. I could tell what he was thinking: Is it really possible to meet a great woman who loves to ride Harleys?

We married months later, for all the right reasons. He calls me his "red-haired fox." As for the fifty-year-old woman who came back from her life-changing journey, she did change—and I like her even better!

CAROLYN FOX

My Love Affair with Vladimir

MY SEARCH WAS ON FOR A CAR. I WALKED UP AND down the aisle, scrutinizing each one, waiting for a sign of recognition, a kindred spirit. Some were too old, too worn, and not well cared for. Some were too young, making me wonder, was there a problem? Then I spied my perfect match. We made contact, his grille forming a rakish grin. I grabbed my husband's arm. "Oh, Don, look!" I had to touch it. The salesman saw that look in my eyes. "I'll get the keys," he said, and went running back to his office. He unlocked the car, and I got in. My excitement grew as I stroked the steering wheel. Only 53,000 miles. Not bad. Burgundy with tan interior. I felt right at home—like it was meant to be. It was a done deal. I was now the proud owner of a three-year-old Volvo.

I've always been of the philosophy that one should name the car one drives. Makes the car feel important and establishes a bond between car and driver. I've come to believe that everything has a consciousness. Why treat your car any differently than you would treat your mother? I wanted my car to know the permanence of our union. I knew immediately that this car was male. Instinctively, I began to call him Vladimir.

One December I noticed other people putting wreaths on the front of their cars. (I think it's a Saint Louis thing, because I haven't seen this anywhere else.) I bought Vladimir a wreath as well. He wears it proudly every December and looks quite handsome. I felt he deserved even more, so for Halloween I bought him a companion—an inflatable skeleton, which I strap into the front passenger seat each October. Vladimir gets lots of other attention as well. He knows I love him—I praise him regularly and pat his dashboard each time we're together. I indulge him with other treats, like better gasoline, deluxe car washes, extra-rich leather cleaner—little things to make him feel special. My last purchase for Vladimir was a mini wind chime, designed to resonate peace and harmony, which I hung from the rearview mirror. The sound is divine.

My husband has made fun of me for years about my devotion to my car. He has a Volvo too—the same model as Vlad, but three years newer. To Don, his Volvo is "just a car," and he pays no attention to his car's physical or spiritual well-being. Don thinks the attention and gifts I lavish on Vladimir are nonsense. He jokingly calls Vladimir's half of the garage the "sacred half." But actions speak louder than words, and the results speak for themselves. Vladimir has needed only routine maintenance, while Don's car has had repeated mechanical problems—he even had to have the transmission rebuilt. Once, I drove his car home alone from a vacation, and it stopped running outside Joliet, Illinois. The car had to be towed to the local dealer and needed *both* fuel pumps replaced. I know in my heart that Vladimir would never do that to me.

Vladimir will be fourteen years old this year and has mileage well into the six digits. We've been together for eleven of those years, and he's never failed to take good care of me. His sense of purpose for service has been impeccable. Don and I looked at new Volvos recently. "He isn't going to last forever," Don snorted gruffly, but I just couldn't part with Vladimir.

Is it true what they say that love makes all things new again? I don't know. Vladimir doesn't look quite as bright and shiny as he once did, but his spirit is as vibrant as the day I drove him home. Looks like we'll be together until death do us part.

SHARON HYLL

Sometimes You Can Go Back

GEORGE IS A BIG GUY. THE KIND OF FELLOW WHO might've been somebody's bodyguard, except that he has the personality of a big teddy bear. Recently retired and divorced, George came into my office to share a story with me about something that had happened to him.

"Reverend Mary," he said, "last Easter you told us that if we would let go of one habit that was limiting us, however small, in one year our life would be transformed. I want to tell you what happened to me.

"For most of my life, I've had a habit of biting the second knuckle on my index finger, like this." He bent the finger and put the knuckle between his teeth. "I even developed quite a callous on both sides of the finger. Well, I decided it was time to give that habit up. I've done pretty well at it all year—but let me give you a little background on this thing.

"When I was six years old, I saw my baby brother hit by a car and killed. He was two years younger than me. I had just run across that street, and he was following me. Just the day before, I was told to watch for cars and to look out for my little brother. We had been very close, and I was heartbroken.

"Sometime after that, I began to bite the back of my right hand between the knuckles of my first two fingers. I constantly had a callous there, about the size of a half-dollar. Whenever I felt angry or frustrated, I'd bite the top of that hand, right there on that spot.

"By the time I was a teenager, I guess I thought that was too childlike to do, and I switched to biting the one knuckle on my hand. I kept right on doing that until Easter of last year. After hearing your talk, I decided it was time to give up that habit.

"This year in March—almost one year after your Easter talk—I was spending the day with my grandson at the park. I noticed that I bit my knuckle that day. *How come?* I was also feeling a lot of love for my grandson as I watched him swing under his own locomotion.

"After I took him home, I went to visit some friends. I was feeling anxious that the laundry I'd meant to do was still in the trunk of my car. As I drove home that evening, my anxiety was rising. I was so rattled that I knew it had to be more than just the unfinished laundry. I had this huge knot in my stomach.

"I thought about my little grandson, who was just about the age my brother had been when he died. And I realized it was coming up on the anniversary of my brother's death, fifty-five years ago! I love that little guy so much, I thought to myself, and I'm afraid he'll be taken away. I knew right then that was just the way I'd felt when I lost my brother. I somehow had it wired up that loving my brother so much had caused me to lose him!

"But this last year, I was changing and not really seeing it. During that day in the park, I was expressing true love for my little grandson —more love than I'd given to my five kids and both my former wives.

"Since that day, I've shared this story with all of them. I've tried to make amends for all the love that I withheld from my family all these years—for fear I'd lose them.

"Reverend Mary, I know if I was still biting this knuckle every time I felt mad, or sad, or frustrated, I wouldn't have uncovered any of this. It was giving up that one habit that taught me so much and let all this love come to the surface. So you see, when you told us our lives would be transformed in one year by taking one little action, you were so right!

"I've been officially retired since the first of May, but now I'm really ready to be retired. This summer I'm just going to play with my grandson. I feel like I've finally got my little brother back!"

REV. MARY MURRAY SHELTON

No Mistakes Here

IT'S NOT EASY BEING MARRIED TO SOMEONE WHO HAS never made a mistake. My husband, Bud, is constitutionally incapable of admitting that he has ever been wrong. I don't think his mouth can form the words "I'm sorry. I made a mistake."

This aspect of his personality is best illustrated by an incident that happened recently.

I was on the phone one evening, talking with my brother, when he asked, "Did Bud tell you I called last night?"

I turned to Bud and said, "Honey, you didn't tell me my brother called last night."

Without interrupting his concentration or even shifting his eyes from the TV set, my husband answered, "Not yet."

ANITA CHEEK MILNER

"When work, commitment, and pleasure all become one and you reach that deep well where passion lives, nothing is impossible."

—Nancy Coey

You'll Be an Artist When You Grow Up

'VE ALWAYS BEEN FASCINATED WITH COLOR. AS A child, I loved to paint and draw with crayons. To my preschool mind, every picture I created was a masterpiece! Then I went to the first grade.

We were asked one day to color pictures, which would be given to the residents of a nursing home to brighten their day. Every child was given one sheet to color. We were also told that a few extra were needed, and anyone who finished early and had done a good job could color more than one. I *wanted* to color more than one. I quickly colored the design with lots of bright colors and raised my hand, sure that my paper would be good enough for me to color another one.

When my teacher came over to look at my work, she scolded me in a loud voice. "Kathleen, that paper is awful. You used too many colors and couldn't even stay in the lines!" I was crushed. I didn't get to color another paper and was forced to sit quietly, holding in my embarrassment, as the rest of the class completed the project.

After that day, I stopped drawing pictures. I dreaded the art class that had been my favorite part of school. Each time I was forced to do anything artistic, I cringed and retreated inside myself. To this day, I do not remember any art project completed after the day my teacher made me feel incompetent and unartistic, although I can tell you all about the many projects I'd completed before that day.

About four years later, our family had a visit from an elderly friend of my mother's. She was a delightful woman, and I spent hours talking to her. Art or creativity was never mentioned. A short while later, my mother received a letter from her friend, thanking her for our hospitality.

The letter contained a paragraph about all of the children in my family. She told my mother how wonderful she thought each of us was, and she proceeded to list what careers she thought we would have when we grew up. I don't remember what was predicted for any of my brothers or sisters, but I'll never forget the feeling of warmth that passed over me as my mother read the letter aloud. It said that I would be an artist when I grew up. An artist!

That afternoon I dug out my old box of crayons and drawing paper. I drew everything I could, nonstop, in every spare minute for the next month. I stopped drawing one day and looked back over all I had created. It looked pretty good, I thought. Good enough that I wished I could show it to my first-grade teacher.

My rekindled artistic spirit eventually took on many new forms and expressions. Today, I travel the world and teach thousands of people a year how to be more creative, how to design beautiful projects, and how to use color in their businesses and their lives. I've written thirty books on the subject and have had hundreds of articles printed. I've even been featured on fifteen videos, have my own television show, and have appeared on numerous other programs.

How different my life, and the lives of those I touch creatively each year, would be if an elderly woman I met only once in my life hadn't told me I'd be an artist when I grew up! She taught me an important life lesson: to honor each person's unique artistic talents. I now encourage others and teach them to color outside the lines.

KATHY LAMANCUSA

XIX

Go with Your Passion

"You are your own promised land,
your own new frontier."

—Julia Cameron

The Dreamer

HEN I WAS NINE YEARS OLD, LIVING IN A SMALL town in North Carolina, I found an ad for selling greeting cards in the back of a children's magazine. I thought to myself: I can do this. I begged my mother to let me send for the kit.

Two weeks later, when the kit arrived, I ripped off the brown paper wrapper, grabbed the cards, and dashed from the house. Three hours later, I returned home with no cards and a pocket full of money, proclaiming, "Mama, all the people couldn't wait to buy my cards!"

A salesperson was born.

When I was twelve years old, my father took me to see Zig Ziglar. I remember sitting in that dark auditorium, listening to Mr. Ziglar raise everyone's spirits to the ceiling. I left there feeling I could do anything. When we got to the car, I turned to my father and said, "Dad, I want to make people feel like that." My father asked me what I meant. "I want to be a motivational speaker, just like Mr. Ziglar," I replied.

A dream was born.

Recently, I began pursuing my dream of motivating others. After a four-year relationship with a major Fortune 100 company, beginning as a sales trainer and ending as a regional sales manager, I left the company at the height of my career. Many people were astounded that I would leave after earning a six-figure income, and they asked why I would risk everything for a dream.

I made my decision to start my own company and leave my secure position after attending a regional sales meeting. There, the vice president of our company delivered a speech that changed my life. He asked us, "If a genie would grant you three wishes, what would they be?" After giving us a moment to write down the three wishes, he then asked, "Why do you need a genie?" I will never forget the empowerment I felt at that moment!

I realized that everything I had accomplished: the graduate degree, the successful sales career, speaking engagements, training and managing for a Fortune 100 company—had prepared me for this moment. I was ready and did not need a genie's help to become a motivational speaker. When I tearfully told my boss my plans, this incredible leader whom I respect so much replied, "Proceed with reckless abandon and you will be successful."

Having made that decision, I was immediately tested. One week after I gave notice, my husband was laid off from his job. We had recently bought a new home and needed both incomes to make the monthly mortgage payment, and now we were down to no income. It was tempting to turn back to my former company, knowing they wanted me to stay. But I was certain that if I went back, I'd never leave. I decided I still wanted to move forward rather than end up with a mouthful of "if onlys" later on.

A motivational speaker was born.

When I held fast to my dream, even during the tough times, the miracles really began to happen. In a short time period, my husband found a better job, we didn't miss a mortgage payment, and I was able to book several speaking engagements with new clients. I discovered the incredible power of dreams.

I loved my old job, my peers, and the company I left, but it was time to get on with my dream. To celebrate my success, I had a local artist paint my new office to resemble a garden. At the top of one wall she stenciled, "The World Always Makes Way for the Dreamer."

APRIL KEMP

"Only those who see the invisible
can do the impossible."

—Author unknown

Paddling Upstream

CHILDREN HAVE ALWAYS BEEN AN IMPORTANT PART
of my life. As a kindergarten teacher for twenty-eight years, I was
surrounded by children—other people's children, for I'd had none of
my own.

In my married life, twenty-five years ago, we tried to have children.
After my divorce, I tried artificial insemination. Still no baby. To someone who had always been drawn to motherhood, it was all the more
heartbreaking when it never happened.

Feeling as though I was desperately running out of time, I decided it
was time to really get serious! This was going to happen. Period. I was
going to take *every* step necessary to have a baby. Every time I came to an
obstacle, I would get past it. Deep inside, I knew I would be a mom.

I retired from teaching and devoted myself to preparing for motherhood. Although the physicians in the fertility clinic said my chances
were growing slimmer, I surrounded myself with people who supported
my dream. I didn't give up even when I felt I was paddling upstream
against a strong current.

Using money from my early retirement, I funded an embryo transfer. While a donor egg was readily available, the sperm proved trickier. I fearfully approached a man I'd been dating a short time. I remember how awkward and emotional I felt telling him about my dream. I asked him to donate his sperm. Tears welled in his eyes. Rather than run, he was honored to be a part of my passionate quest.

I continued dreaming of having a child. I meditated about having a child. I created affirmations like "I am healthy, happy, and pregnant!" I made a huge poster covered with photographs of babies and pregnant women. It was in a prominent place in my home, so everyone who came in could see and believe with me.

The embryo implantation was successful—I did not expect anything other than that! My pregnancy was problem free. The C-section went smoothly, and on March 29, 1995, Zachary Lee Roth entered my life.

There's an analogy I strongly relate to. I'm like a salmon. The salmon has one goal: to get back to that spawning ground and lay her eggs. It will thrash through the rapids and over the rocks. It gets battered, but not beaten. No matter what, that determined salmon will get there or die. I'm definitely that salmon—and I made it!

I'm hard to reach these days. I'm busy playing with my young son. It's a miracle to watch him grow and change each day. It's a miracle I'm on my own, yet able to create this beautiful young child.

When I got to that place where I could see what I had to have, nothing could stop me. Having a baby was miracle enough. What made it a major miracle was having my baby at age fifty.

HARRIET ROTH

The Magic of Anger

ᘓᑫᕈ

UDDENLY THE CLASSROOM DOOR FLEW OPEN. IN MARCHED the vice principal, better known as "The Tyrant." You could hear an undercurrent of groans as The Tyrant folded her arms in front of her buxom bosom and lifted one eyebrow so high it looked as if it could emerge from the crown of her cranium. The Tyrant was no ordinary lady. In fact, she was no lady at all, but rather the epitome of "I'm Not OK; and Neither Are You."

I pondered what game she was about to play, as I attempted to carry on with my lesson. My students were enthusiastically involved in a discussion of a popular psychology of the day, based on Thomas Harris's *I'm O.K., You're O.K.* and Eric Berne's *Games People Play.* I really loved interacting with my students and had become their "noon-hour counselor."

Instead of watching the dynamics of the class, The Tyrant fixed her icy stare at me. After a grueling thirty minutes of intense scrutiny, she got up and started to walk out. We were all primed for a huge sigh of relief, when she suddenly did an about-face and lurched at me. Her jaw was clenched, and she wildly jabbed her finger in fury, preparing to dissect her victim of the day. She snarled with such vengeance that I could taste her bitter breath. "Who do you think you are, Mrs. Field? Watch what you say to these students. Remember, you are not a psychologist."

As the anger welled up inside me, it felt as though my blood pressure soared beyond the measure of any instrument. My adrenaline surged and my pulse skyrocketed. My eyes filled with tears, and my heart beat to the frenzy of a primitive war dance. It was all I could do to keep a lid on my boiling insides.

After The Tyrant had completed her abusive mission and finally stalked out, the students rallied to my defense. One cried, "She shouldn't be let out without a keeper!" Another added, "She needs to be tamed. She took apart my purse today in the lavatory, even though I asked her to stop because I don't do cigs or drugs." It was the quavering voice of a usually shy boy that really got to me. "She's just jealous because we come to you with our problems instead of her."

As I drove home that evening, still feeling like Mount Vesuvius ready for the grand eruption, the stored-up tears flowed like hot lava that burned without comfort. When I finally crawled into bed, I could not sleep. Over and over again, the taunting words of The Tyrant resounded: *Remember, you are not a psychologist. Who do you think you are? You are not a psychologist. You are not . . ."*

The endless night finally gave way to a brilliant dawn. As the morning star illuminated my face, a light went on in my brain, and I heard myself shout, "Why *not* a psychologist?" Passion replaced my anger, and I found myself in the car, driving to the university. Before the sun gave way to the full moon, I had registered for my first course in clinical psychology.

Our teachers come in many forms. Sometimes we are jolted toward change by those least likely to have a positive impact. The Tyrant, in her quest to quench my spirit and put me in my place, failed at the first task while succeeding brilliantly at the second. My spirit soared as the fire of my anger became the fuel for my newly chosen path.

Many years have passed since that transition in my life. Yesterday, the door of my office opened. In walked a new patient, looking like a teakettle ready to steam. "Dr. Field," she said, her eyes filled with tears, "I'm a schoolteacher. I've had such a terrible day. I have this tyrannical principal. She bawled me out in front of the whole class. I'm so humiliated. I can't take it anymore!"

Compassion welled up within me as I said, "I believe I can help you."

ELEANOR S. FIELD

An Influential Lunch Date

ʃʃ

I WORE A RED PLAID PLEATED SKIRT, A WHITE BLOUSE with a Peter Pan collar, white bobby socks, and penny loafers at the Cathedral of Saint Raymond's school. In the sixth grade, I was convinced I knew exactly how our school should run. I was frustrated by the lack of school spirit. I decided it was my mission to save the school.

At the end of a crisp autumn day, I marched down to the principal's office and asked the ancient secretary to see Sister Muriel. Looking very stern in her drab gray suit, Sister Muriel asked what I needed. Words spilled out of me about how we needed more school spirit. She cut me off and asked if I would join her for lunch the next day. Obviously she recognized my keen intellect! There was a bounce in my step the whole way home.

"I'm having lunch with the principal!" I declared to my friends. "Are you in trouble?" "How boring!" exclaimed my pals. As usual, my friends thought I was insane. They thought only teachers could change things like school spirit.

Sister Muriel had pulled a huge red leather chair next to the desk for me. Once I climbed up, my toes barely touched the floor. Carefully, I spread my napkin over the desk and arranged my baloney sandwich, Cheetos, and a carton of chocolate milk. Sister Muriel had done the same with her tuna fish sandwich, pretzels, and Oreos. I couldn't believe a nun ate Oreos!

While munching on pretzels, Sister Muriel asked me to explain, in detail, my concerns. I rambled passionately on about school spirit. After several minutes, she leaned forward and asked, "What do you want to do about it?" Uh-oh. I didn't know. Slowly, I began to give her ideas—ending each one with a question mark in my voice. After each proposal, she would ask me, "What resources can we use? How would we carry it out? Would the other students support it?" Together we weeded out the silly ideas and elaborated on the good ones. Once we identified three strong prospects, she asked me to pick my favorite one. Sister Muriel leaned back in her chair and asked me if I was really committed to this project. With the enthusiasm of an innocent child, I exclaimed, "Yes, Sister!" She looked me straight in the eye and said, "OK, you can do this." I believe I flew home that day.

Over the next three years, I ate many lunches while sitting in that huge red chair. Sister Muriel made me feel important. With each lunch, I expressed myself better. I learned to predict what she might ask. It became a game to see how prepared I could be. Eventually I was able to come to lunch with a few solid ideas and an action plan. Sister Muriel listened to me, let me try things, let me fail, and let me try again. I thought I knew everything going into those lunches. But it was during those lunches that I learned everything.

Much later, as a first-year teacher, I was convinced that I knew exactly how the school should be run. Deeply concerned about the lack of school spirit, I decided it was my mission to save our school. Armed with ideas, I flew into my principal's office. "Tom, we must have lunch!" I exclaimed. The next day, we sat together over lunch and discussed my ideas. We agreed on a plan, and Tom gave me a green light. I believe I flew back to my classroom.

When I casually mentioned to a tenured teacher that I was going to see Tom, she explained to me that principals are very busy people, that teachers can't really change anything, only administrators can cause change. I thanked her for her insight and went to see Tom anyway. Over the years, Tom and I have become good friends. He's encouraged my confidence to share ideas with him.

Looking back now, I'm grateful that Sister Muriel and Tom took the time to listen to an enthusiastic young person. I know they were very busy, yet they still found time for me. There are moments in time that create who we are. It is from these moments that confidence is created or destroyed.

I have come to believe that anyone, regardless of age or position, can offer ideas and cause change. I hope that someday someone comes to me with an idea, and I am able to invite that individual to lunch.

MARGUERITE MURER

Shut Up and Dance

MARTHA GRAHAM, THE HIGH PRIESTESS OF MODERN dance in America, once said, "I am a dancer, and I believe that we learn by practice—whether that means we learn to dance by practicing dance or learn to live by practicing living. Life does not have to be interpreted—it has to be experienced."

I studied dance for years. I would come to class early and spend an hour or more warming up and striking regal poses for the admiring mirrors on the studio walls. I marveled at my perfect alignment and fabulous extensions. The analytical interpretation and technical perfection held me spellbound. Alone in that studio, I was Margot Fonteyn dancing a pas de deux with Rudolf Nureyev. . . . I was Isadora Duncan, scarves flying, scandalizing all of Europe with her sensual interpretations.

Yes. In my imagination, I was awesome!

Until class began.

Then the admiring mirrors turned into leering spectators. I'd catch a glimpse of my less-than-perfect image, and cringe and gasp at what I saw. With all the students' eyes upon me, I changed from a prima ballerina to an awkward student.

Can you relate? Have you ever fancied yourself Pavarotti or Maria Callas in the shower, but outside of that steamy chamber you'd be mortified to even chime in on a chorus of "Happy Birthday"?

Frustrated, my dance teacher would turn to me and say, "Mari Pat, you must give yourself up to the movement—dance full out—unafraid of the consequences!"

I would nod, pretend I understood, and once again timidly take my place on the dance floor. This went on for months.

Because cold muscles are dangerous for a dancer, we arrived at the studio during winter bundled from head to toe. As we worked and warmed up, our clothes came off in layers. One day we'd been working at the barre for about an hour when a fellow dance student stripped off his sweatshirt, to reveal a T-shirt emblazoned with his life philosophy. The words across his chest shouted: SHUT UP AND DANCE.

I was so stunned that I nearly collided with him. The words pierced me like a thunderbolt. So simple! So true!

At that moment, I learned that life is happening right now. This is the real thing! It's time to stop planning, posturing, and postponing. It's time to stop *talking* about a dream—and start *doing* my dream. I finally let go of my negative self talk and striving for perfection. I released my inner music. On that day, I became a dancer.

MARI PAT VARGA

> "When you hold back on life,
> life holds back on you."
>
> —Mary Manin Morrissey

Someday

ঔৈ৯

ID YOU EVER KNOW ANYONE WHO HAD A DREAM SO infectious that everyone believed in it? I had a friend like that in college.

Suzy Brown was a beautiful, bouncy blonde with huge flashing green eyes and a laugh that could stop a rainstorm. She wanted to be a clown —a real live Barnum & Bailey clown—and she practiced every day. Suzy would dress up in funny old clothes, turn somersaults, lean backward until I thought she would break, and strut around the room, singing, "I've a bright-red nose, big shoes of brown, and I will be the world's best clown!"

And she might have been . . . if she had tried.

When I saw Suzy a few years later, she was not in the center ring, not wearing a polka-dot suit, not making people laugh. She was living alone in a tiny apartment, tied to a low-paying job that she hated and too busy to see the circus when it came to town. She was twenty-five years old, but she seemed sixty-five. You know what she said? She said, "It's not over, Kay. Someday I'll have another chance. Someday I'll go to the circus. Someday when . . ."

Like Suzy, I had a dream. My dream was to be a speaker who could inspire people to do and be whatever they wanted. But first I needed the confidence to stand in a room filled with people, open my mouth, and have something . . . anything . . . come out. But I was so scared, I couldn't lead a silent prayer! My brain may have started working the day I was born, but it sure stopped when I tried to speak in public!

For years, I said I wanted to develop my speaking skills. But I was busy, I was broke, I was sick, I didn't know how. When you're afraid to do something, one excuse is just as good as another.

One day, after telling so many others about my dream and preparing for it for so long in little ways I didn't even recognize, I ran out of excuses. I knew I *had* to walk through my fear of speaking.

The first time I tried to make a speech, there were only ten people in the room, and I knew every one of them well. I also knew my speech well, but when I stood up to speak, every function in my body failed. My memory stopped. My eyes glazed over, and I couldn't see my audience anymore. My heart tried to pound its way out of my chest. My body went into rigor mortis. My deodorant stopped working! I took a deep breath, became light-headed, faced my friends—and very calmly fainted!

Ever so slowly, I *did* learn to speak. I even won a few speech contests. With every success, I became braver. And with every loss, I became stronger. I eventually became a finalist in the International Championship of Public Speaking!

Remember my friend Suzy Brown? My beautiful and talented friend died of cancer at the age of thirty, without ever being part of the circus. Her "someday" never came. The last time I saw her, she said, "Kay, I only wish I had another chance to try." Putting your dreams on hold is like putting your life on hold.

Two dreams . . . two endings . . . I took the first step, Suzy put her dream on hold. If Suzy could talk to us right now, I'll bet she'd say, "Don't be afraid to reach for the stars; that's why God put them out so far."

KAY duPONT

XX

A New Way of Being

"You cannot discover new oceans, unless you have the courage to lose sight of the shore."

—Author unknown

You Don't Have to Come Home from Work Exhausted!

⌘

STUDYING WITH DR. MARGARET MEAD, I NOTICED THAT she enjoyed a different quality of energy. She worked circles around the rest of us, even though she was thirty-five to forty years our senior! One day I asked, "Margaret, how can you enjoy such abundant energy, when the rest of us are dragging?"

She stopped and thought for a moment, scratching her head as she did so, then replied with a grin, "I suppose it's because I never grew up . . . while fooling most people into believing that I have!"

Taking what she said to heart, I began to sift through the joy of my childhood. Just remembering playing kick the can on a summer's night would revive me with that special energy we all experienced as kids.

So what might happen if I got even bolder and claimed some precious dreams that never happened? I never told anyone I wanted tap-dance lessons as a child, wanted to dance in a recital wearing a beautiful costume and shiny black tap shoes.

I grew up in Houston, next door to an adorable little girl named Linda Hovey. She was petite and looked a lot like Shirley Temple. I was big, gawky, and teased with the nickname "Miss Moose" by my older brother and his friends.

So, years later, it took all the courage I could muster to go into a neighborhood shoe store and order size 9B tap shoes.

"How old is the kid with 9B feet?" the clerk asked with amazement.

"Soon she will be fifty," I answered in a quiet, embarrassed voice.

Late at night, after my family went to bed, I would put on a videotape by Bonnie Franklin called *Let's Tap* and claim my fantasy of becoming Shirley Temple onstage.

One night my husband, Larry, woke up and came through the den on his way to the kitchen for a bowl of Grape-Nuts. Catching me in the act, he said, "Hey, you're almost good at it!" We both laughed, and I shared my ideas about living our dreams. He had enjoyed playing the saxophone and clarinet as a boy, so we searched through the want ads and found a wonderful old clarinet.

We were absolutely amazed that we could come home from our workday totally drained and exhausted, yet after twenty minutes of music for Larry and a few shuffle-ball changes for me, we both would experience a miraculous rejuvenation. Inspired by our discovery, we decided to give ourselves a surprise 104th birthday party (his fifty-fourth and my fiftieth). The surprise would be a joint recital, and all our friends would be invited to perform something they enjoyed as a kid or dreamed of doing.

We couldn't believe the energy that led up to that magical night. Friends arrived with costumes, props, and scripts, surrounded by mystery. Like young children, we each fought the delicate balance of fear tinged with excitement as we waited our turn to perform. Ordinarily, when adults perform, we expect to have rehearsed until we are perfect. But kids rehearse until they are bored or tired and then say, "Pretend I'm really good!" That night we pretended, and we clapped wildly for each other.

In the ten years since that life-changing night, I have risked sharing my childhood dream and dared to tap-dance badly for many audiences. They delight in my childlike courage as I ask for a standing ovation at the end, "like you might give Barbra Streisand when she was the best she has ever been." There are always tears in the crowd, our kid selves begging us to make room for them in our busy lives.

When I do these outrageous performances, I end with a childhood game, I Dare You! I say, "I dare you to spend some time with childhood dreams and fantasies. Then find your own creative way to claim them."

One very dignified, six-foot-six CEO thanked me after I received a standing ovation at his company's annual meeting. "All my life I have secretly wished I could tap-dance," he said. "I'll soon be sixty-eight, and today you've given me the courage to claim that lifelong dream!"

ANN McGEE-COOPER

From Under the Boot Heel

N MY TWENTY YEARS AS A PARAMEDIC, I HAVE BEEN charged with performing duties that require enormous amounts of bravery. I was about to learn a new kind.

Several years ago, I sat in a dilapidated office housed in a condemned hospital building in the center of a nondescript town in south Texas. I lit a cigarette (this was back in the days when one could smoke in a building) and watched a large cockroach climb up the wall in front of my desk. I began my 457th day of acute self-pity.

Tim, an EMT coworker, strolled in and flicked the ugly bug onto the floor, slamming down on it with the heavy heel of a patrol boot. Even with that pounding, the bug wouldn't die. Sort of like me, I thought. Stomped on unmercifully, and I keep coming back for more.

In the year since my divorce, there had been few happy days. My entire existence seemed to depend solely on my life-saving duties. Responding to an emergency was the only time I knew my heart was beating. My thoughts turned once more to the core of my problem. *If only I could find a nice man . . .*

I suddenly felt ill. What was I thinking? Am I to waste my entire life waiting for Prince Charming? He certainly had not been around during the first thirty-seven years.

I stood up and walked past Tim and out to the street. Standing on the curb, I surveyed my surroundings. "Oh my God!" I said to myself while continuing my slow turn. "There is nothing to see here, no view, no green trees or water, no spiky mountains. Not even a hill. Why am

I here?" The question was the internal combustion I needed. I smiled and felt hope welling up within me. Standing there on the curb of Center Street, dressed in my uniform, I laughed until tears streaked my face.

That night I pulled out a yellow legal pad. On it I wrote: "WHAT I WANT." Under the heading, I listed eight items: 1. to live in a beautiful place with a 360-degree view; 2. to make a good salary; 3. to once again own a red sports car; 4. to never see a cockroach again; 5. to have a wonderful job teaching EMTs and paramedics; 6. to be proud of myself; 7. to never, *ever* need a man again, except for plumbing repairs; 8. to spend my next forty years in peace and happiness. I worked until the wee hours of the morning, polishing my résumé, and then I sent copies to Emergency Medical Services offices in four northwestern states.

Over fifty people attended my going-away party, and each of them asked the same question. "Wendy, how can you just pack up and go to Alaska without knowing anyone there?" Some of the women said, "I could never go off to the wilderness all alone." One man informed me that there were seven men to one woman in Alaska. "You're going to get a husband, right?"

"Yeah, right."

The truth is, I had chosen to enjoy my own company for a while. Something I had never really done.

In one week, I would become the Emergency Medical Services Coordinator for Southeast Alaska. The job required travel by boat and float plane to outlying areas—the bush. I was to spend time in these isolated communities teaching classes on emergency services. I never knew such a career existed, and it was as if I had designed the position myself.

As I looked around at all the doubting faces that day, I felt absolutely no fear. Just joy. Two suitcases and four boxes of training materials were all I had packed. I purged myself of all belongings.

As I said my goodbyes, I realized it took no bravery to pack up and move to Alaska. The bravery had occurred when I made my list and resolved to fulfill it. I recognized that I could control my own destiny. The weakness was in waiting for change instead of creating it.

Who do I need? Me. Who do I depend on? Me. Who do I love? Me. Who makes me happy? Me. Selfish, you say. Darned right. And there are no cockroaches in Alaska.

WENDY NATKONG

Firewalk—Warming My "Soul"

✑

M Y FRIEND ROBERT PHONED TO SAY HE'D JUST EXPE-
rienced a "firewalk." Excited, he encouraged me to do it too, saying,
"It was amazingly easy—like walking through a doorway of fear." I
was impressed with Robert's personal triumph of "mind over matter."

I had spent years believing I wouldn't achieve results unless I was
willing to roll a large boulder uphill in the process. Maybe this walk
was just the boost I needed.

The workshop began with the lighting of a huge pile of wood. The
temperature of the wood would reach 1200–1300 degrees. That's hot
enough to melt aluminum. Yet we were expected to walk on the glowing embers barefoot without burning our feet!

We were instructed to become aware of our body sensations and our
thoughts, to *know* whether or not it was safe for us to walk across the
embers. If we noticed our body was tense, or we thought: I'm afraid I
will be burned, we shouldn't walk. If, however, our body and mind felt
relaxed, and we thought: Yes, I trust I'll be safe, then we could go for
it. We were being taught to trust our intuition.

A visualization process turned out to be the most revealing part
of the evening. We were asked to think about any fears we might
have about walking on fire and to visualize our *worst* fear realized.
In my mind, I imagined my feet severely burned, but I was shocked
to realize that wasn't my *worst* fear. My worst fear was of lying in a
hospital bed, explaining to my sister how I had got burned. I was
really afraid of what she would think of me. I could hear her exclaim,
"Frances, why in the world did you pull this crazy, stupid stunt?" I

had never known I cared so much about what other people thought of me.

We were then asked to visualize what would happen after we faced our worst fear. I experienced telling my sister what I had done and why. I saw her comforting me and expressing her love. Another revelation. Of course she would love me no matter what!

The firewalk instructor gave us four simple, yet very important, steps to follow for crossing the coals without getting burned (and for living our lives):

1. Know where you're starting from.

2. Know where you want to go.

3. Design a plan to get you there.

4. Follow the plan.

It was time to go outdoors and face the fire. "Am I going to trust my intuition, or am I going to hold back in fear?" I asked myself. I stood there feeling worn out, discouraged, and defeated from years of holding myself back. I was determined to break free! I made the commitment to trust myself and walk.

With that first step, I changed my life. I could feel a release as I stepped forward. I was doing what I wanted to do without the fear of what others would say. I proved to myself that fear doesn't have to stop me from being who I want to be. This was a breakthrough—I was actually walking barefoot on red-hot coals.

My feet began to feel very hot as I completed this powerful walk and stepped off onto the cool, wet grass. I used the garden hose to wash off the ash and cinders and went indoors, where I could examine my feet in the light. They were not burned or blistered at all. My intuition had served me well.

Since the firewalk, I have been more aware of the signals in my body and my mind whenever I need to make a decision or take a risk. My intuition has become a useful tool for making even the smallest choices in my life.

When my heart speaks now, I always listen. I check in with my intuition and design a plan I can follow. Each step of the way, I make sure I'm staying on track. I accomplish my innermost desires and experience much more ease and harmony in my life.

Yesterday I walked with fear. The firewalk warmed my soul and rekindled my spirit. Today I walk with confidence and joy, and amazing miracles have become a regular part of my life!

FRAN FISHER

> "Every time you heal a part of yourself,
> you bring more light into the world."
>
> —Author unknown

Doorway of Destiny

T WAS 10:30 A.M., AND I WAS ALREADY LATE FOR MY
appointment. I had a busy day ahead of me; my mind was cluttered
with the many tasks I wanted to accomplish. As I hurried down the
crowded street in Seattle's Pioneer Square district, oblivious to my
surroundings, I suddenly stopped, cemented in my tracks. Out of the
corner of my eye, I noticed a flash of gold. Very slowly, life as I had
known it began to change, and I was about to step from one field of
reality to another.

I stood there with my heart pounding and my body sweating. I was
unable to continue onward. Looking around, I saw nothing unusual—
only a dirty brick building and a man curled up in the doorway. I
didn't recognize him at first. In fact, it took me a few moments to
figure out why I even stopped.

I never would have known him by the long, salt-and-pepper hair
and scraggly beard. The torn gold polyester shirt and dirty brown pants
were unfamiliar to me. I had never seen the ripped shoes and green
military overcoat he had rolled himself in to keep warm.

The gold ring had caught my attention. His hand clung to the coat he was using as a blanket. The sunlight caused the ring to flash just as I walked by. How well I remembered that gold signet ring. I had seen it daily as a child.

Slowly, I realized the man sleeping in the doorway was my father. *My dad.* As I looked at this man whose ears and neck were covered with lice, memories of a handsome, charming man came flooding back. I remembered how much he was sought after as a dance partner at elite country club dances. I recalled how important it was for him to be immaculate, clean-shaven, and fashionably dressed.

It was as though a movie of my life passed in front of my eyes. I remembered the many parties; heard people laughing, drinking, and pretending. I also recalled the violent fights at the dinner table, night after night. The incest. The sarcasm. My parents' divorce. I remembered the good times. I saw Dad as we found the golden Easter egg at the club. The poem we wrote that won the honor of being published. Dad's remarriage. The private school. I saw the treatment center and felt the hope of recovery. It all flashed before me.

I stood there, grief-stricken and ashamed as the memories of yesterday came flooding back. I felt again the humiliation and embarrassment I had felt for so long. Angrily I asked, "Why, God, why my family? What's the purpose of all this? Why was my family hit so hard with alcoholism, drugs, and abuse? Why?"

I stood there, looking at my father, with tears running down my face. The depth of pain seemed unbearable, and yet it was in this moment that I surrendered. I began to experience the most freeing and healing moment of my life.

I began to understand. Before me was an eloquent expression of a life that had rediscovered its own soul. I believe we each choose our journey and discover what life is about in our own way. Others cannot do that for us.

I had spent years analyzing, criticizing, judging, and condemning my father. I had focused on trying to change him.

In that moment of truth, I began to understand that it was I who needed to change. I needed to move from holding on to letting go. I needed to move from judgment to compassion. I needed to honor his path of discovery. I needed to see both of us differently.

My father is one of the most talented and creative men I have ever known. His pathway of self-discovery was alcoholism, abuse, and, now, living on the street.

In that moment, I asked myself if I was willing to acknowledge my God-given creative talents and step boldly into my greatness. Or was I going to let bad habits, alcohol, and fear of others' opinions rob me of my dreams.

Although I was badly shaken, I continued to look at the gifted man curled up in the doorway. I realized it is not about right or wrong, should and should not. We each choose our response to life's challenges and learn what we learn.

I took one last look at my father lying in the doorway, wiped my tears, and whispered to myself, "Thanks, Dad, for teaching me about compassion."

JODY MILLER STEVENSON

He Loves Me, He Loves Me Not?

Ave never tells me he loves me. Sometimes I don't think he even cares," my good friend Bonnie told me over lunch.

Knowing the couple well, I told her, "Bonnie, he really adores you. It's obvious."

"You really think so? After twenty-seven years of marriage, things aren't like they were the first year or two."

"I know how you feel, but why don't you try something?" I asked. "When you get home, start looking for evidence that he adores you instead of evidence to prove he doesn't. Just for twenty-four hours. OK?" Bonnie was quick to agree.

Bonnie phoned me the next day. "Your idea worked," she almost shouted. "When I got home, Dave asked, 'How was your lunch?' I thought to myself: He wants to know because he adores me. When he called me to come see the sunset, I thought: He's doing this because he adores me. In the middle of the night, I woke up and couldn't get back to sleep. Dave asked if anything was wrong and started rubbing my back.

"Some funny things started to happen. First, I noticed what a great guy he was. How else are you going to feel toward someone who adores you? And *then*, a little later, when he was grumpy, I thought: He's grumpy, but that's all right, because I know he adores me."

"Good for you," I said.

"Wait. There's more. I began to feel differently about myself too. I'm not such a bad person. In fact, I'm adorable." She giggled.

Bonnie learned she had the power to alter her perceptions. She could have gone home to the same old marriage, with her same old attitude, and things would have looked the same old way. Because she would have been looking to confirm he didn't love her, Bonnie would have missed all the love that was there.

Once, Bonnie used to ask, "Does he love me? Or does he love me not?" Now she is amazed to discover all the creative ways her husband finds to give her the answer that was there all along: "He loves me."

CHRISTINE B. EVANS

"When we dim our light, we invite mediocrity."

—Kris King

What Do You Want to Do with the Rest of Your Life?

ᴊᴾ

I'LL NEVER FORGET MY COLLEGE GUIDANCE COUN-
selor, Cathy Martin. I met her when I transferred to Northwestern
University as a sophomore.

Cathy invited me into her office and asked, "What do you want
to do?"

I thought I was ready to respond boldly to the question. Proudly I
announced, "I want to be in broadcasting."

Cathy seemed unimpressed by my declaration. She asked, "What,
specifically, do you want to do in broadcasting?"

"I'll do anything."

"So will a lot of other people," she said sharply. "Broadcasting is a
very competitive field. You need to know exactly what you want to do
in order to succeed. You need to decide right here and now what it is
you want to do."

I looked Cathy squarely in the eyes and stated with conviction, "I
want to be a television news anchor and reporter."

She smiled. "Good," she said. "Now you know what you want to do. When you leave here, you tell everyone who you know what you want to do with your life—that you want to be a TV anchor and reporter. And on those days when you're feeling uncertain, you share that uncertainty with your family, with your friends, with me. But as to the rest of the world, you address them with certainty in all that you do."

I walked out of Cathy Martin's office. I had direction. I had a mission—to become a broadcast journalist *extraordinaire*. In December 1973, I graduated half a year early, to get a jump on the June graduates. Within several months, after countless rejections, I got that first job as a TV reporter. In fact, I was almost the first, as well as the youngest, female coanchor in the United States at the time. I went on to become a coast-to-coast TV news reporter, anchor, and talk show host.

When it came time for me to move on in my career, I thought back to how Cathy Martin motivated me to set a goal, to become all that I can be, to achieve my dream. I decided to take my broadcasting background and become a trainer and motivational speaker, sharing my secrets on how to make better presentations and enhance one's image, thus helping people to get the results they want by winning every audience. In essence, I became a coach. Once again, Cathy Martin's wisdom allowed me to achieve what I wanted to do. It all happened to me! Pushing through our fears and self-doubt can be a prolonged process or a simple decision. Cathy Martin taught me to decide—and to go for it.

Not long ago, a woman named Carol came to see me, seeking advice about the direction of her career. As I searched my mind for what would be most helpful to her at this important time in her life, Cathy Martin's words came flooding back.

"What do you want to do?" I asked her. Carol was ready to respond to the question. Proudly she told me, "I want to give talks to groups."

Acting unimpressed by her declaration, I asked, "What, specifically, do you want to speak about?"

"I'll speak on most anything uplifting."

"So will a lot of other people," I said sharply. "Speaking is a very competitive field. You need to know exactly what you want to speak about in order to succeed. You need to decide right here and now what it is you want to do."

Carol looked squarely in my eyes and stated with conviction, "I want to validate people's pain and make them feel better. I want people to love themselves and go for their dreams. I want to be a professional speaker giving talks on self-esteem."

I smiled. "Good," I said. "Now you know what you want to do. When you leave here, you tell everyone who you know what you want to do with your life—that you want to be a professional speaker who gives talks on self-esteem. And on those days when you're feeling uncertain, you share that uncertainty with your family, with your friends, with me. But as to the rest of the world, you address them with certainty in all that you do."

Carol left our meeting full of determination and confidence. Four years later, I learned she had become a sought-after professional speaker on self-esteem.

I can't help but wonder when she will pass on the invaluable advice my guidance counselor so generously shared with me so many years ago.

LINDA BLACKMAN

"Official" Hugs

❧

ONE SUNDAY I PASSED HUG CARDS OUT TO THE CON-
gregation. It may sound corny, but each of the Hug Cards reads: "Good
for One Free Hug." While people laughed and made light of them, I
witnessed person after person becoming softer and enjoying the process
of giving to one another.

A shy Sunday-school teacher in the church works for the Internal
Revenue Service. I've always pictured an IRS office as bureaucratic,
gloomy, and cold, with mounds of paperwork. She noticed how all the
hugging we did at church was good for us. When growing up, she was
taught to be a private person. Years ago, if anyone had tried to hug
her at church, she would have burst into tears of vulnerability and
embarrassment. Not so today.

She wondered what would happen if she gave out Hug Cards at the
IRS. On her birthday, she took in a whole stack of the "Good for One
Free Hug" cards to work. After she had passed the cards around to each
office, amazing things began to happen. People she recognized but had
never met came from floors above and below her to ask if she was the
lady who was giving out birthday hugs. A certain Bill even wanted to
know if there was an expiration date!

Two years after the Hug Cards were introduced, a part-time employee returned to work for the new tax season. And she was carrying
her Hug Card! She said she had brought it along on her first day so she
could be welcomed back to the office with a hug. Another employee,
who was transferring to Colorado Springs, had saved his Hug Card,
and he produced it on his last day to collect hugs from his IRS friends.

Bill, who had been especially enthusiastic about the card, later contracted cancer. When he retired early, not one person was embarrassed to give him a hug before he left.

It may be unusual to associate hugs with the IRS. Yet one person who was willing to take a risk clearly made a difference. People began thinking of themselves and of others differently. "Official IRS Hugs" became commonplace in her office.

Just think how our world would improve if we were all willing to hand out Hug Cards with no expiration dates and no conditions. The ripple effect of a hug would be much greater and last longer than an IRS refund check!

REV. MARY OMWAKE

XXI

Tenderness and Compassion

❧

"To keep a lamp burning, we have to keep putting oil in it."

—Mother Teresa

"We are not held back by the love we didn't receive in the past, but by the love we're not extending in the present."

—Marianne Williamson

Breaking Free

જ્જી

WHEN THEY CALLED MY NAME TO DISEMBARK AT THE Women's Federal Correctional Institute in Lexington, Kentucky, I was devastated.

The federal marshals grinned. Knowing I had believed I was being transferred from a maximum-security prison in California to a minimum-security camp in Bryan, Texas, they had purposely waited to call my name last. As I struggled down the steel steps of the aircraft in my shackles, my throat tightened, and I lost my voice. I couldn't blame the marshals—to them, I was just another inmate, a convicted felon.

Under armed guard, the other prisoners and I were led to a bus whose windows were caged over in chicken wire. It was April, but there was still a bite to the Kentucky air. I shivered, but only partly because of the cold. I knew Lexington was the most violent women's prison in the system. My mind remained stuck on one thought: Why, God? Why have you dropped me out of the palm of your hand?

I'd been in prison eight months. Following the pattern of most survivors of long-term sexual and physical abuse, I didn't know how to say no to my father when he asked me to commit fraud. I was convicted; he was not. I pleaded guilty and was given the maximum sentence allowed for my offense—twenty-one months.

When I had begun my prison sentence, I soon realized that the violence, the chaos, and the hypervigilance I was witnessing were simply reflections of what I had experienced throughout my childhood. I knew my life had to change. I asked for and was sent books of Truth, and I began writing affirmations. When I heard the voice of my father in my mind saying, *You are a nothing,* I replaced it with the voice of God saying, *You are my beloved child.* I wrote affirmations that didn't feel true but held the vision of what I knew to be true: that God loved me unconditionally and that I was a worthwhile person. Over and over, day after day, I began changing my life, thought by thought.

Arriving at FCI Lexington, I entered the dark night of my soul. I felt betrayed and frightened. What was the point of praying and affirming if I ended up in a worse situation than before? As the bus approached the gates of the prison, the twelve-foot double fences with razor wire on top were hints of what I would find inside the walls. I tried to pray. I really did. But all I felt was an immense sadness that once again, no matter what I did, nothing worked.

The guard who handled my paperwork commented, "You're here on an Infraction 313." I kept my head down, still not finding my voice. When I was strip searched and given my new uniform and bedroll, I was also handed a booklet of the rules and regulations of FCI Lexington. Quickly I turned to the back of the booklet, looking for the infraction numbered 313: "Lying or providing a false statement to a staff member." My heart began to pound even louder, for I knew I had been transferred for something I did not do. Once again, I felt trapped in a situation where I was powerless to convince others of the truth. After all, I knew there were only two rules between the guards and the inmates: one, inmates never trusted a guard, and two, guards never believed the word of an inmate.

As the women were led to their respective housing units, I noticed the units all had names reflecting the Kentucky outside the walls, such as "Bluegrass." One by one or in groups, all the inmates were turned over to the guards in the housing units, until finally there was just me. The guard led me to an elevator in the main unit, which housed the cafeteria and the commissary. I could not believe the huge number of women gathered both in the yard and in the unit. They pressed against each other and me. Many looked me over, some called and whistled to me. It was not friendly. The guard would not allow any other inmate in the elevator with the two of us, and for a brief moment I caught his eyes in fright. Would he hurt me? No, he just looked away. He gently pushed me off the elevator on the third floor, where he rapped loudly on a steel door. A guard came to let us in, and I marveled at the smallness of the unit. I saw only two women, and they were in wheelchairs. Where was I? The guard assigned me a room upstairs. I still had not spoken. I met several women on the stairs and heard the television blaring in the television room. I felt panic building inside, and only one thought sustained me as I climbed the stairs: "Get Gary on the phone."

My husband, Gary, had stood by me throughout the ordeal, totally supporting me in my recovery. He always believed in me, and in his eyes I was guilt-free. Instead of concentrating on my incarceration, Gary's letters and phone calls focused on the day I would come home to Kansas. He was my only link to the outside. Before I left California, I had called him with the good news that I was being transferred to Bryan, Texas. We were both excited, as we'd been able to see each other only once during my incarceration. In Texas, we could have regular visits.

There were five women and five iron beds in the room I was taken to. Dumping my gear on the one unmade bed, I turned to the woman in the bed closest to me and found my voice. "Where's the phone?" I demanded. She told me it was downstairs by the guard station. I left my gear on the bed and went back down the stairs, to wait an hour and a half for my fifteen-minute phone privilege. By the time Gary answered the phone, I was at a breaking point, and for the first time in almost a year, I cried. "I'm in Lexington, Gary!" I wailed. "And I think I'm going to die here!"

Gary had heard my stories of Lexington, passed on by inmates who were lucky enough to get transferred out. When he heard my voice, he began to cry too. He told me later he had never felt so helpless. I was in the hands of the federal prison system. "Don't cry, baby," Gary pleaded. "I can't do anything for you, but I can write to you. Look around and tell me the name of your unit, and I'll write to you tonight." Drying my tears, for I would not let another inmate see me cry, I stuck my head out of the phone booth and looked for a sign, such as "Bluegrass." Then I saw it. There, above the guard's station, was a simple sign that read: WELCOME TO RENAISSANCE. Slowly I began to smile, and I felt a warm rush of peace flow through me. I knew that no matter what the appearances, I was right where I was supposed to be. The "coincidence" of my unit being named Renaissance was a simple, clear reminder to me that I was still and always will be in the palm of God's hand. I was fine; I simply had more to learn. "Gary," I whispered, "it's OK. I'm going to be all right. The name of my unit is Renaissance—'Rebirth.' " I almost cried again, in joy. Gary calmed down somewhat in response to my voice, but our time was up, so I couldn't reassure him further. That would have to come later.

As I made my way back up the stairs, I knew God had not forgotten me, nor was I truly in the hands of the Federal Bureau of Prisons. I was right where I was supposed to be. I was safe. But suddenly I tensed. I realized I had breached an important rule in prison: I had been rude to my cellmates by not introducing myself to them before demanding the location of the telephone. Politeness and manners carry a very high priority in prison; with so many people crowded together, even a perceived lack of respect has an extreme price. I wondered if I would be facing my first fight at Lexington very soon.

As I stepped into the room, I noticed that someone had made my bed and that my clothes were missing. I looked at the woman in the bed next to mine. I should have known. When you have so little, even an extra pair of pants or a T-shirt has great appeal. I assumed the bed was made as an exchange for the clothes. I sighed and opened my locker, just to stall the moment of confrontation. I knew I would have to fight for my clothes.

But instead of an empty locker, what I found were my clothes neatly hung up, as well as a supply of toothpaste, deodorant, shampoo, and even lotion. The women in the room, who had so little themselves, had shared with me, who had even less. I bowed my head and smiled. I was more than safe; I was blessed. As I later learned, Renaissance is a medical unit for older and infirm inmates. Why I was sent there is still a mystery, since I was neither ill nor elderly. But I was safe. And that 313 infraction? The guard was mistaken. I had been transferred to be "closer to home." The Lexington facility wasn't as close to my home in Kansas as Bryan, Texas, would have been, but it was still a major improvement over California.

I introduced myself to the women in the room and thanked them for their generosity. None of them would admit to having given me anything. After taking a shower, I pulled back my sheets to get into bed and noticed one more act of kindness. One of the ladies had taken the time to baby-powder the sheets, making them silky instead of stiff and scratchy. I felt an overwhelming love build inside me and I thought: God, my God, you love me enough to have someone baby-powder my sheets.

I served the next five months in Lexington and was transferred to a halfway house in Kansas City to complete my sentence. I continued to study inspirational teachings and affirm the goodness I saw in myself and others.

When I finally came home, I asked Gary, "Do you see the changes, the life changes, I have made since I entered prison?" He responded, "No, what I see is the person I saw and knew to be there all along."

BARBARA ROGOFF

Grace

CHANGING THE WAY WE PERCEIVE INCIDENTS IN OUR life can change the way we respond to them.

A few years ago, I decided to add a ten percent grace factor in my life, and it has resulted in tremendous changes, all positive.

Assume a ten percent grace factor in your life:

Assume you'll pay ten percent more than your share of a dinner check shared with friends. Grace in your friendships is certainly worth that.

Assume that the bargain you got will cost ten percent less somewhere else tomorrow. Grace reduces stress.

Assume that you'll get cheated about ten percent of the time and that you'll lose about ten percent of your property one way or another. It costs to add grace to your life. It's worth it.

When you travel in another culture, assume a twenty percent grace factor. Then if you feel cheated by a taxi driver or someone else, it won't ruin more than a few minutes of your trip. Traveling in other countries requires grace.

Public grace will, in private, reduce tension, improve your perception of the world, improve your relationships, and increase your joy.

You'll end up with more of everything.

JENNIFER JAMES

Dedicated to Nealy

***

I REMEMBER THE DAY WE WERE DRIVING THE HOUR'S distance down our country road, back from town and a day of errands. It was just my son, Alec, and I. We made small talk for a short time, then he leaned his head against the side window and rested. He was fourteen years old, and conversations with Mom no longer came easily.

Some time later, he startled me by breaking the silence. "Mom," he said, "I tried to pull her out of the way of the car, but I couldn't reach her in time."

My God, I thought, he still feels responsible for her death. "I know, Alec," I said. "It's not your fault."

He was referring to the night nine years earlier when Bill and I were out for dinner and the kids were home with a sitter. They were playing outside, and our two-year-old daughter was struck by a car near the house. Alec was closest to her and tenderly scooped her lifeless body into his arms, willing her to live. He held her for some time, but it did no good. The sitter called for help. In the panic and confusion, Alec's grandmother hastily yelled at him, "Why didn't you get her out of the way?" He just couldn't *think* why he hadn't gotten her out of the way.

The whole family did a lot of grieving and counseling. Alec and I hadn't spoken of her in a long time. I assumed that after all this time, he had worked it through.

Now I realized that no amount of "It's not your fault" comments from me or the counselor had relieved Alec's mind. Oh, God, I thought, I cannot face her death again. The pain is too deep. And yet here's Alec sitting across from me, still filled with guilt and self-blame. His pain is still living and breathing in his mind, eating away at his heart. He had taken on the responsibility for a tragic accident that was not his fault. I didn't know what I was going to do, but I made the commitment to do *something*.

The next morning, my conversation with Alec was still fresh in my mind as we drove by our local grade school. Suddenly I got an idea. I asked Alec to go with me into the kindergarten classroom, to observe for a while. He couldn't figure out why I wanted him to come with me.

"So we can learn about responsibility," I said.

When we walked into the room, the kids were busy painting, coloring, and pasting.

I noticed Alec's expression when we walked into the room. His look seemed to say, "I'm a fourteen-year-old guy . . . what am I doing here?" Very quickly, however, I noticed his eyes soften, and he began to take notice and delight in the kids' laughter and innocence.

Easing into the conversation, I said, "Alec, would you ask that little girl over there to help you with your homework?"

"No, Mom. She's just a kid," he replied.

"Well, maybe we should ask Tommy over there to run to the store for us. I'm starved."

"Come on, Mom," he said. "He's not old enough to do that."

"Well, if one of the children in this room had an accident and was dying, would you expect that another child could prevent the child's death?" I asked.

"Mom, a kid can't do that," Alec said without thinking.

"Alec, you were five years old when Nealy had a horrible accident. I know that you were in no way responsible for that accident, and no one, not even you, could have saved her. What's more important is that you now know that too."

Alec looked at me for a time without saying a word. The realization of what he had just learned for himself was sinking in: he was not responsible for Nealy's death. A new kind of peace washed over my precious young man.

SUSAN P.

Hot Dog! Thou Art!

ᴊᴘ

I WAS EIGHTEEN YEARS OLD, AND I WAS THE GOLDEN girl. A junior in college, I was president of the college drama society, a member of the student senate, winner of two off-Broadway critics' awards for acting and directing, and director of the class play. In class, my mind raced and dazzled as I tossed off quick answers in class and impressed my teachers and fellow students. Socially, I was on the top of the heap. My advice was sought, my phone rang constantly, and it seemed that nothing could stop me.

I was the envy of all my friends, and I was in a state of galloping chutzpah.

The old Greek tragedies warn us that when hubris rises, nemesis falls. I was no exception to this ancient rule. My universe crashed with great suddenness. It began when three members of my immediate family died. Then a friend whom I loved very much died suddenly of a burst appendix while camping alone in the woods. The scenery of the off-Broadway production fell on my head, and I was left almost blind for the next four months. My friends and I parted from each other, they out of embarrassment and I because I didn't think I was worthy. My marks went from being rather good to a D-plus average.

I had so lost confidence in my abilities that I couldn't concentrate on anything or see the connections between things. My memory was a shambles, and within a few months I was placed on probation. All my offices were taken away; public elections were called to fill them. I was asked into the adviser's office and told that I would have to leave the college at the end of the spring term, since clearly I didn't have the "necessary intelligence to do academic work." When I protested that I had had the "necessary intelligence" during my freshman and sophomore years, I was assured with a sympathetic smile that intellectual decline such as this often happened to young women when "they became interested in other things; it's a matter of hormones, my dear."

Where once I had been vocal and high-spirited in the classroom, I now huddled in my oversize camel's-hair coat in the back of classes, trying to be as nonexistent as possible. At lunch I would lock myself in the green room of the college theater, scene of my former triumphs, eating a sandwich in despondent isolation. Every day brought its defeats and disacknowledgments, and after my previous career I was too proud to ask for help. I felt like Job and called out to God, "Where are the boils?" since that was about all I was missing. These Jobian fulminations led me to take one last course. It was taught by a young Swiss professor of religion, Dr. Jacob Taubes, and was supposed to be a study of selected books of the Old Testament. It turned out to be largely a discussion of the dialectic between Saint Paul and Nietzsche.

Taubes was the most brilliant and exciting teacher in my experience, displaying European academic wizardry such as I had never known. Hegel, gnosticism, structuralism, phenomenology, and the intellectual passions of the Sorbonne cracked the ice of my self-doubting, and I began to raise a tentative hand from my huddle in the back of the room and ask an occasional hesitant question. Dr. Taubes would answer with great intensity, and soon I found myself asking more questions.

One day I was making my way across campus to the bus, when I heard Dr. Taubes addressing me: "Miss Houston, let me walk with you. You know, you have a most interesting mind."

"Me? I have a *mind*?"

"Yes, your questions are luminous. Now, what do you think is the nature of the transvaluation of values in Paul and Nietzsche?"

I felt my mind fall into its usual painful dullness and stammered, "I d-don't know."

"Of course you do!" he insisted. "You couldn't ask the kinds of questions you do without having an unusual grasp of these issues. Now, please, once again, what do you think of the transvaluation of values in Paul and Nietzsche? It is important for my reflections that I have your reflections."

"Well," I said, waking up, "if you put it that way, I think . . ."

I was off and running, and I haven't shut up since.

Dr. Taubes continued to walk me to the bus throughout that term, always challenging me with intellectually vigorous questions. He attended to me. I existed for him in the "realest" of senses, and because I existed for him, I began to exist for myself. Within several weeks, my eyesight came back, my spirit bloomed, and I became a fairly serious student, whereas before I had been, at best, a bright show-off.

Dr. Taubes acknowledged me when I most needed it. I was empowered in the midst of personal erosion, and my life has been very different for it. I swore to myself then that whenever I came across someone "going under" or in the throes of disacknowledgment, I would try to reach and acknowledge that person as I had been acknowledged.

I would go so far as to say that the greatest of human potentials is the potential of each one of us to empower and acknowledge the other. We all do this throughout our lives, but rarely do we appreciate the power of empowering others. This gift can be as simple as "Hot dog! Thou art!" Or it can be as total as "I know you. You are God in hiding." Or it can be a look that goes straight to the soul and charges it with meaning.

I've been fortunate to have known several of those the world deems "saints": Teilhard de Chardin, Mother Teresa of Calcutta, Clemmie, an old black woman in Mississippi. To be looked at by these people is to be gifted with the look that engenders. You feel yourself primed at the depths by such seeing. Something so tremendous and yet so subtle wakes up inside that you are able to release the defeats and denigrations of years. If I were to describe it further, I would have to speak of unconditional love joined to a whimsical regarding of you as the cluttered house that hides the holy one.

Saints, you say, but the miracle is that anybody can do it for anybody! Our greatest genius may be the ability to prime the healing and evolutionary circuits of one another.

JEAN HOUSTON

Ritual: a tradition, a time-honored practice; a rite.

Tootsie Roll Ritual

RITUALS ARE A WONDERFUL WAY TO CONNECT WITH those I love. Meaningful rituals provide predictability, stability, and roots.

My favorite childhood ritual occurred at my grandfather's house. As a young girl, I would get to Grandpa's farmhouse, scramble out of the car, throw open the front door, and race, as fast as my little legs would carry me, to the pantry at the back of the house. There I would wait excitedly. Tall and lanky Grandpa Schulte, always dressed in his striped bib overalls, would slowly and silently stroll to the pantry as well. He'd reach high up on a shelf, take down the "magic" box, and, with a big smile, stoop down to my level. I would reach in and grab as many Tootsie Rolls as my little fists could hold. This unconditional offering was symbolic to someone growing up in a house with five brothers. Everything in my life seemed to have limits. Grandpa's Tootsie Rolls were an exception.

Dad often remembered the wonderful relationship he had with his grandfather. He remembered how he had watched me run to his father to collect fistfuls of Tootsie Rolls. Now that I was grown and married, he longed to be the revered grandpa, handing out the Tootsie Rolls.

When I became pregnant with my first child, I carefully wrapped a package to send to my dad. I lovingly placed it in the mail.

I was told my father wept with surprise and joy when he opened the package. It contained a box stuffed with Tootsie Rolls.

MARY LoVERDE

"Imagination is the highest kite one can fly."

—Lauren Bacall

Waste Not, Want Not

ﾉﾉﾉ

ONE YEAR IN THE LATE FIFTIES, MAMA CROCHETED OUR Christmas—neck scarves, berets, and mittens. We raised Angora rabbits in chicken-wire cages kept in the garage; from their fur Mama made our gifts.

I remember the Saturday a large package arrived from Sears Roebuck. It was a spinning wheel. While the five of us kids listened to our favorite radio shows—the Nelsons, the Green Hornet, the Lone Ranger —Mama spun the fur into thread.

"Just imagine how warm the angora will keep the children this winter," she said to Papa.

"The way you dress them, I'm afraid they'll die of *underexposure*. You haven't let them build up a lick of resistance," Papa said, teasing.

Parents of the fifties suffered two world wars, a depression, and Korea. They were frugal and conservative and squandered little. "Charity begins at home" was a slogan, as was "Waste not, want not." I remember Mama always borrowing from Peter to pay Paul. It was a long time before I knew who those fellows were.

When Mama died this past June, I found myself drawn into a tunnel of childhood remembrances. Strange things surfaced, like the taste of the Denver mud Mama applied to my chest when I had a cold. She heated the mud in the lid on the burner, then spread it on my chest. To ward off the evil spirits of virus and bacteria, she made us take cod-liver oil potions. Our lips were greasy with fish lard and our breath smelled like seafood for hours.

We saved money every way possible, which meant that Mama acted as our nurse and our doctor. In a past life, I think she was a medicine woman, a shaman, or a witch. She had a cauldron of remedies. Papa worked out of town, inspecting power lines. The pay was poor, but both he and Mama wanted us to have nice things like other kids. They did the best they knew how, cutting corners and skimping on things.

One Monday, the year after we received our neck scarves and mittens, I found Mama staring and twisting her thumbs as she sat in the old pink rocker.

"What's wrong, Mama? "

"Just worried about Christmas. There's no extra money for gifts, I'm afraid."

Traditionally on Monday nights we gathered around Mama and Papa's bed and prayed the rosary. Mama suggested we ask for God's help. We gathered in the bedroom, gripping our rosary beads. "A family that prays together stays together," she said.

It didn't seem like our prayers were heard, for the next day our Philco upright radio went on the blink. Now we wouldn't be able to listen to our shows. Most of the neighbors had black-and-white televisions, but it would be another two years before Papa would buy us a little portable TV. We sat around at night playing blackjack, Monopoly, and Chinese checkers. Sometimes we fought, accusing each other of cheating. All of us were edgy about Christmas, but I've always had a lot of faith and truly believed in the power of prayer. I held tight to the image of a magical Christmas morning—everyone would have gifts.

On the weekends, Papa came home, and he and Mama held conferences. When they weren't conferring, Papa was in the garage, tinkering. I knew he could do some things well, but often his ideas were less than professional. Once, installing a light switch in the kitchen, he put the box on the outside of the wall instead of the inside. Another time, he invented an automatic dog feeder, which he wanted to patent. Dog food rotated on conveyor belts. I never understood the point. On the patio we had an old car-seat chair with pipes for legs—Papa's idea of constructing furniture.

From Friday night, when he came home from work, until Sunday afternoon, when he left, he was in his shop. This went on for weeks. We were all curious. The clock ticked: Christmas is coming—Christmas is coming. Then finally it came.

I was the first one up. We'd decorated the tree the night before, with tinsel, glass balls, and bubble lamps. I plugged the lights in and lay on my stomach, looking at the few gifts that were under the tree. I'd been saving my allowance and had a package of razor blades wrapped for Papa and some stockings for Mama. I gave my brothers marbles— bought one sack and divvied them up. My sister would get a new headband. I felt good about having gifts for everyone. While I counted packages, my sister slipped into the room.

"What's that?" she said, rubbing her eyes.

"What's what?" I asked.

"That," she said, pointing to a huge *something* in the corner of the living room, covered with a sheet.

"I don't know," I said.

At the unveiling. my sister and I gasped. Under the sheet was the most beautiful dressing table and stool we had ever seen. An antique mirror was attached to the back. It had cubbies for our barrettes and bobby pins, and there was even a drawer in the stool. We were thrilled. This is what Papa had been doing in the garage. In a strange way, I felt I knew this piece of furniture, that it belonged. The boys had homemade toolboxes and their own sets of tools from Papa's spares. Mama had a new coffee table, the top made from old black and white ceramic tile that had been stored in the garage.

All day, my sister and I took turns sitting at the dressing table, putting on lipstick and earrings and brushing each other's hair. I remember running my hand along the smooth polished wood, almost embracing it. This was the best gift ever—an answer to my prayers for a magical Christmas. When my sister dropped a bobby pin, I bent over to pick it up and noticed some gold writing on the side of the dressing table. It read *Philco*.

LINDA ROSS SWANSON

Intensive Caring

As a critical care nurse, I knew from years of experience that the scene before me was not a hopeful one. There was no movement, no audible breath sounds. IV poles surrounded him like so many pencil-thin trees, offering their various fluids in hope of sustaining life. I read his chart and noted that he was no longer responding to the efforts of medicine. Now, as he lay here in the ICU, it was only a matter of time until his body was put to rest.

Slowly, I walked around the bed. I was somewhat preoccupied with my thoughts about the finality of life, medicine, life supports, and dying. I methodically labeled all the IV tubes, so that I knew which bottle led to which arm with what medication. Deep in thought, I barely heard her walk in. She gave no sign that she even saw me as she quickly walked to the bedside, leaned over, and smoothed the man's hair. I immediately felt like an intruder in a very private relationship.

"Any change?" She smiled as she asked, not looking at me but keeping her gaze on the man.

"I wish I could say yes." I watched as she took one of his hands and eased herself down in the chair next to him, never abandoning her vigilance on his unresponsive face.

"How long has it been since you were able to hold each other?" I had to ask. Her longing was so great that my question seemed not intrusive but necessary.

"Too long," she said, tears following the familiar path down her face. "It was so sudden. His heart . . ." Her sobs ended the sentence as she moved even closer to the bed.

"Would you like to hold him? Would you like to gather him into your arms and cuddle? Is your relationship close like that?"

For the first time, she looked at me. Curious, hopeful, and self-conscious. A sob escaped with her answer. "Yes, I would love to hold him."

I quickly moved to the bedside, arranged tubes, bags, and machines, then motioned to her. Hesitantly she came to my side, and then she slipped cautiously into the small bed beside her husband.

Then I became self-conscious, an uninvited witness to their intimacy. I quickly turned my back and pulled the curtains partway around the small cubicle, enclosing them in a private space.

As I busied myself with nursing duties, I could hear her murmuring sweet nothings, reassuring him, reassuring herself, and unknowingly reassuring me. I turned to readjust an IV drip and caught a glimpse of her running her fingertips gently down his cheek, then softly kissing him.

I didn't try to hide my tears as I helped her out of the bed and held her close. "I miss him so much," she whispered. "I've wanted to hold him for so long that I ache. We have always cuddled and been close. I *knew* he wanted to hold me one more time too. . . . Thank you."

Not long after, while she sat holding his hand, his spirit left to go on its journey.

Once more, I held her.

PATTY ROSEN

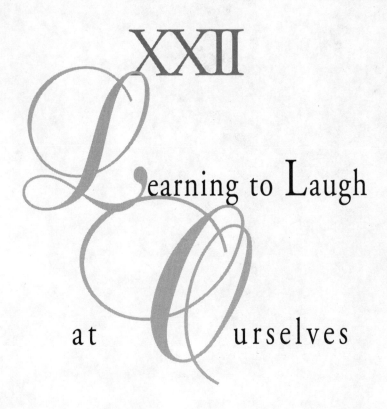

XXII

Learning to Laugh at Ourselves

ᒐᑭ

"Don't get your knickers in a knot.
Nothing is solved,
and it just makes you walk funny."

—Kathryn Carpenter

The Last of the Big, Big Spenders

ɔʃʃ

FIVE DOLLARS AND FIFTY-NINE CENTS. . . .

"Ma'am! That will be five dollars and fifty-nine cents," said the young thing with the big hair standing behind the cash register at McDonald's. She tapped her chrome-plated, inch-long nails on the counter in annoyance. She was the perfect counterpart to the foil message draped behind her: "Joy to the World! Happy Holidays!"

I dug through my purse. I hadn't intended to stop here for dinner, but my five-year-old son had insisted.

"Let's see, five and fifty, five and fifty-five, five and fifty-eight . . ." I held my palm out to her, imploringly. From behind me, a man tossed a penny onto the counter.

Alms for the poor? Hey, OK. Anything to speed the process along.

Balancing the tray on one hand, I navigated to the table already staked out by my son. With the ease of a veteran McDonald's habitué, he opened the box, located the holiday-theme toy, and began to munch his way through thousands of calories' worth of greasy, salty french fries. Two fistfuls later, he nonchalantly wiped his hand down the front of his clothes and announced, "I gotta go to the bathroom." Hence the name "fast food."

But today I didn't worry about the effects of fast food on my son's digestive system. Today I was on Cloud Nine, because the night before, I had hosted the perfect Christmas party. I moved through McDonald's in dreamy reminiscence of the triumph I had enjoyed just last evening. Last night I had done the impossible, the suburban wife's Olympian feat: the flawless, Martha Stewart, eat-your-heart-out Christmas party.

"You realize we must show our new members the heights to which they can aspire," Myrtle, the hospitality committee chair, had said to me in early November. "Seeing a veteran member who has, well, *made it* gives them added commitment to our organization." She had paused to sniff delicately, then added in a whisper, "I am sure they will be very, very impressed by your . . . hospitality."

And they were. By December 15, the house was spotless, dressed in its holiday finest. By sheer force of will, and great planning, I had even managed to groom myself to the max before the first dinging of the Westminster chimes from the doorbell.

Usually, my modus operandi consists of sliding through the foyer and snatching frantically at the door, while pulling up sagging panty hose with my spare hand. Halfway through past galas, I would manage to sneak away and reappear with makeup, a trick that always causes the heavy drinkers to cut back.

But not last night. Last night I appeared before the first guest as the hostess with the mostest, immaculately dressed, cool, and calm. Last night was snooty, snobby perfection.

I tossed the tray contents into the trash receptacle and steered Michael to the john. As he dried his hands under the blow dryer, he turned to me and said, "I can't wait to go back and finish my food. I'm really, really hungry."

Oops! The food was in the garbage. Michael began to howl.

"I'm hungry! I'm starving! And my toy is gone too. *Aaauuuuuhhh!*" He raised his voice several decibels.

"Well . . . I don't have any money," I said quietly and desperately.

He howled, "Get me my *foooood!*"

I made an executive decision. I reached into the trash. Fishing around frantically, I pulled up a half-eaten burger, a handful of lettuce, and a Happy Meal box. I peered inside. Yep, it was his. I turned to hand it to him and looked up into the face of Myrtle, standing silently beside another genteel woman.

"Goody good," said Michael with glee. "I'm so, so hungry."

Myrtle smiled thinly. Her lipstick was on slightly crooked, I noted with satisfaction as I picked a wilted piece of lettuce off my wrist.

"Oh, Joanna, I was just telling Mrs. Freeman here about your home. It is so . . . so . . ."

"Elegant? Expensive?" I supplied, stuffing the lettuce into the trash.

"Yes . . . oh . . . uh," and Myrtle's gaze shifted to my son and his burger.

The woman beside Myrtle was entranced. Rarely have I seen anyone so stunned. She and Myrtle stood there quietly, waiting for the beads of perspiration to form as I tried to explain my predicament.

I decided to deny them the pleasure.

"Well, my dear departed mama always said that if you look after the pennies, the dollars will take care of themselves. Come along now, Michael. We have other trash cans to explore. Mama is a little hungry herself."

JOANNA SLAN

Coats That Don't Fit

❧

I WAS INVITED TO FLY IN A HELICOPTER TO AN OFF-shore oil rig. I had never been in a helicopter, and I definitely had never been on an offshore oil rig. I tried to control my excitement. I arrived hours early at the Lompoc airport. Eventually about twenty of us were milling around, most of them men who work on the rig. These big, burly guys are called roustabouts.

Our tour guide arrived. Or should I say drill sergeant? He immediately ordered us outside for the weigh-in. Weigh-in? When I signed up, no one had mentioned a weigh-in. The only kind of weigh-in I undergo takes place in the far north corner of my closet, where I have hidden my scale and a flashlight. There, all alone, I turn on the flashlight, zoom the room to make sure there are no spies, weigh myself, and get out of the closet fast. Now, that's my kind of weigh-in.

Hoping not to be noticed, I attached myself to a group of roust-abouts, and we walked outside. When I saw the scale, I knew I was in trouble. It sat in the middle of the runway and had a platform so large we could have all done a rip-roaring square dance on it. The arrow pointing to the pounds was at least six feet tall. Our drill sergeant shouted, "Jack Nife, step up on the scale." Uh-oh. Jack Nife was number one on the sign-in log, I was number four. I had a very short time to figure out how I was going to weigh in without anyone noticing where the arrow landed. That familiar voiced shouted out, "Patsy Dooley, step right up."

Without a moment's hesitation, I jumped up on that scale, grabbed an imaginary mike, and began singing "Let me entertain you, let me see you smile," as I did a fast two-step shuffle across the scale. I jumped off the other side and bowed. From the expressions on their faces, I knew that none of them had paid any attention to that arrow in the sky. Some of them, however, were no doubt reconsidering going on this adventure with me.

The drill sergeant handed us lifesaving-type coats. When I put mine on, I knew right away I had a problem. It didn't fit. After several abortive tries to zip my coat, I decided, "Oh, pooh, I'll just wear it *casual.*" Our drill sergeant began to inspect the troops. When he got to me, he stopped abruptly. "All coats must be zipped and secured before anyone boards this helicopter." He shouted so loud that I was sure everyone on the offshore oil rig knew I was coming—and I was coming with an *unzipped zipper!*

Determination set in, but no amount of scrunching, tugging, pulling, mental imaging, or praying was going to make that coat fit. Finally, I pulled the bottom of the coat up around my neck. I huffed and puffed as I inched the coat down from my shoulders, and engaged the zipper. It was like crawling into a girdle backward! I was so busy, I didn't notice that a group of guys who work the rig had surrounded me. As I manipulated the zipper, they reached up, grabbed the bottom of the coat, and yanked. I was poured into the coat. I could not bend. I could not breathe. Lack of oxygen was causing my brain to become somewhat rattled. My heart, liver, and corpuscles were all busy meeting each other. The guys cheered. I couldn't get a cheer out.

The drill sergeant then announced that tucked up inside the back flap of the jacket was a thing called the "diaper." In case of an emergency, we were to bend over, reach up between our legs, unsnap the "diaper," pull it through our legs, and snap it to the front of our coats. My eyes locked in on the drill sergeant. He must have seen my panic, because a hint of mercy seemed to appear in his eyes. He cleared his throat. "Normally, we practice this maneuver," he bellowed. Then he looked at me. Everyone looked at me. "But I think we'll skip it this trip." Everyone sighed. I could not sigh. I was having this mental picture of my roustabouts, who had formed an emotional responsibility for my well-being, circling me in the water, trying to assist me with my diaper, as we all went down for the third time.

However, thanks to a little help from my friends, all went well that day. It took me a while to see the humor in the situation, but eventually I could look back and laugh as hard as my roustabouts had. What a spectacle I must have been, trying to get into that coat.

Later, as I thought about it, I was able to see an analogy. Changes in our lives usually feel like my lifesaving coat did, tight and uncomfortable. Whether the change is marriage or divorce, a baby or a graduation, a new job or a layoff, it is uncomfortable at first, and we all struggle. Sometimes, however, when the struggle seems especially intense and lonely, God sends "roustabouts." They hug me when I cry. They pick me up when I fall. They cheer as I make changes and congratulate me when I stick to my goals. Each new "coat" has been good for me. I've grown through the struggles and have been blessed because of the roustabouts in my life. Because of them, I can continue to put on coats that don't fit.

PATSY DOOLEY

Fifty Is Nifty

ℐℛ

ON MY FIFTIETH BIRTHDAY, MY OLDER DAUGHTER GAVE me a pin that said: 50 IS NIFTY. I wore it to work that day, and what fun it was! All day, people kept saying things to me like, "Anita, you don't look fifty " or "Why, Anita, you can't be fifty" and "We *know* you can't be fifty."

It was wonderful. Now, I knew they were lying, and they knew I knew, but isn't that what friends and coworkers are for? To lie to you when you need it, in times of emergency, like divorce and death and turning fifty.

You know how it is with a lie, though. You hear it often enough, and you begin to think it's true. By the end of the day, I felt fabulous. I fairly floated home from work. In fact, on the way home, I thought: I really ought to dump my husband. After all, the geezer was fifty-one, way too old for a young-looking gal like me.

Arriving home, I had just shut the front door when the doorbell rang. It was a young girl from a florist shop, bringing birthday flowers from a friend. They were lovely. I stood there holding the flowers and admiring them, and the delivery girl stood there, waiting for a tip.

She noticed the pin on my jacket and said, "Oh, fifty, eh?"

"Yes," I answered, and waited. I could stand one last compliment before my birthday ended.

"Fifty," she repeated. "That's great! Birthday or anniversary?"

ANITA CHEEK MILNER

ℐℛ

> "The way I see it, if you want the rainbow,
> you gotta put up with the rain."
>
> —Dolly Parton

A Wise Old Sage

ON AN EXCEPTIONALLY TRYING SUNDAY EVENING, I HAD been responding to the temperamental mood swings of my son, Eli. Although Eli is thoroughly charming, he is also a typically willful five-year-old. It had clearly been a day of power struggle, as he gave new meaning to the phrase "difficult child." I had bitten the bait far more times than I care to admit.

I've read those books designed to shape the ultimate parent. I have vowed to achieve the totally unnatural responses they advocate. To be the Unpushable-Button Mother has been my goal. For most of that day, it worked.

Perhaps nothing more than my own exhaustion roused me by his bedtime. If I could just get him into bed and make it downstairs, I knew everything would be all right again. I could return to the safety and security of my high-pressured career in the morning—with significant relief!

I can't recall exactly when my brilliant little negotiator finally shoved me over the edge. Maybe it was the request for yet another glass of water. Or just one more book. Or his urgent need to locate a tiny Lego aqua shark he had not played with in over a month. But out it flew, loud and clear: "Eli, *just shut up!*"

I turned in anger, fleeing to the sanctuary of my favorite reading chair in the living room. I was thoroughly beaten and disgusted with myself. With my adrenaline flowing, I was certain there should be laws against people like me becoming a mother! (So *this* is how women lift cars off their children! Or drop them onto them, depending.)

Ten minutes later, as calmness and sadness settled where fear and anger had been, I opened my eyes to find a quiet visitor at my feet. As Eli climbed into my lap, he leaned forward and said gently, "I want to whisper something to you."

Anticipating an endearment, I held him close. "What . . . you . . . said . . . wasn't . . . very . . . nice," he informed me. His tone was paced and deliberate, with a touch of sass that said I'd been nailed.

Welcoming his honesty, I agreed.

"You're right, sweetheart, and I'm sorry. I try *never* to say words like that, because they hurt your feelings. I was feeling angry, tired, and upset, but that's no excuse. Can you forgive me?"

With a nod of his head and a grin, he leaned against me for a five-minute cuddle. I watched him relish his middle-digit "suckie finger" on his left hand. So hard to be five . . . one moment a wise old sage, the next a little babe again. No wonder they're tormented creatures.

Back in his bed, sitting bolt upright with his legs extended in the way only small children can achieve, he glanced at me sideways with his characteristic sparkle.

Experience should have cued me, but I never saw it coming. Eli fluffed his covers onto his lap, smiled his sweetest smile ever, and put our hellish Sunday to bed. "Well, Mama, it's good we had this discussion tonight."

JACQUELINE GILLIS ELLIOTT

Preserving Miz Wells

IF THERE'S ONE THING WE GREEKS LIKE TO DO, IT'S eat. We also like to cook, which is why some ninety percent of Greek immigrants to the United States open restaurants.

My grandmother arrived in Virginia as an immigrant bride in 1900, which meant there was not a single person she could talk to in her city except for her husband. The language barrier created a second, even more desperate, problem. She could not invite other women over for tea so that she might show off her prowess in the kitchen. In desperation, she had six children.

When her second daughter, Connie, began school, Grandmother's chance to invite a guest for food suddenly materialized. Connie had a fight in the second grade with a little boy, and the teacher, Miz Wells (that's the Virginia pronunciation) confronted her. "Well, Connie, just go home and tell your mama I'm coming to see her at four-thirty this afternoon."

Connie rushed home and announced the impending visit. Grandmother received the news with a mixture of joy and terror. Here, at last, was someone she could stuff to death. With two hours' preparation time, she flew into a frenzy. She threw a baklava into the oven, sliced a ham, brought out a wheel of cheese, and dipped thirty olives out of brine into a bowl. This would be for the main serving, which comes after a respectable length of time.

The first serving—the best homemade preserves you have—is presented the moment the guest enters the door. By tradition, the preserves are piled generously into a bowl in show-off fashion, even if only one guest is expected. Along with them come a spoon and a glass of iced water, so that the guest can take one helping, hold it over the water, and eat it. In the back of the tray are six to eight small glasses filled with homemade wines and brandies. The guest takes her choice.

Grandmother's preserves, brought from Greece, were candied green walnuts in a rich and powerful syrup. One walnut would last you several weeks. Two could kill you.

When Miz Wells arrived, Grandmother admitted her and shouted (because you always talk louder to foreigners), *"Seet down."* Then she rushed to the kitchen and returned with the preserve tray. She shoved it under Miz Wells's chin and ordered, *"Eat!"*

Miz Wells whimpered, "Well, ah don't know if ah kin eat all this, but I certain'y will try!" And she picked up the bowl and ate all twenty-two of the preserved green walnuts. As Grandmother watched in stunned silence, her guest then drank the water. Dazed, Miz Wells regarded the small glasses and asked, "What's in all these li'l glasses?"

Down went the ouzo. The seven-star brandy followed. After she consumed the remaining six firewaters, she walked stiff-legged to the door. She never called again, and Grandmother formed her opinion of American educators that afternoon. "Bunch of drunks, coming in here and eating everything in the house!"

HOPE MIHALAP

Head Majorette

ON ONE OF MY MORE SELF-ASSURED DAYS IN MY THIR-teenth year, I volunteered to be the head majorette for our small-town drum-and-bugle corps, the Applearrows. Although I had not yet mastered the art of baton twirling and stumbled during marching drills, I rationalized that my gymnastic abilities well qualified me for this prestigious position. Did I mention that I was also arrogant?

The big parade day arrived, and I proudly began flipping, cartwheeling, and marching my band along the crowded parade route. Family, friends, and even favorite teachers had come to cheer me in my new endeavor. This was a rare mountaintop experience for me; and I was savoring every aspect of this dream come true.

Suddenly I felt a frantic tap on my shoulder and heard an irritated voice in my ear. It was my band director. He spun me around just in time for me to see the disappearing backs of my band members as they marched two blocks away in the other direction.

Lessons I learned that day:

1. Don't take yourself too seriously.

2. It takes more than guts and arrogance to be a leader.

3. A good leader looks over her shoulder now and then to make sure the "arrows" are pointing in the right direction.

4. However fast you run, it's really hard to catch up with a group that is marching in the opposite direction!

CANDIS FANCHER

Contributors

*B*urky Achilles is a writer and recipient of a Walden Fellowship. She is working on her first novel as well as a book of inspirational short stories. She and her husband are raising a daughter and a son on the brink of teenhood. (503) 638-4100.

*E*mory Austin, Certified Speaking Professional, was recently featured in *Industry Week* magazine, along with fellow speakers Colin Powell, Margaret Thatcher, and Terry Anderson. She is a Phi Beta Kappa Communications graduate of Wake Forest University and has keynoted in almost every industry, to rave reviews. For information regarding Emory's presentations and tapes, please call (704) 663-7575.

*U*rsula Bacon fled Nazi Germany with her parents and spent the next nine years in China. She was interned along with 18,000 European refugees by Japanese occupation forces in Shanghai for four years. She emigrated to the United States at the end of World War II. Ursula is married to author Thorn Bacon, and they operate a small publishing house and write books. She is the coauthor of *Savage Shadows* and the author of *The Nervous Hostess Cookbook.* (503) 682-9821.

*M*aggie Bedrosian, MS, business owner and executive coach, specializes in helping people produce focused results with natural ease. Author of three books, including *Life Is More Than Your to Do List: Blending Success & Satisfaction,* Maggie hosted television's *Spotlight on Business.* She is past president of the American Society for Training &

Development, Washington, D.C., chapter. Audiences enjoy her light-hearted programs at business gatherings, or on cruise ships, and at the Disney Institute. (301) 460-3408.

*L*inda Blackman, a consultant, trainer, and professional speaker, shows executives how to make more effective presentations to all audiences and teaches company spokespersons the secrets of handling the media. She is a former coast-to-coast TV reporter, anchor, and talk show host. Linda knows how to transfer the power of the spoken word to you. (412) 682-2200.

*J*oan Borysenko, PhD, is the president of Mind/Body Health Sciences, Inc., and the author of several books, including *Fire in the Soul*, a *New York Times* bestseller; *Minding the Body, Mending the Mind;* and *Guilt Is the Teacher, Love Is the Lesson.* She cofounded and is a former director of the Mind/Body Clinic at New England Deaconess Hospital and was an Instructor in Medicine at Harvard Medical School. One of the architects of the new medical synthesis called psychoneuroimmunology, Dr. Borysenko is herself a cell biologist, a licensed psychologist, and an instructor in yoga and meditation. (303) 440-8460.

*M*ildred Cohn graduated from college with honors at age sixty-eight. She resides in Fort Lauderdale, FL.

*W*endy Craig-Purcell is the senior minister at the Church of Today in San Diego, CA. Wendy was a skater with the Ice Capades before becoming the youngest ordained minister in the Unity movement. Her ministry is characterized by her personal strength and an attitude of open and unconditional acceptance. (619) 689-6500.

*P*atsy Dooley is a humorist and motivational speaker who thrives on challenges and change. Through her twenty-five years in the business world, she creates funny and value-packed programs to show people how to add humor to their lives. Her gift of connecting humor with reality, and of sensing business climates, affords a fresh originality to her programs. She brings her own unique stories and humor for her audiences' enjoyment and growth. (805) 489-1091.

*K*ay duPont, Certified Speaking Professional, is executive vice president of The Communication Connection, an Atlanta company that custom designs communications and relationship programs for organizations all over the world. (770) 395-7483.

*E*dith Eva Eger, PhD, an Auschwitz survivor, is a licensed psychologist and a keynote speaker, workshop leader, and consultant. She tailors her presentations to the unique requirements of business, government, military, health care, religious, civic, community, and educational organizations. Dr. Eger's unforgettable presentations bring dynamic new perspectives to the universe of human behavioral issues facing all people and organizations today. (619) 454-8442.

*S*hirley Elkin, MSEd, is a professional speaker and trainer based in Decatur, IL. She presents keynotes and leads seminars on Body Language in the Business World, Change Your Thinking—Change Your Life, and Professional Presentation Skills. She has a master's degree and worked in secondary education prior to becoming a speaker and trainer. (217) 875-1721.

*J*acqueline Gillis Elliott is a freelance writer living in West Linn, OR. She received her master's in physical therapy in 1977. Positions she has held include therapist, consultant, university instructor, rehabilitation manager, and director of quality services. She credits her husband, Dave, her son, Eli, and many geriatric clients with contributing healing doses of humor and inspiration to the most ordinary moments of daily living.

*C*hristine B. Evans, MA, a marriage and family therapist, has been in practice for twenty-three years in Sebastopol, CA. She is a keynote speaker and leads women's support groups and workshops on shame and empowerment. She wrote *Breaking Free of the Shame Trap: How Women Get into It, How Women Get Out of It.* John Gray, author of *Men Are from Mars, Women Are from Venus,* says of her book, "An important and strong book and a necessary support for validating women's feelings at a time when it is most needed." (707) 829-5901.

*C*andis Fancher, MS, CCC in Speech Pathology, is the founder of Inner Sources. Her well-known "Pleasure Pause" seminars energize participants to adopt more positive lifestyles. Her inspiration came from her own life-threatening illness and the loss of a family member. She sees the immediate benefits of integrating humor into patient care. Her clients include hospitals, professional organizations, public agencies, and commercial businesses. (612) 890-3897.

*E*leanor S. Field, PhD, is a licensed psychologist, marriage and family therapist, and hypnotherapist in private practice in Tarzana, CA. She is the coauthor of *The Good Girl Syndrome* and has participated in many radio and television interviews, including *Donahue, Hour Magazine,* Tom Snyder, and Michael Jackson. Dr. Field is on staff at the Encino-Tarzana Regional Medical Center and consults on pain control and depressive disorders. She is a member of the National Speakers Association and speaks on motivational topics and "The Mind-Body Connection." (818) 708-3559.

*F*ran Fisher is a Certified Personal and Professional Coach and president of Living Your Vision, which provides guidance and coaching for individuals and small-business owners. "We each have a unique divine design that desires to be fulfilled," says Fran. She blends the art of visioning, the structure of planning, and her intuitive ability to help clients fulfill their heart's desires. (800) 897-8707.

*C*arolyn Fox is currently writing a book about her spiritual and personal growth from her motorcycle adventure through all fifty states. (514) 957-5631.

*E*dwene Gaines is a Unity minister known for her life-changing seminars such as: Prosperity Plus Workshop; Integrity, Commitment, Riches and Honor; Rites of Passage; The Firewalk; and Celebrating the Goddess Within. For a list of her tapes and materials, contact: (800) 741-6790.

*P*atricia Forbes Giacomini is a freelance writer residing in Denver, CO. (303) 733-7220.

*L*ola D. Gillebaard lives in Laguna Beach, CA. A recipient of the Reader's Digest Writers Award, she is a professional speaker and a past president of the Greater Los Angeles Chapter of the National Speakers Association. Her one woman show, *Life's Funny That Way,* has been acclaimed all around the country. Lola is a humorist, a college associate professor, an author, and a corporate keynoter. She believes that laughter is the handshake of good communication and that humor in business is serious business. (714) 499-1968.

*L*ynne Goldklang, MA, MFCC, is a psychotherapist in private practice in Los Angeles. She gives seminars on humor and healing and is coauthoring a book, *Count It as a Vegetable and Move On,* all about stressing less and enjoying life more. (213) 874-5097.

*A*nn V. Graber (aka Westermann) is a gifted counselor. She holds a Master of Divinity in Interfaith Ministerial Counseling and earned her Diplomate in Logotherapy from the Viktor Frankl Institute of Logotherapy. As a consultant/educator, Ann works with individuals and groups using meaning-centered therapeutic approaches. Her inspiring audiotapes, *Images of Transformation,* are available by calling (314) 947-6175.

*P*am Gross is the founder and vice president of CareerMakers, a life-planning and career management firm in Portland, OR. She is the author of *Want a New, Better, Fantastic Job? (The How-to Manual for the Serious Job Seeker).* Pam Rollerblades, swims, reads theology and fiction, and enjoys hiking in old-growth forests. (503) 244-1055.

*D*onna Hartley is a motivational, informational speaker. She is known for *Fireborn—9 Skills for the '90s,* her true-life story, featured on PBS, and for her *Get What You Want* video series. She can be reached at (916) 581-2005.

*K*athlyn Hendricks, PhD, ADTR, has had a lifelong passion for transformation and the power of consciousness. She directs the Hendricks Institute, which conducts trainings and workshops in relationship and body-centered transformation throughout the United States and in Europe. She is the coauthor of nine books, including *Conscious Loving* and *At the Speed of Life,* and has appeared regularly on national television with her husband and partner, Gay Hendricks. (805) 565-1870.

*J*an Hibbard has a background in social services and real estate and is presently marketing wellness products for Nikken International. She lives in Portland, OR, with her husband and two children. (503) 244-5752.

*C*onnie Hill is founder and president of The Fulfillment Center, Inc., a service company that provides organizations with warehousing services to distribute and fulfill requests for product and literature. Hill started The Fulfillment Center in 1988 with $100 and one client. Today she operates a 15,000-square-foot facility and has twenty-five clients. Hill lives with her husband and two teenage boys in San Rafael, CA. (707) 224-6161.

*J*ean Houston, PhD, is an internationally known psychologist, scholar, philosopher, and teacher, who has developed revolutionary ways of unlocking the latent human capacities existent in each human being. The author or coauthor of over fifteen books—including *Public like a Frog; Life Force; The Possible Human; Godseed; The Search for the Beloved;* and *The Hero and the Goddess*—she has also worked in human and cultural development in over forty countries. Her school of spiritual studies, modeled on the ancient mystery schools, is now in its twelfth year. (914) 354-4965.

*B*arbara Marx Hubbard is an author and a world-renowned futurist, social innovator, speaker, citizen diplomat, social architect, and prophetic politician. She has led a life of perseverance and commitment to a single purpose: To understand, communicate, and encourage the evolutionary potential of humanity. Barbara has written *The Hunger of Eve; The Evolutionary Journey;* and *The Book of Co-Creation: The Revelation: A Message of Hope for the New Millennium.* With her partner, Sidney Lanier, she has cofounded the Foundation for Conscious Evolution. For information, call (415) 454-8191.

*S*haron Hyll, DC, is a chiropractic physician in private practice in Saint Louis. She focuses on chronic disease management, integrating body, mind, and spirit into her practice. Acupuncture and nutrition are also extensively used. She lives with her husband, two stepchildren, two cats, one dog, and two Volvo wagons. (314) 256-7616.

*K*imberly Jacobsen is Planning Director for Wasco County, OR, and a mother. (514) 298-5169.

*J*ennifer James, PhD, holds a doctorate in cultural anthropology and master's degrees in both history and psychology. She is a columnist for the *Seattle Times* and one of Seattle's most popular commentators. A renowned lecturer worldwide, she is the author of five books, including *Success Is the Quality of Your Journey*, which has sold over 100,000 copies. (206) 243-5242.

Berniece Johnson, who is not a contributor but who is featured in the story "Angel on Patrol," is a police officer. She aspires to be the first black female country singer. (503) 240-4917.

April Kemp, MS, is an award-winning motivational speaker and sales trainer. She is dynamic, with a high-energy delivery style dedicated to the education of audiences nationwide. Her company specializes in motivational keynote speaking and teaching women the art of selling. Along with her husband, April developed a motivational software product, Motivational Mind Bytes™. (800) 307-8821.

Marlene L. King has an MA in art therapy (cum laude). She is executive vice president of Exhibitron Corporation and co-owner of FutureQuest Co. She writes, edits, and conducts seminars and classes in the field of dreamwork. Her dream-based oil paintings have been shown at Planetfest, Illuminarium Galleries, and Northwoods Galleries. She is a member of the Association for the Study of Dreams and the American Art Therapy Association. (541) 471-9337.

Kathy Lamancusa, CPD, CCD, MSF, writes and presents Family Lifestyle, Creativity, and Creative Skills programs designed for parents, teachers, and students. Over one million copies of her books and videos have been sold, her column appears in magazines nationally and internationally, and she can be seen on television on the Discovery Channel, the Learning Channel, PBS, and Home & Garden Network. Her own show, *At Home with Flowers*, is a "how to" lifestyle program appearing on PBS around the country. For information on seminars, presentations, books, and videos, call (330) 494-7224.

*G*ladys **Lawler** is a ninety-three-year-old poet living in Kansas City, MO.

*I*rene **B. Levitt,** MGA, an instructor and professional lecturer in handwriting analysis at the college level since 1985, is president-elect of the National Speakers Association, Arizona chapter. She provides document examination, vocational analysis, criminal investigation, jury screening, and personality assessments. She is an expert on graphotherapy and is working with inner-city teenagers to help improve their self-esteem. She is a member of the Governors' Commission on Prevention of Violence Against Women. To order her book, *Brainwriting,* or the audiotape/booklet *A Key to Your Personality—Using Handwriting Analysis,* call (602) 661-9199.

*M*ary **LoVerde,** MS, ANP, is a professional speaker and founder of Life Balance, Inc. Her passion is researching new ways to balance career success with a happy and healthy family. She has produced an audiotape series entitled "June Cleaver Never Fried Bacon in a Bill Blass Dress" and is the author of the book and videotape *Your Family's Greatest Gift,* soon to be published. (303) 755-5806.

*P*hyllis **Mabry** has published poetry and articles during her twenty years teaching in secondary education. She serves as a writing judge for the National English Council and is currently working on her first novel. (217) 428-1166.

*A*nn **McGee-Cooper,** EdD, author, lecturer, business consultant, and creativity expert, is a widely recognized leader in the emerging field of brain engineering. Her work has been featured in such major publications as the *Chicago Tribune, USA Today,* and *International Management.* She has authored three books, *Building Brain Power, You Don't Have to Go Home from Work Exhausted!* and *Time Management for Unmanageable People.* Her Creative Time Planner is now available through Day-Timers. She can be reached at (214) 357-8550.

*M*ary Jane Mapes, Certified Speaking Professional, professional keynote speaker and seminar leader, specializes in interpersonal communication and managing personal change. She is known for thought-provoking, cutting-edge programs that appeal to the head and touch the heart. She is from Kalamazoo, MI, and can be contacted by calling (616) 324-1847.

*D*anielle Marie, entrepreneur, business consultant, and author, acts as a Chief Imagination Officer on many boards, helping companies grow creatively. In her book, *Straight from the Heart,* authors, celebrities, and others share their philosophies on making a difference in the world. The book inspires readers to see how we all can make a difference. (602) 368-8526.

*S*helly Marks, MS, is coauthor of *Miscarriage: Women Sharing from the Heart.* (619) 469-6267.

*A*lex Merrin is an intuitive personal growth coach, whose passion is supporting people in conscious evolution. A senior associate of the Hendricks Institute, she is director of the institute's Personal Supervision Program, working with individuals, couples, and corporations. (503) 228-7784.

*C*onnie Merritt is a writer and a humorous and engaging professional speaker, who speaks in fifty cities a year on dealing with difficult people, change, and building your business. She is currently working on three books, *Finding Love Again: The Over-Forty Dating Survival Manual; Ten Smart Conversations to Make Your Marriage Work;* and *Tame the Lions in Your Life: Dealing with Difficult People and Tough Times.* (714) 494-0091.

*H*ope **Mihalap** is an author, an actress, and a radio personality, and is the voice behind hundreds of national commercials. As a professional speaker, she has received the prestigious international Mark Twain Award for Humor, won also by Bob Hope and others. She is one of only twenty women in the world to be awarded the National Speakers Association's Council of Peers Award of Excellence. She has an ear for accents and an eye for hilarious situations. (804) 623-0429.

*S*usan **Miles,** a photographer and writer, is currently studying for a degree in art therapy. (503) 282-6266.

*A*nita **Cheek Milner** is a lawyer, a humorist, and a stand-up comic. She enrolled in law school in her forties, passed the California bar exam at age fifty, and is now known as "The Change-of-Life Attorney." Anita keynotes to groups all over the United States, presenting "Laugh and Stay Healthy." (800) 747-9130.

*J*ann **Mitchell** is a feature writer for *The Oregonian* in Portland. She has received national awards for her coverage of social issues, features, humor, and mental health. Her popular Sunday column, "Relating," provides insights into our relationships with others and ourselves. She is the author of four books: *Codependent for Sure; Organized Serenity; Home Spiritual Home;* and *The Holiday Survival Guide.* She also lectures frequently on self-development. (503) 221-8516.

*M*ary **Manin Morrissey** holds a master's degree in psychology. Her growing global audience is a tribute to her inspirational speaking and teaching ministry. She counsels and leads seminars reaching thousands each year as founder and spiritual leader of the Living Enrichment Center, often referred to as a model of the 21st Century Church. She is the author of *Building Your Field of Dreams.* (503) 682-5683.

*M*arguerite Murer is an educator, a professional speaker, and an inspirational writer. Her keynote addresses, seminars, and workshops are noted for their electrifying interaction and explosive insights. (817) 273-5234.

*W*endy Natkong works as a paramedic in Juneau, Alaska. A freelance writer, she is currently working on her second novel. (907) 789-7825.

*S*heryl Nicholson is the president of her own consulting firm, More Than Survival! "Gifts of the Heart" is an edited excerpt from her seminar, published in April 1991 in *Esteem*. She can be reached at (813) 684-3076.

*M*ary Omwake has been the senior minister of Unity Church of Overland Park in Kansas since 1989. Under her leadership, the congregation has grown from under 200 to 1,500 members. Prior to attending ministerial school, Mary received a BA in psychology from California State University, Irvine, and completed her graduate work in education at the University of California. The church's Outreach Program has reached more than 2,500 children, inner-city adolescent girls, and gang members; it also provides care to 2,500 adults in nursing homes and abuse shelters. (913) 649-1750.

*R*osita Perez, author of *The Music Is You*, has received the Council of Peers Award for Excellence, was named Speaker of the Year by the National Management Association, and has been given the two most coveted awards from the National Speakers Association. She changed careers at forty, when she picked up her guitar and decided she could do meaningful, life-transforming programs by using music and self-disclosure from the platform. Her commonsense approach and use of humor have led to her being described as a "revitalizer" at national conventions around the world. (352) 376-0133.

𝒫enelope Pietras is a freelance writer and editor in Colorado. She conducts memoir-writing workshops and is currently working on a novel. (303) 791-3981.

𝒟iann Roche is an agent for commercial artists and photographers. Although based in Kansas City, she represents these talented people on a national level. Diann's goal is to bring integrity and peace to every person she meets or with whom she speaks. (816) 822-2024.

ℬarbara Rogoff is a writer and cocreator of the workshop for adult survivors of abuse "Beyond Survival into Triumph." She has a prison ministry that incorporates techniques to quiet the chaos, find hope in the present moment, and thereby attain personal freedom. She lives in Stilwell, KS, with Gary, her husband and best friend of nineteen years. (913) 897-7250.

𝒫atty Rosen is a writer, lecturer, facilitator, consultant, and Nordic ski instructor. She was formerly a registered nurse and certified nurse practitioner, and was clinical director for a chapter of Planned Parenthood and Urban League Family Planning. She sponsored the Oregon Death with Dignity Ballot Measure. (541) 389-7280.

ℋarriet Roth, MSEd, is an infant massage instructor through the International Loving Touch Foundation, Inc. She draws from twenty-eight years' experience as a kindergarten and first-grade educator with a master's degree in education as well as an Early Childhood Certificate. Harriet has a passion for teaching children. (503) 520-0352.

ℳary Murray Shelton is senior minister of the Huntington Beach Church of Religious Science in southern California, and is dean and director of the Holmes Institute: A Graduate School for Consciousness Studies. A minister since 1986, she currently serves on the International Board of Trustees for the United Church of Religious Science. Originally trained in theater, she uses storytelling as one of the ways to bring messages of truth into real-life terms for our everyday living. (714) 969-1331.

*J*oanna Slan is a mother, wife, and professional speaker. She may be found at better trash cans near you or onstage, presenting to large and small groups of people. Joanna speaks on topics she has yet to figure out, like balancing one's life, communications, having fun, and peacefully coexisting with difficult people. Meanwhile, keep your eyes open for Joanna's book, *If Mama Ain't Happy, Ain't Nobody Happy: How Women and Their Families Can Live Life with More Joy and Less Stress.* (800) 356-2220.

*J*ody Miller Stevenson, author of *Soul Purpose* and *Soulutions,* draws from twenty years' experience teaching thousands of people nationally how to "discover their unique and special purpose for existence." Her specialty is assisting others to create and manifest their personal vision while mastering the transition process. Her delight is coaching people as they awaken to their potential and their personal passion. Jody is currently a counselor in private practice, speaking nationally and leading seminars on creative expression. (503) 977-2235.

*S*uzy Sutton, Certified Speaking Professional, is a speaker, trainer, and entertainer. A working actor in film and TV commercials, she produced and hosted the Philadelphia radio and TV show *We Can't Stop Now* for sixteen years. She is the author of *Practical Steps to Speaking Up and Out,* and the coauthor of *Build a Better You.* (215) 493-4766.

*L*inda **Ross Swanson** is a freelance writer who frequently publishes essays and poetry. "Waste Not, Want Not" is an excerpt from her upcoming book, a collection of essays and vignettes about life with her manic-depressive mother. (503) 292-4755.

*M*ari **Pat Varga** is a professional speaker and workshop leader who specializes in interpersonal communication, presentation skills, and peak performance. Mari Pat has inspired, entertained, and challenged business audiences since 1985. (312) 989-7348.

Acknowledgments

MY HEARTFELT THANKS GO TO THE CONTRIBUTORS OF this book. Their individual and collective enthusiasm and their willingness to tell their favorite uplifting stories created the beauty herein.

Many thanks and the warmest regards to my agent, Maureen Walters, and my editor, Becky Cabaza, for the ease with which this project flowed. My deep gratitude goes to my review board: Clara Harwood, Ginny Warren, and Phyllis Weter. Their love of the project, their support of me, and their objectivity brought a unique perspective and individual "taste" to the stories they felt would have the most impact on readers. The stories they helped select represent a cross section of inspirational experiences important to women from around the country.

I would also like to thank: Patty Rosen for her friendship and beautiful editing; motivational speakers Maggie Bedrosian, Joanna Slan, Linda Blackman, and April Kemp for their encouragement and suggestions; writer Penny Pietras for her ability to add tenderness to a story; Mary Omwake and Barbara Rogoff, where it all began. Special thanks go to Kathie Borstel, Linda Kemp, Marilyn Guldan, Ursula Bacon, Carole Greenberg, Karen Howells, Janet Reigel, Cathy Kinnaird, Karen Weight, M. J. Evans, Debbie Rosas, and Rev. Bruce Robinson for their support, feedback, and friendship. Thanks to my family—especially to Dad, for being interested enough to read every story!

Not all of the hundreds of stories contributed are in this book, but they all touched my heart. Here are a few women I want to pay special tribute to:

- Jane Adams lost her twelve-year-old daughter, Susan, in a tragic automobile accident. Six years later, she was invited to speak at the high-school graduation ceremony for Susan's class. This invitation allowed Jane the opportunity to be Susan's mom one more time on a more positive note.
- Diane Hunsaker is no stranger to hardship. She lost both her parents as a young girl. Diane learned that *determination* makes the difference in getting something done. Once married, with a family of her own, Diane longed to attend college. She returned to school while working full time. Diane attended classes for fourteen years—one hour per day, during her lunch hour! She graduated recently at age fifty, and is now in a master's program —this time attending night classes.
- Sandra "Kandy" Mandel was in the process of writing her story when she died of cancer. Her courage, compassion for others, and sweet spirit are sorely missed by all who knew her.

Applause to my husband, Eric. His clarity of direction, vision, and values continue to be an inspiration to me. He is my life partner and my teacher. Thank you, Eric, for your belief in, encouragement of, and love for me.

The greatest reward from compiling this book has been the new friendships of sixty-eight women from around the country. I respect and admire their work, and I'm honored to have their stories in *Chocolate for a Woman's Soul.*

Permissions Acknowledgments

From *Chocolate for a Woman's Heart*

"The Minister and Me" is an excerpt from *Only the Angels Can Wing It, The Rest of Us Have to Practice,* by permission of Tomas Nelson Publishers, Nashville, Tennessee, © 1995 by Liz Curtis Higgs.

"United States of Motherhood" is an excerpt from *I'm Too Blessed to Be Depressed: Stories to Move You from Stressed to Blessed,* with permission of Joanna Slan, © 1997 by Joanna Slan.

"Healing with Love" is an edited excerpt from *Building Your Field of Dreams,* by permission of Bantam Books, a division of Bantam Doubleday Dell Publishing Group, Inc., New York, New York, © 1996 by Mary Manin Morrissey.

From *Chocolate for a Woman's Soul*

"A Legacy of Love" is an edited version of "A Mother's Unexpected Legacy of Love." Reprinted from *Miracles* magazine with permission of Joan Borysenko, PhD.

"Hot Dog! Thou Art!" is an excerpt reprinted by permission of The Putnam Publishing Group/Jeremy P. Tarcher, Inc., from *The Possible Human* by Jean Houston. Copyright © 1982 by Jean Houston.

"Flower Power" is an excerpt from *The Music Is You,* Knox Publications, with permission of Rosita Perez, CPAE.

"Gifts of the Heart" is an edited excerpt from *Esteem* magazine, with permission of Sheryl Nicholson.

"Thanks for the Miracle, Sis" is reprinted from the "Relating" column, *The Oregonian,* with permission of Jann Mitchell.

"Grace" is a reprint from *Success Is the Quality of Your Journey,* Newmarket Press, with permission of Jennifer James, PhD.

More Chocolate Stories?

O YOU HAVE A SHORT STORY YOU WANT PUBLISHED that fits the spirit of *Chocolate for a Woman's Heart & Soul*? I am planning future editions using a similar format, which will feature love stories, inspirational stories of all kinds, divine moments, kid stories, and humorous events that teach us to laugh at ourselves. I am seeking heartwarming stories of one to three pages in length that feed and lift the spirit, and encourage us to go for our dreams.

I invite you to join me in these future projects by sending your special story for consideration. If your story is selected, you will be listed as a contributing author, and you may include a biographical paragraph of your choice. For more information, or to send a story, please contact:

Kay Allenbaugh
P.O. Box 2165
Lake Oswego, OR 97035

For more information, please check out my Web site!
www.chocolateforwomen.com